WHY NOT WOMEN?

A FRESH LOOK AT SCRIPTURE ON WOMEN IN MISSIONS, MINISTRY, AND LEADERSHIP

4/8/02
Dear Wendell
Good reading

Love Harlan

WHY NOT WOMEN?

A FRESH LOOK AT SCRIPTURE
ON WOMEN IN MISSIONS,
MINISTRY, AND LEADERSHIP

LOREN CUNNINGHAM
DAVID JOEL HAMILTON
WITH JANICE ROGERS

YWAM PUBLISHING
P.O. BOX 55787   SEATTLE, WA 98155

YWAM Publishing is the publishing ministry of Youth With A Mission. Youth With A Mission (YWAM) is an international missionary organization of Christians from many denominations dedicated to presenting Jesus Christ to this generation. To this end, YWAM has focused its efforts in three main areas: 1) Training and equipping believers for their part in fulfilling the Great Commission (Matthew 28:19). 2) Personal evangelism. 3) Mercy ministry (medical and relief work).

For a free catalog of books and materials write or call:
YWAM Publishing
P.O. Box 55787, Seattle, WA 98155
(425) 771-1153 or (800) 922-2143
www.ywampublishing.com

Why Not Women? A Fresh Look at Scripture on Women in Missions, Ministry, and Leadership
Copyright © 2000 by Loren Cunningham and David Joel Hamilton

Published by Youth With A Mission Publishing
P.O. Box 55787
Seattle, WA 98155

Illustrations by John Darnall
Cover Photo Credits: Jack Vander Merwe (top center) Psalm Wilson (lower right)

Publisher's Cataloging-in-Publication
(Provided by Quality Books, Inc.)

Cunningham, Loren.
    Why not women? : a fresh look at scripture on women in
missions, ministry, and leadership / by Loren Cunningham
and David Hamilton ; with Janice Rogers. --1st ed.
    p. cm.
    Includes bibliographical references.
    ISBN: 1-57658-183-7

    1. Women in Christianity--History. 2. Women in
church work--History. 3. Women in the Bible. 4. Bible
--Study and teaching. I. Hamilton, David, 1956-
II. Rogers, Janice. III. Title.

    BV4415.C86 2000   261.8'344
                             QBI00-821

ISBN 1-57658-183-7

Printed in the United States of America.

We dedicate this book to our daughters and granddaughters. May they never experience limits on their God-given destinies.

ACKNOWLEDGMENTS

We wish to thank the many people who helped make this book a reality. We especially want to thank

Curtis and Lucy Allen
Larry Allen
Retha Badenhorst
Juanita Barton
Cindy Bentch
Baron Bettenhausen
Tom Bloomer
Randy Bremer
Linda Bridges
Bob and Millynne Brown
Darlene Cunningham
John Darnall
Bob Dowds
Evangelical Sisterhood of Mary, Phoenix, Arizona
Anete Ferreira
Robin Fischer
Jeff Fountain
Dawn Gauslin
François Gibert
Len and Phyllis Griswold
Christine Hamilton
Keith and Marilynn Hamilton

John Henry
Verdun and Mary Alice Hering
Catherine Clark Kroeger
Aimee Krol
Sarah Lanier
Barry and Renee Malina
Howard Malmstadt
Dennis and Carrie Martinoski
Jimi Miller
Matt Misselbeck
Barbie Odom
Jim Rogers
Mike and Carol Saia
Carol Scott
Dean Sherman
Ron and Judy Smith
David and Sharon Swarr
Paul and Bertha Swarr
Larry and Carolyn Todd
Carolyn van Cise
Pam Warren
Gerrit and Celeste Wolfaardt

Contents

FOREWORD

Today I met a woman named Jenny. She is a leader. She leads a local ministry. She has responsibility for one of the departments of a national network. She is part of the council of pastors and institutional leaders who meet to strategize in South Australia.

Is her apostolic pioneering a contradiction of the Scriptures? Are her prophetic teachings a usurpation of the biblical domain of men? The male leaders in the city seem to deeply appreciate her, yet I am aware that an undercurrent of doubt exists in this generation. Women like Jenny usually carry painful memories. Nearly all have at some time been devalued or rejected.

Who can resolve this? Is there anybody whose wisdom is built on a lifetime of practical experience? Is there a scholar whose work will hold up to scrutiny, somebody whose knowledge of the language of the text and ancient culture is sufficient to show clearly and finally what the Bible says about gender?

This is a tall order! However, the book you find in your hands is an effort by two men to give us fresh biblical insights into this difficult subject. The partnership between Loren Cunningham, founder of one of the world's largest mission societies, and David Hamilton, a dedicated student of the Word, at last gives us the integrity and experience we need in exploring this volatile subject.

Over the past forty years since he cofounded Youth With A Mission with his wife, Darlene, Loren has released hundreds of thousands into ministry: young people, women, and persons from developing nations. He has in word and in deed broken through generational, gender, and ethnic barriers. He has invested in others in such a way that they have discovered their destiny in God. He's encouraged them to walk into the call of God and exercise their God-given gifts.

Loren Cunningham stands as one of the premier leaders of Christian missions in our time. To my knowledge, he is the first person in history who for the sake of the Gospel of Jesus Christ has ministered in every single country on earth. He holds the whole world in his heart as no other man I know. His constant travels and ministry across the full spectrum of the Body of Christ have given him a unique perspective of the potential of the church to complete the Great Commission. He is also able to discern those things that hinder the church from fulfilling God's greatest dream.

It is out of this broad missions perspective and Loren's many years of equipping and promoting other leaders that he has the practical authority to address the crucial issues of this book. He has opened the door for so many key women leaders within the Body of Christ. Few are more qualified than he is to answer the question, "Why not women?"

Loren's coauthor, David Hamilton, is also a veteran missionary who has ministered in more than one hundred countries. David loves languages. He has not only learned several modern languages but also has studied the original languages of the Bible. As to the subject of this book, I have never found anyone who has studied this subject as comprehensively and in-depth as David Hamilton. He has pored over all the key Bible passages regarding women. He has also studied this issue in Greek and Roman history and literature from the ancient times of Homer into the times of the early church. He's similarly studied the Jewish rabbinic literature of the Mishnah and the Talmud as it dealt with women. He has more than four hundred books and articles cited in the bibliography for his master's thesis on this subject.

For all these reasons, I suspect that no one in the past two thousand years has studied this particular subject in the detail that David has. Despite this and his natural brilliance as a scholar, David is one of the most humble men I know. It is on the basis of his character and Christ-likeness that I commend him to you.

JOHN DAWSON

Founder of International Reconciliation Coalition
Adelaide, Australia

1.

It's High Time!

By Loren Cunningham

I have a dream of a spiritual awakening sweeping the world through this emerging generation, the millennium generation. I see the Gospel finally being spread to every person in the world, with every nation and every people group discipled with the teachings of Jesus Christ.

An old apostle, Simon Peter, also had this dream. He saw the beginning of its fulfillment on the day of Pentecost.[1] An old prophet, Joel, predicted that in the last days this dream would come true as sons and daughters would prophesy.[2] An old king, David, had the same dream, saying that a great host of women would proclaim the Good News.[3]

In the near future, the red-hot core of the spiritual awakening will be those now entering university and younger, a generation connected worldwide, not just through music and fashion but by common thoughts and by instant communication through the Internet. This connection will help speed the message given by Jesus two thousand years ago.

As I envision this, I see every little girl growing up knowing she is valued, knowing she is made in the image of God, and knowing that she can fulfill all the potential He has put within her. I see the Body of Christ recognizing leaders whom the Holy Spirit indicates, the ones whom He has gifted, anointed, and empowered without regard to race, color, or gender. This generation will be one that simply asks, "Who is it that God wants?" There will be total equality of opportunity, total equality of value, and a quickness to listen to and follow the ones the Holy Spirit sets apart.

This new generation will not be bound by traditions hindering women from obeying God's call the way my generation has. Instead, they will take a fresh look at the Word of God, knowing that the Holy Spirit will never do anything that contradicts His Word. As this emerging generation studies the Bible free of cultural blinders, they will see that the Lord has always used both women and men to proclaim the Good News and to prophesy the Word of God to their generation.

CATCHING THE JET STREAM

Sometimes we have to be willing to go in a new direction. Perhaps I can use an example. As I write this, I am on my third round-the-world ministry trip this year. I've discovered something during more than forty years of nearly constant travel. I experience less jet lag when I go west with the sun than when I head east against its direction. When I cross time zones headed west, my mind isn't fighting to stay behind in the country I just left. However, when I do head east, I catch the jet stream, and my airplane goes faster, even though traveling in that direction goes against my mindset, against my mental habits.

I believe this is similar to what the Lord is wanting to do with this new generation. Instead of following comfortable old ways, mindsets, and traditions, it will turn and catch the jet stream, following the quickening winds of the Spirit to see a rapid fulfillment of the Great Commission, the dream of the old prophet, the apostle, and the king—the dream of God Himself.

It will be very difficult for the older generation to make sweeping application of the truths in this book. There are too many cultural bondages, too many obstacles to the dream. For instance, I was in the capital city of a certain nation where I learned about a vital prayer movement that had been led by women in one of the homes. The women had prayed for various leaders and had seen dramatic results. The prime minister's wife came to know the Lord. Several members of the cabinet had come into the very house where the women were praying and had given their lives to Jesus. Then the prayer movement stopped. Why?

Some people began teaching in that country that women must not be in public ministry. They said that women couldn't have prayer meetings unless a man was present. They taught that women were more likely to become deceived than men. Women had to have "spiritual covering" to pray as a group. The women agreed to this, but none of the men ever showed up to give them covering. The prayer meetings were canceled. An effective work of the Holy Spirit was stopped.

This story illustrates what our spiritual enemy is doing all over the world, although usually in more subtle ways. As I travel, typically through thirty or forty countries each year, I see similar situations everywhere. This attack, which has been going on for centuries, is a leading crisis in the church for the twenty-first century.

Some say that the issue of women in ministry is the most divisive issue to confront the church since the Reformation. Bible-believing people are coming down on opposite sides of this argument, often with more heat than light in their discussions. Others try to ignore it altogether, thinking it is not their battle but a controversy between fringe elements.

This issue is hardly one involving a fringe element or a side concern. It's an issue that goes to the very heart of the church. When we look at this issue of women and their role, we are entering humanity's most ancient battleground—the war of the serpent against the woman. There are several aspects of the serpent's strategy concerning women that we need to look at together.

1. THE ATTACK AGAINST THE GOSPEL WORKFORCE

The devil knows his time is limited. He is doing everything he can to delay the completion of the Great Commission. One of his tactics is simply to cut the number of workers.

I see this issue of women in ministry from the vantage point of being a leader in missions for four decades. Two-thirds of all Bible-believing Christians are women. Fredrik Franson said, "When two-thirds of the Christians are excluded from the work of evangelizing, the loss for God's cause is so great that it can hardly be described."[4]

Jesus said we should open our eyes, look at the fields, and see that the harvest is plentiful but the workers are few.[5] Why would anyone look at the huge harvest we face and the tiny workforce trying to gather it in and seek to eliminate any workers whom God would call?

We don't need fewer workers. We need more! But the enemy is trying to cut back on the number of workers for the harvest in every way he can. I believe he is behind the confusion in the church about women and their active participation in ministry. And sadly, some people are unknowingly part of this strategy as they allow tradition and the misunderstanding of certain scriptures to prevent or blunt the ministry of women.

2. THE ATTACK AGAINST MEN AND THEIR MINISTRIES

The temptation to keep women from obeying God's call on their lives is an attack on males in the Body of Christ. On the surface, this attack appears to be only against women, but when we look deeper, it is also against men. The enemy appeals to the pride of men by saying that women are not their equal, not worth as much. Although some cultures call this attitude "macho," it's nothing more than pride. In the coming chapters of this book, David will expose how the forces of darkness used Aristotle, Plato, and other ancient philosophers to spread the idea that women were inferior, even subhuman. This attitude was echoed by some Jewish rabbis of ancient times who exchanged the God-given equality of woman in the Garden of Eden for a view that gave women far less value. All of this appealed to the pride of man.

The sin of pride is the refusal to accept who you really are. Pride enters in when you think you are better than others. It is the basis for racism, nationalism, and many other "isms." Pride is choosing to believe a lie about yourself. And pride can ultimately destroy you. Lucifer fell from his place in heaven because of pride, according to Isaiah 14. Now the devil attacks men through pride, telling them they are better than women. Because of some anatomical difference, he tells them, they can hold certain spiritual ministries that women cannot.

You can see the results of this attack on men in churches throughout the world. Go into a church in Asia, Africa, Latin America, Europe, North America—anywhere. You will find far more women than men. And the real prayer warriors, those on the cutting edge of intercessory prayer ministries worldwide, are usually women. Why? Because men have believed the lie that they are somehow spiritually superior to women. A man's pride destroys his intimacy with God and effectively stunts the growth of his ministry.

Sometimes leaders have tried to bring better balance by appealing even more to male pride. The church has given special titles, status, attire, and money to men to lead congregations made up mostly of women. In many parts of the world, I have seen a solitary male who receives a salary leading a church filled entirely with women.

Also, the Body of Christ has often elevated people who weren't ready for leadership, putting untried young males over more spiritually capable women. One missionary woman in Asia was passed over for leadership year after year, being placed under younger and younger men, even though she showed outstanding leadership qualities. She said, "For sixteen years I was told I had potential!"

When we begin to discover the revelation of God in this area, we will begin to free men to become who they were chosen to be alongside women in spiritual strength and numbers. Our churches will be balanced with men and women walking with God.

3. The Attack Against Women

Ever since the Garden of Eden when God told Satan that the seed of the woman would bruise his head, the devil has been ferociously attacking women all over the world.

In countries based on biblical principles, however eroded, women fare much better than those in countries with little Christian heritage. But even in Europe and North America, women suffer more injustices than men. In the United States, women still earn only 74 percent of the salary that men earn for doing the same job.[6] Many of these women are struggling to support themselves and their children, thanks to a spiraling divorce rate and "deadbeat dads" who don't pay child support. Add to this the fact that about 400,000 teenage girls will become mothers this year in the USA and will raise their babies without the help of the young man who fathered the child.[7] These women are still better off than the more than 100,000 women who will be raped this year in the USA.[8] Many more are molested as little girls—approximately one in every three girls is sexually abused before she grows to maturity.[9]

No one knows whether wife abuse is on the increase or is simply being more accurately reported. But more than 800,000 women will be beaten by their husbands or boyfriends in America this year. More than 1,000 will not survive.[10]

However bleak this picture seems, if you go to countries with little Christian heritage, it becomes even worse. According to World Vision:[11]

— 450 million women are physically impaired due to childhood malnutrition. In many societies, girls and their mothers eat only after the men and boys are fed.

— Women make up half the world's population but own just 1 percent of its wealth. Seventy percent of the 1.3 billion living in poverty are women.

— A girl is twice as likely not to be educated as a boy.

— Two million girls, mostly in Africa and the Middle East, are mutilated through female circumcision to diminish their sexual desire. Little girls who survive the procedure grow up to face painful sex, possible infertility, and a greater chance of dying during childbirth.

According to *Time* magazine:[12]

— In Brazil, it is justifiable homicide to kill an unfaithful wife.

— In Russia, a woman's office job can include having to sleep with the boss.

— In India, a husband and his parents sometimes conspire to kill his young bride after they have collected her dowry, freeing the young man to marry again and get another dowry. There are six thousand cases of this a year, and growing.

No Identity

When it comes to the suffering of women, there is one area of the world that weighs especially on my heart: some of the countries of North Africa and the Middle East.

In a North African airport several years ago, I saw something that continues to haunt me. I was passing down an elegant corridor of duty-free shops filled with luxury goods. Suddenly, a swarthy man with a stubby beard came down the hallway of the airport, dragging a young woman with a six-foot cord tied around her waist. He yanked her behind him as if he were pulling a cow, yelling abuse at her. I saw her face—I don't know why she wasn't veiled—an attractive, intelligent face filled with embarrassment. I looked around, wondering what to do, thinking a guard or policeman would intervene. But even though there were at least forty people in this secured area, including guards, no one paid any attention. No one gave the slightest sign that the man was doing anything out of the ordinary. Then he was gone, dragging the woman quickly down the hallway.

Who was this woman? Had the man come to this nation from some other Arab country to purchase a wife? Or had I just had a fleeting glimpse of the international slave trade, which continues even though it's illegal? And why was I apparently the only one in that crowded airport to feel any concern? I can still see that young woman's face—expressing humiliation and desperation. I can still feel the gall of my frustration—my complete helplessness to rescue her.

On another occasion, I flew on Swiss Air into the capital of one of the most conservative Middle Eastern countries. When I boarded the plane in Zurich, it was filled with men and women wearing typical Western clothing. Just before it landed, however, the women started filing into the airplane's restrooms. When they came out they were covered from head to foot with thick black veils—*chadors*. I couldn't see who was who anymore. The women had no faces. They had no identity. They were just anonymous figures shrouded in black.

I've been struck by the absence of women in public places in several Middle Eastern nations. Those I did see were covered from head to toe. Always silent, they passed quickly down the street like ghosts. Many religious authorities prefer to keep women inside all the time. In Afghanistan, the Taliban government has passed laws against girls going to school and against women working outside the home. The Taliban has gone so far as to require that women's ground-floor windows be painted black! Some of these women, now imprisoned in their own homes, are highly educated. Those without husbands have no way of supporting themselves. According to reports, many commit suicide.

For those who break religious rules concerning women (*purdah*), punishment is severe and is often carried out by the woman's closest family members. In *Nine Parts of Desire*, a British journalist tells of the execution of a young woman in a parking lot of the capital city of Saudi Arabia in 1977. A documentary on the BBC about her killing led to the British ambassador's being kicked out of the country. What was the woman's crime? She had tried to flee the country to avoid an arranged marriage.[13]

A few years ago, I read a book called *Princess*,[14] coauthored by a Western reporter and an anonymous member of a wealthy Middle Eastern family. In the book, the woman tells of a leading family gathering at their poolside to watch the father drown one of his daughters. The daughter's crime? She had secretly dated foreigners.[15] *Princess* tells of the stoning death of a thirteen-year-old girl who was gang-raped in her own home. Her attackers went free.[16] Another young woman was sealed inside an isolation room on the top floor of her family's mansion for the rest of her life. The room was specially constructed to deaden the sounds of her screams.[17]

Not all Muslims treat women terribly. In fact, many give women honor and respect. I personally believe that these inhumane practices come not from the teachings of any modern religion. They are inherited culturally, passed down from the earliest ages—from teachings by the ancient Greeks. But these modern-day practices are allowed, even legally endorsed, in several nations in the Middle East.

In some nations, female rape victims are imprisoned for adultery while their attackers go free.[18] "Honor killings" of women and young girls are also on the rise. A woman doesn't have to be guilty of doing something immoral to be killed. Her father, her husband, her brothers, and her uncles may kill her simply because she is the subject of gossip. No one knows the exact number of honor killings, but in just one region of one of these nations, 350 young women—some as young as twelve—were murdered in one year. The preferred method of killing women to restore honor to the family is either to burn them alive or to throw acid on them.[19]

The Secret Holocaust

A few years ago, I found an article in a back section of the *New York Times* with the title "100 Million Are Missing."[20] The article explained how demographic scientists can predict how many males and females will be born anywhere in the world. But recent statistics show that as many as 100 million little girls are missing in today's generation worldwide—killed by their families because of their gender. Many millions of these missing girls are from India or China, where mothers routinely have abortions when they learn they are carrying a girl. "Everyone wants a son, so they get an ultrasound test and if it's a girl they have an abortion...ultrasound has brought great joy."[21] Other girl babies are carried to term, then left outside to die of exposure.

According to the article, another reason for the 100 million missing girls is death by neglect. In many countries of the developing world, if a son gets sick, the family does everything possible to get medical help. If a little girl gets sick, she is often allowed to die.[22]

It's important to note that the *New York Times* article showed that these missing girls are from the populations of predominantly non-Christian countries. Even in very poor but Christianized countries of sub-Saharan Africa, the Caribbean, and Latin America, the number of females growing up with the males is normal.[23] It is only the countries with limited Christian heritage that are slaughtering so many young babies because of their gender.

Think about it, though. I found this article in the back pages of the newspaper. One hundred million humans are killed, and the story didn't merit front-page treatment! Instead, the vicious attack on women is allowed to quietly continue throughout the world.

The degradation of women isn't a problem just of faraway countries with little Christian heritage. The problem is everywhere. Read these quotes from noted people in countries of the West:

- Prominent author Kurt Vonnegut said, "Educating a woman is like pouring honey over a fine Swiss watch. It stops working."
- Former U.S. Vice President Spiro Agnew said, "Three things have been difficult to tame: the oceans, fools, and women. We may soon be able to tame the ocean; fools and women will take a little longer."
- Former tennis pro Bobby Riggs said, "Women are about twenty-five percent as good as men, so they should get about twenty-five percent of the money men receive."
- Former President of Poland Lech Walesa said, "Women are to have fun with. In politics I prefer not to see a woman. Instead of getting all worked up, they should stay as they are—like flowers."[24]

4. THE ATTACK AGAINST THE CHARACTER OF GOD

When bias against women is perpetuated by Christians, the message it sends is that God is unjust. A woman of the past who felt this injustice was the famous nurse Florence Nightingale. Nightingale wanted to be a missionary, but there were no opportunities for her. She said, "I would have given [the church] my head, my hand, my heart. She would not have them."[25]

That was the nineteenth century. A few years ago, I was in Zimbabwe preaching at a Christian conference. Afterward a young woman and her husband came up to speak with me. The woman had just completed seminary, graduating at the head of her class. Now she was not allowed to teach or preach. Her husband said, "This is so unfair!" I had to agree.

When Christian leaders act unjustly, it reflects on the character of God. Unbelievers watch and decide that if Christians are like that, their God must also be unjust. After all, if God gives gifts to a person, then prohibits her from using them, doesn't that make Him unjust?

Justice, like judgment, must begin in the house of God.[26] This issue of freedom and equality for women will be decided with or without the church. It is my deep conviction that for God to be glorified, the people of God must take the leadership. If we don't, we will miss the greatest opportunity since people fought for the freedom of slaves. If we don't seize this opportunity now, the church will fall behind for generations.

5. THE ATTACK AGAINST THE IMAGE OF GOD

The devil is not only attacking the character of God but also doing all he can to destroy the image of God. He knows that male and female together are created in God's image.[27] He is attacking homes and marriages because he knows that husbands and wives acting together in unity portray the unity of the Trinity. The enemy is also stirring up difficulty between men and women in the workplace. Male and female relationships were broken in the Garden, and since then, the devil has been doing everything he can to heighten the conflict.

Satan is seeking to drive a wedge between men and women with the radical feminist movement, playing upon the hurt and rejection that women have suffered. Because females and males together complete the physical expression of God's image in humanity, the devil is promoting homosexuality and lesbianism. God gave us gender differences, which we are to protect and rejoice in. Satan is using rejection and emotional wounds to destroy the revelation of the image of God.

Many Christians fear women preachers because they associate such change with radical feminism. But I agree with Pastor David Johnson from the Christian Missionary Alliance who said, "All my life I heard that [the acceptance of] women preachers was a spineless accommodation to feminism. However, the elimination of women from ministry is actually a sinful accommodation to a culture that isn't all that different from the male-dominated Jewish culture Jesus came to blow up. It's not that feminism is affecting the church—it's the church which has allowed culture to rob it of Christ's redeeming work for women."[28]

If young women involved in militant feminism were shown how radical Jesus was in the way He treated women, thousands would find Him as their Savior and Redeemer, the source of the justice they seek.

When we look at these five attacks of the enemy, we could be discouraged. But Jesus came to destroy the works of Satan.[29] Jesus came to restore God's original design and purposes for men and women.

Jesus Put Women in the Spotlight

In the three greatest events of Jesus' life, His birth, death, and resurrection, women were in the spotlight.

His Birth

In a later chapter, we will examine the ancient world's belief that the father was the only source of life for a young child. The ancients believed that male semen contained tiny human beings that had been formed in a man's head. This belief led to the Greek "headship" concept. The woman was only the "soil" for the miniature human to grow in until birth. Of course, if you think of women as nothing more than dirt, you will treat them like dirt.

God took that idea and stood it on its head by having Jesus be born with only a woman as His earthly parent. Think about it! Mary was the only human source for Jesus' DNA.

His Death

Jesus' death was the central reason He came to earth, His most important ministry. In the Old Testament, people were commissioned—ordained for ministry—by the anointing of oil. Samuel took great pains to do this in secret for David. If King Saul had discovered the ceremony, he could have killed them both. But the ceremony had to be done. It was important. Samuel's anointing of David was the outward sign of God's calling David to do something significant.

Who anointed Jesus? Who commissioned Him for His most significant ministry on earth? It was two women. His cousin John baptized Him, but two woman "ordained" Him. In the last week before his death in Lazarus' home, Jesus was anointed by Mary.[30] A few days later, another woman entered a house where Jesus was dining. She poured the entire contents of an alabaster jar containing expensive ointment over His head. Jesus said that because she did this, her act would be spoken of everywhere the Gospel was preached.[31] He put her in the spotlight.

His Resurrection

After the Resurrection, Jesus again honored women, appearing first to Mary Magdalene. Women were the first to find the empty tomb. Jesus told them to go and tell the others that He was alive.[32] So women were the first to hear Jesus' command to go and tell.

Women ministered alongside men during apostolic times, a fact we will see plainly illustrated in later chapters of this book. But as the centuries went by, the church became more influenced by surrounding cultures than by the Word of God. It was only in unusual times of revival that women were again allowed the freedom to obey God and minister.

WOMEN IN REVIVAL MOVEMENTS

When God begins a dramatic work of His Spirit, women are often in the forefront. Historians say that in most spiritual awakenings, women are accepted as ministers in the early stages. Later, as revival excitement cools into organizational structure, the women are squeezed out.[33]

One of the greatest spiritual awakenings of history was experienced by the Moravians in the eighteenth century in eastern Germany. It was a move of God that spread to the whole world as men and women went out as missionaries. Moravians were the first Protestant missionaries. The Moravians held a twenty-four-hour prayer vigil for the unreached of the world that lasted more than one hundred years. A few years ago, Darlene and I visited Herrnhut, where it all began. We stood in their simple museum and looked at the paintings on all the walls. There were the heroes of the Moravian missionary movement; so many were women.

The spiritual awakening that transformed England and America was led by George Whitefield and John and Charles Wesley in the late 1700s and early 1800s. The Wesley brothers had a remarkable, godly mother named Susanna. Besides spending time every day in earnest prayer, Susanna found time to teach each one of her nine surviving children. Mrs. Wesley preached to more than two hundred people every week in prayer meetings, which she led in her husband's parish. No wonder her son John used women leaders for the small groups called "classes," which spread their revival so effectively. Wesley said, "Since God uses women in the conversion of sinners, who am I that I should withstand God?"[34]

In the early part of the nineteenth century, God again moved in revival in America through Charles Finney, who invited women to pray and speak in public worship. When Finney started Oberlin College, it was the first college in America to allow women to study alongside men. (It was also the first college to be racially integrated.) Finney was the first Protestant leader to train women in theology. In 1853 one of his former students, Antoinette Brown, became the first woman ordained in America.[35]

Another evangelical leader of the nineteenth century, Dwight L. Moody, was eager to allow women to preach. Moody Bible Institute offered its pastor's course to women up until 1929.[36] A. J. Gordon, the founder of Gordon College, wrote in defense of women in public ministry.[37] A. B. Simpson, who started the Christian Missionary Alliance (CMA), included women in all levels of his leadership. Besides women pastors, evangelists, and teachers, four of the CMA's first eight vice presidents were women.[38]

Two influential women in the Holiness movement of the nineteenth century were Phoebe Palmer and Hannah Whitall Smith.[39] Palmer's book *The Way of Holiness* was in fifty-two editions by 1867. Smith wrote *The Christian's Secret of a Happy Life* in 1875. The book is still a well-loved classic for Christians all over the world. Smith played a leading role, teaching men and women through the printed page as part of the Keswick Higher Life Movement in Britain, which brought many thousands of people into a closer walk with God.

Other moves of God saw women being released. The Wesleyan Methodist Church ordained its first woman in 1863. General William Booth used women in preaching and leadership roles throughout the Salvation Army. The Church of the Nazarene and other Holiness churches starting up in the late nineteenth century also ordained women.[40] After the Pentecostal revival began in Azusa Street in Los Angeles in the early twentieth century, several women preachers became well-known. Just one of many was Maria Woodworth-Etter, who held some of the largest evangelistic crusades in America until her death in 1924.

WOMEN MISSIONARIES—TAKING ON THE HARDEST JOBS

It was in missions, however, that women really began to shine. There was what Dr. Ralph Winter called a "burst of female energy"[41] into missions. Not many know that famous women's colleges such as Bryn Mawr, Radcliffe, Wellesley, and Smith were founded to train women as missionaries.[42]

By the beginning of the twentieth century, there were forty evangelical missionary organizations led by women.[43] Armies of women missionaries went out, not only evangelizing but also starting hospitals and schools, including an eight-thousand-student university in Korea and one of the best mission-run medical schools in the world in Vellore, India.[44] Women missionaries were the first to translate the Bible for hundreds of language groups. And they did it in the most rugged, remote places. As one writer said, "The more difficult and dangerous the work, the higher the ratio of women to men."[45]

Twice as many women as men marched into China as missionaries. Because women were hindered from teaching men in the Bible schools, they taught women in their homes and by the rivers as they washed their clothes. They produced so many Chinese "Bible women" that to this day, women are more prominent than men in the unregistered churches of China. Forty thousand of the fifty thousand house churches now in China are led by women.[46]

I love reading stories of women heroes in missions. God seemed to delight in using women in the most impossible places, facing the most terrible odds. Gladys Aylward, known as "The Small Woman," worked in some of the most difficult regions of China. She was turned down by every missionary society, so she went to China without any financial backing, traveling from London by train and crossing war zones in Russia and Central Asia. Her years of ministry in China won her a reputation for fearlessness. One time, she went into a bloody prison riot all alone and stopped it cold, using nothing but her authority in Jesus.

Hudson Taylor's wife, Maria, led groups of women missionaries deep into China on long preaching journeys where no Westerner had ever gone.[47] Southern Baptist missionary Lottie Moon was so successful at evangelism, church planting, and the training of indigenous pastors in north China in the late 1800s that her leader said, "I estimate a single woman in China is worth two married men."[48]

When we look back on what Jesus did to release women and what the Holy Spirit has done in periods of revival and missionary fervor, we must determine to do everything in our power to release those whom God is calling today. We must make sure we are not unwittingly part of the enemy's plan to weaken the workforce. We must remove the obstacles so that this new generation can follow God's leading.

When Jesus raised Lazarus from the dead, his friend came out from the tomb alive but still bound up in the burial shroud. Jesus told those standing around to loose him and let him go free. Lazarus needed someone's help to free him. Multiplied thousands of women today are alive in Jesus but still tied up by the burial shroud of human tradition—tradition that says they are second-class citizens—and cultural ideas that tell them they cannot carry out the highest callings of God's kingdom.

It has been two thousand years since Jesus came to proclaim liberty to the captives. It's time to set the women free. It's high time!

2.

HOW WE KNOW
WHAT WE BELIEVE

By Loren Cunningham

*B*efore we look at the question of whether or not women should be in public ministry, we need to understand our foundations for understanding, interpreting, and applying truth. Behind every question of faith or practice is a presupposition—a premise. If you start with an incorrect premise, you may end up with a logically sound argument, but you will have a conclusion that simply isn't true.

START WITH A SOUND PREMISE

Mark Twain said that it's not what a man doesn't know that's the problem. It's what he thinks he knows that is in fact not true. For many centuries, everyone believed the world was flat. It was sound logic for people to fear falling off the edge if they sailed too far into the ocean. Sound logic, but untrue because it was based on a false idea to start with. A wrong premise.

We can do the same thing when we single out a verse of Scripture, presuppose what the author meant, and then build a superstructure of belief on that foundation. It may sound logical but may not be true.

We are all still growing in our knowledge of the truth. I don't think there is a man or woman of God alive today who would claim to have all truth. Paul said we know things in part.[1] None of us would say that we have learned everything God wants us to know in the Bible.

If I am growing in faith and knowledge, I know more truth today than I knew at this time last year. We, the people of God—individually from the time of our salvation onward and corporately as the church over the centuries—are being transformed as we learn more and more. The Word of God calls this process having our minds renewed by the washing of the Word.[2] That is, God reveals His Word to us, showing some behavior or attitude, even a cherished belief we've been taught all our lives, that needs to change.

We all go through this as we come to understand and apply more truth into our lives. Paul said we are spiritual Jews and heirs of Abraham.[3] But none of us have arrived to receive our full inheritance, either in behavior or in knowledge of the truth. Instead, we are in a process of being transformed by the Holy Spirit, being changed from glory to glory into the image of Christ.[4]

KNOWLEDGE IS NEVER ENOUGH

Knowledge of the truth starts when we first become Christians. We accept God's grace through Jesus' death on the cross and His resurrection. At salvation, we obey the truth that we are given. Each new believer has a different amount of spiritual understanding. Some have grown up in Christian homes but have never obeyed the truth. Others have had little knowledge of the Bible; when they obey the understanding they have, the Holy Spirit gives them more. Knowing a lot of Scripture has never saved anyone. It's only when we start obeying the truth that we come into relationship with God.

In some categories, we have more spiritual understanding today than the men and women of God of the past. Abraham had less knowledge of the truth than we do, yet he was righteous in the sight of God because he lived up to the light he had. In Ephesians 3:2–13 and Colossians 1:26–27, Paul talks about mysteries that were hidden from righteous men and women that are now revealed. Hebrews 11 tells of those who died before seeing what we see. Will we meet them in heaven? Certainly. Noah, Abraham, Ruth, and David were just as saved as you and I. They had saving faith as they looked forward in faith to the Cross, to the time when Jesus would be the perfect sacrifice for sin.

We are the beneficiaries of the Holy Spirit's revelation in the past. We have both Old and New Testaments, plus the lives and teaching of many generations of God's people. God is leading His people into more and more understanding of the truth over the centuries. For instance, has it ever bothered you that slavery wasn't expressly forbidden in either the Old or the New Testament? Why was that?

God's revealed Word is designed to help us think through its implications. Mindless repetition of Scripture is no sign of true knowledge. God wants us to think through the Scriptures and arrive at the implied conclusions. The Bible lays down principles of truth, but it may take time for the people of God to realize how to apply those principles in everyday life. The Bible even talks of times of ignorance that God overlooked.[5] In other words, God didn't immediately confront everything that was wrong in society, such as slavery. He gave us truth in His Word, but we have the responsibility to think through the implications.

When Jesus was on earth, He didn't talk about abolishing the institution of slavery. However, when He said we should love our neighbors as ourselves,[6] He undercut the roots of slavery. We cannot buy and sell someone while loving that person as we love ourselves. In fact, if you read the Old Testament, thinking through its implications, you'll realize that God wasn't in favor of slavery then, either. God revealed the same truth to Moses that Jesus quoted.[7] From the time that Moses first told God's people they were to love their neighbors as themselves, the truth that slavery was wrong was there, waiting for the people of God to see it.

Paul told slaves to obey and serve their masters as if they were serving the Lord. At first glance, this seems terrible to us. Was Paul endorsing slavery? No. In the next breath Paul said, "And masters, treat your slaves in the same way."[8] You can't enslave people while serving them as if they were the Lord.

In a similar way, Paul urged Philemon to accept Onesimus, his former slave, as a brother, asking him to treat Onesimus the same way he would treat Paul.[9] These statements and others in the Bible would one day, centuries later, bring all Christians to understand that slavery was never God's will for any nation.

HOW THE RIGHTEOUS WIN CULTURE WARS

We hear a lot about culture wars in the media of the West—the war of public opinion over such issues as abortion, euthanasia, and rights for homosexuals. But people's opinions aren't changed by angry demonstrations, violence, war, or political means. Jesus told us to disciple nations.[10] This happens as we, the people of God, learn from Him. We bring our lives into line with what He has shown us, first modeling the truth (salt) and then teaching it to others (light) as they respond.

As the righteous remnant grows in number, as more and more individuals' lives are transformed, a nation eventually becomes influenced. Opinions change, and people begin to accept some things as right and other things as wrong. For example, most nations today believe a marriage is between one man and one woman. Having more than one wife was never expressly forbidden in Scripture. But when Paul said having one wife was the standard for spiritual leaders, he revealed a principle. The foundation for that principle—total unity between a man and a woman—went back to the Garden of Eden when God said a man was to leave his father and mother and cleave to his wife. The two would become one flesh.

In another example of nations being discipled, the whole world finally agreed that slavery was wrong. It is now outlawed in every country of the world. The last to outlaw slavery was Mauritania in 1980.[11] But this took many years. The people of God didn't always believe that slavery was wrong. However, as the righteous body of knowledge grew and expanded over the centuries, people changed their opinions. Jesus laid the ax to the roots, but it took centuries for legalized slavery finally to wither and die.

How a Nation Becomes Free

Jesus said, "You will know the truth, and the truth will set you free."[12] As the righteous remnant in a society grows in grace and knowledge, it has more and more freedom in its land. First, individuals become more and more free as they obey God and learn more truth. Society around them benefits as more people come to know the truth and apply it in their lives. Freedom increases in the land, along with peace and prosperity. New forms of government emerge, giving more rights to more people. Just and fair laws allow wealth to be generated, multiplied, and shared with more and more individuals.

The prosperity of the West that the world envies is partly the result of a righteous remnant of the past who grew in its knowledge of

God's ways. In Switzerland, in the Netherlands, and in the New World, Christians searched the Scriptures for godly models of government, education, and commerce. Some of these were Englishmen who fled religious persecution in the early 1600s, settling in the Netherlands. These separatists, who came to be called the Pilgrim Fathers, studied the Bible in the Netherlands under a Dutch pastor for fifteen years, searching out biblical principles for how to run a country. Then they boarded the *Mayflower* for the New World and contributed significantly in the founding of the United States. They applied what they had learned from the Bible in their homes, their schools, the marketplace, and their government. We still enjoy the fruit of their efforts today, even though the righteous foundations that they laid down are being attacked.

This is the way entire nations and civilizations can be transformed. This is what Jesus told us: to go and teach all nations to observe all that He has commanded us.[13] God always uses the righteous remnant, His minority. Jesus compared this righteous minority to yeast,[14] which permeates all of society. We are called to be that righteous remnant, living models of the truth, laying down our lives if necessary.

Look at Canaan where Abraham was sent. It was a land filled with idolatry. One particularly gruesome Canaanite practice was the worship of Molech, represented by a large stone statue. Fires were built at its base until the idol was red hot. Then parents came and laid their infant son or daughter in its hollowed belly, worshiping Molech while their baby screamed and burned to death. Can you imagine a land of greater darkness, of worse cultural custom and belief?

Canaan was also a land where homosexuality and every sort of sexual perversion were accepted and rejoiced in. Some of the people groups were consumed by venereal disease. When God led Abraham into the land to possess it, that included changing it into a land of blessing. A land is blessed whenever God's righteous remnant models righteous behavior, confronts cultural beliefs that are against God's revealed truth, and persuades the lost to follow Christ and His ways.

IN EUROPE, IT STARTED WITH A WOMAN

Another example of God's righteous remnant was Lydia, whom Paul found in Philippi, a Greek city in the Roman Empire and a place of great darkness. Lydia was the door opener for Paul. She opened her heart to the truth, becoming Paul's first convert in Europe. Soon other believers were added to Lydia, and they became the righteous remnant for Philippi.

Throughout the centuries, the Holy Spirit has guided the people of God into an increasing, clearer understanding of truth. Whenever the church went off course, God sent a faithful witness to bring correction. One of these course corrections came at a time when the church believed that salvation could be purchased through the sale of indulgences (buying prayers to shave time from purgatory for themselves or their loved ones). God spoke to a man named Martin Luther. Luther was crawling on his knees in penance, trying to find forgiveness for his sins. Suddenly, God spoke to him, and Luther understood the verse of Scripture that says the righteous shall live by faith.[15] Through Luther, more people came to know that you couldn't buy salvation. The Reformation and other renewal movements followed, both in Protestant and in Catholic circles, correcting many wrong beliefs and behavior.

WHEN WE LOVE GOD, EVERYONE BENEFITS

Revivals throughout history were accompanied by fresh understanding of truth, followed by reforms of all sorts. In Geneva, Switzerland, John Calvin initiated education for all classes, not just the elite. If everyone had to read the Bible to know God better, everyone had to be able to read. Calvin also applied scriptural truths to other areas of society. His teaching led to the growth of the middle class and economic reforms. He taught that all work was holy, and this Protestant work ethic led to prosperity all over western Europe and strongly influenced America's founding fathers.[16]

We have already mentioned the move to abolish slavery. This began during the closing years of the eighteenth century in a revival movement led by the Wesley brothers and George Whitefield. William Wilberforce was a young man whose heart was stirred during this awakening. He promised the Lord that he would devote his life to abolishing slavery. For years, his little prayer group prayed for his election to Parliament. When Wilberforce was finally elected, he pursued his cause for thirty years. No one wanted to listen, because slavery was too important to the economy. Yet, every year for decades, Wilberforce gave speeches in Parliament urging a law to free the slaves. Finally, though others initially jeered, the moral issues eventually prevailed over financial concerns. The year after Wilberforce died, the law banning slavery was finally passed.

A few decades later, revival broke out in America under the ministry of Charles Finney. The early abolitionists came from these revivals. Abraham Lincoln was one of the people who had been influenced by Finney's message against slavery. But for many Americans, financial concerns outweighed moral concerns. Freeing the slaves simply cost too many people too much money. Eventually, after the Civil War broke out, President Lincoln signed the Emancipation Proclamation, freeing slaves in the USA.

Other reforms came out of these revivals of the eighteenth and nineteenth centuries. People's eyes were opened to the horrors of child labor. Before Christians campaigned against the practice, small children spent long hours down in Britain's coal mines, dragging heavy wagons through tunnels hundreds of feet below the ground. Because a sudden cave-in could kill a valuable horse, children were used as beasts of burden. Animals were expensive; children were cheap.

Reformers also came to believe that mental hospitals and prisons should be places of humane treatment. If we were all created in God's image, no one should be left in squalor and pain. Still others fought against the growing tide of alcoholism. Before General William Booth and the Salvation Army came against this evil, the pubs of England had step stools to allow small children to climb up to the bar and order their gin.

Following a spiritual awakening in 1819 in Geneva, Switzerland, Henry Dunant's conscience was quickened to the plight of casualties and prisoners of war. Before then, wounded prisoners were often left to die on the battlefield. Dunant and some friends from his church formed an action group, which became the International Red Cross. How many centuries went by and how many people were left to die before God's people realized they should go out to the battleground and help the wounded?

A MINORITY OPINION

Another old truth, newly discovered, was the Great Commission. This discovery happened in Germany in the eighteenth century. Eighteen centuries earlier, Jesus had given the command to take the

Gospel to every person on earth. Yet a large part of the earth was unevangelized, and most Protestants believed they were to stay within their borders, within Christendom. Then a group of religious refugees in Germany—the Moravians—came to understand the duty of the church to obey Matthew 28:19–20, Mark 16:15, and many other passages of Scripture. They began to go out as missionaries. Some even sold themselves into slavery to reach slaves in the West Indies.

A young man named William Carey read about the Moravian missionaries and became convinced that God was calling him to take the Gospel to India. Carey went to his denominational leaders in England, asking for their endorsement to set up a mission society. One of his leaders replied, "Young man, sit down. When God pleases to convert the heathen, He'll do it without consulting you or me."[17] Hardly any Christians believed as William Carey did, but Carey went to India anyway. Others followed his example of obedience, and the trickle became a wave of missionaries going out—to China, to the islands of the Pacific, to India, to Africa, and to Latin America. Eventually, most of the church came to believe what one young man believed almost all alone.

This has been the formula for reform in society: People repent of their sins in a revival; then God gives them more understanding; obedience to that understanding leads to more freedom, joy, and fulfillment; this is followed by still more understanding from the Holy Spirit.

Why did centuries go by before slavery was ended, before the horrors of child labor and alcoholism were exposed, or before the Great Commission was taken seriously? Perhaps we, the church, were unwilling to see the truth in God's Word. We have listened more to our culture than to the Lord or to His Word.

WHAT ABOUT WOMEN'S RIGHTS?

Another reform that came out of the revivals of the nineteenth century in America was the women's suffrage movement, the campaign to allow women to vote.[18] In 1920 women in the United States were finally allowed to choose their political leaders after a struggle lasting more than seventy years. Their sisters in many other countries had already received that right. To my knowledge, every nation based on Christian principles now allows women to vote.

Other rights followed as the doors of universities were opened to women. Women were able to become scientists, doctors, and lawyers.

Isn't it ironic, though? Although the women's rights movement was born in Christian revivals of the nineteenth century, recent activists for women's rights see the church as a prime enemy.

ABSOLUTE TRUTHS AND RELATIVE STATEMENTS

The Bible contains absolute truths as well as relative statements—that is, teaching given relative to a particular time, place, and situation. For example, 1 Corinthians 11:14 says that a man is dishonored or shamed if he has long hair. Was this an absolute truth for all time, for all men everywhere? If so, how can you explain God's telling Samson to let his hair grow long as a sign of his special calling?[19]

Paul's instruction concerning men's hair length is an example of a relative statement of Scripture. Paul was addressing an issue of a time that we do not fully understand. Many of the details have been lost with the passing of time. However, it is clear that Paul's instructions were important to those in that time and culture.

When it comes to cultural beliefs, our attitudes die hard. Much of what we believe doesn't come from the Bible but springs from our culture—things we learned when we were very young children. Christians are often more outraged by breaches of culture than by disobedience to Bible absolutes. For instance, it is sad that American Christians are horrified by vulgarity but aren't nearly as shocked when people use God's name in vain. Censors on American TV bleep out four-letter words describing bodily functions, but bywords that include God's name—a practice forbidden in the Ten Commandments—are considered okay for broadcast because they do not offend as many.

It is important not to offend people by cultural insensitivity. To do so will often close the door to the Gospel. That's what Paul was telling the men of Corinth: If they had long hair, they were committing a cultural blunder that would bring dishonor to Jesus.[20] If Paul had been speaking to Christians in Thailand instead of Christians in ancient Corinth, he might have reminded them that crossing their legs and leaving one foot pointing at another individual would bring dishonor to Jesus. The statement about long hair was a statement relative to a particular custom in a particular place and time.

THE TRAP OF LEGALISM

The Bible doesn't give us a one-size-fits-all code for behavior, dress, worship modes, music style, or proper entertainments to be imposed upon every culture we come across. Whenever man has attempted to make relative truths in the Bible into absolutes, the result has been legalism.

Sometimes the results of legalism are almost funny. After I married my beautiful wife, Darlene, I became more aware of this. When we arrived at a new country, missionary wives would let her know the rules. Darlene had to avoid sleeveless dresses. Her short hair was also a problem, but Darlene disguised that with an artificial hairpiece. In one country where these rules existed, one woman was suspicious of the length of Darlene's hair. "Exactly how long is your hair, Mrs. Cunningham?" she asked.

Darlene told her she could sit on her hair. The woman nodded her approval. Then Darlene went on to say she could even stand on her hair! The woman's eyes grew wide in admiration. But then Darlene couldn't resist. "In fact, I can even throw it across the room!"

Neither these missionaries nor the churches that sent them believe in these rules anymore. But they have to conform to the rules set down by missionaries forty, fifty, or sixty years ago. The rules have become absolutes. A woman cannot go to heaven if she wears sleeveless dresses or has short hair.

The Pharisees were men who loved the Scriptures. They were men of the Word. Very few Christians have memorized as much of the Bible as they did. But the Pharisees still didn't have truth. Am I saying the Bible isn't true? No, not at all. However, studying the Bible without listening to the Spirit of God can lead to legalism and spiritual death. The Pharisees didn't recognize the Truth when He was staring them in the face! They had the letter of the law, which kills.[21] They didn't have the life, which comes when the Spirit of God opens the Word to you.

THE TRAP OF LIBERALISM

The opposite danger occurs when people take the absolute truths of the Bible and change them to fit the times. We should never look to the world to define truth for us. God's absolutes never change, because they come out of His nature, His character. There isn't even a shadow of turning with Him, according to James 1:17.

When you take absolutes of truth and make them relative, you get liberalism. One of the more extreme examples of this has been the Jesus Seminar, where modern theologians come together and vote on which verses of the Gospels are true. The Bible says that that makes the

Word of God to no effect[22] and promises a strong punishment for anyone who does that.[23] We are not to use our culture as a standard by which we measure Scripture. Instead, we are to let the Bible be the standard by which we measure our culture.

So how do we know which statements in the Bible are absolutes and which are statements relative to a particular time and place and situation? Jesus said the Holy Spirit would guide us into all truth.[24] He said that those whose hearts were committed to obey God would recognize the truth.[25]

There are two foundational guidelines to follow when you're considering issues of faith or practice.

THE FIRST GUIDELINE: KNOW GOD

There are never new truths. Truth is eternal, originating in the person of God. Even the Bible isn't our foundation for truth. The God who inspired the writing of the Bible is our foundation. You can know the Bible from cover to cover, try to obey everything in it, and still be as lost as the Pharisees were. The letter of the law kills. The Spirit gives life. The Bible didn't come before God. God came before the Bible.

It's even possible to make our study of the Bible an idol, leading us away from the God of the Bible. God is who He is, and His character, revealed in the Bible, is the foundation for truth. Therefore, when the Bible says, "Be holy, because I am holy,"[26] we are to be holy. The Word also says that God is righteous in all His ways and kind in all His deeds.[27] When God tells us to be righteous and kind, it comes from His character. Justice is also important to God. He tells the judges that He is watching them in their courts to see if they are upholding His justice.[28]

The more we come to know God and what He is like, the more we'll understand the Bible and how to apply its principles to everyday life. This is why we need to read our Bibles with humility, asking God for revelation. He is waiting to open His Word to us. There are no new truths, but we can gain new understanding of truths that have always been there in Scripture.

THE SECOND GUIDELINE: USE SCRIPTURE TO UNDERSTAND SCRIPTURE

We must never judge a verse in isolation. Instead, we must look at the entire Bible to make decisions on individual issues. Taking what we know of God and His character, we hold one scripture up to the light of other scriptures. Does a verse of the Bible seem to make God unjust, unwise, or unloving? This isn't possible, for we know that God is always just, wise, and loving. The entire Bible shows that. If it appears otherwise in a particular passage, the problem must be with our interpretation. God and His Word are infallible; our interpretation of His Word is not.

The same is true of God's other character traits: God will never be untruthful, He will never be unrighteous, He will never be unfaithful, He will never be unmerciful. Paul told Timothy to learn how to handle the word of truth accurately.[29] If we handle God's truth accurately, Scripture will never contradict God's character.

WAS GOD UNJUST TO WOMEN?

Paul said in 1 Corinthians 14:34, "Women should remain silent in the churches. They are not allowed to speak, but must be in submission, as the Law says." Was Paul giving an absolute truth or a relative statement, that is, a teaching to correct a specific situation at the church in Corinth?

If Paul was stating an absolute, saying that women should keep silent in church, he certainly was contradicting what the Spirit said through Joel: "And afterward, I will pour out my Spirit on all people. Your sons and daughters will prophesy....Even on my servants, both men and women, I will pour out my Spirit in those days."[30] Also, Peter quoted this promise from God on the day of Pentecost.[31]

If Paul was saying that women should always keep silent, he was even contradicting himself. Just three chapters earlier, in 1 Corinthians 11:5, he told women to pray and prophesy. Publicly testifying of Jesus is what prophecy is all about, according to Revelation 19:10. First Corinthians 14:3 (NASB) explains that prophecy is supposed to edify (teach), exhort (correct), and console (encourage). When Paul told the women how to pray and prophesy, he was expecting them to do this out loud and in public.

On the other hand, if Paul was giving an absolute, telling all women everywhere to be quiet in church, we should apply his demand to *all* sound coming from women in church. Women not only should be banned from preaching but also shouldn't sing, pray aloud, give a praise report, or even make an announcement. They shouldn't even laugh at the preacher's jokes, cough, or shuffle their feet! Does that seem ridiculous? Consider some of the lengths women have had to go to so as to fulfill what has been taught as an absolute of Scripture.

Sophie Mueller is one example. She went out as a missionary to Colombia in the late 1940s. She worked near where the Orinoco and Amazon Rivers come together, starting at least five hundred churches. But since she had been taught that a woman should keep silent in the church, she taught her converts outside. When it rained, this dear pioneer missionary taught her students under a lean-to. Was this necessary? Is the church a building? Of course not. The church is the people.

Or take the example of Watchman Nee, a Bible teacher from China whose books are still devotional classics. Nee was converted under the preaching of a Chinese woman evangelist named Dora Yu and was greatly influenced by several other godly women—both Chinese and foreign missionaries—who taught him the Word.[32] But later, Nee received teaching from Christians outside China who prohibited women from teaching or preaching. As a result of the teaching against women preachers, which Nee adopted for a time, the work of several effective women evangelists in China was stopped. However, on at least one occasion, men hid behind curtains to listen as gifted women preachers taught the Bible to other women.[33] Can you imagine men hiding behind curtains, listening to a woman teaching from the Scriptures, taking notes, and then going out to preach to others? Somehow plagiarism from this woman—the theft of her ideas—was considered more righteous than allowing her to preach to men!

It gets complicated when man adds his rules to God's Word. Legalism often leads to incredible mental acrobatics. For instance, one of the Ten Commandments tells us to keep the Sabbath holy. We would all agree the Ten Commandments are absolute truths for all time, for all people everywhere. But exactly what did God mean when He said to rest on the seventh day and keep it holy?

Jewish rabbis took several centuries to come up with elaborate guidelines for obeying this commandment. You couldn't work on the Sabbath, but what did that mean? Since traveling was considered work, they came up with what they called "a Sabbath's day walk." You could walk only so far and no more. If you walked farther, it would be work and you'd be sinning.

The people asked the rabbis, "What do you mean? Walk from where?" The teachers decided it meant you could walk only the prescribed distance from your home. Then someone else asked, "But what about the baker? He doesn't have a home. He lives over his shop." The rabbis clarified the Sabbath walk as walking only so far from one's possessions.

In the following years and centuries, good law-abiding Jews found a way to be righteous and still be the first to get their goods to market following the Sabbath. A farmer would start out with his goods, go the prescribed distance, lay one bundle down, then mark off the Sabbath walk from that possession with his others before laying them down and going back to retrieve the first bundle. He'd repeat this process over and over, alternating the bundles, walking all night long, laying down possessions and going back to retrieve them. He could go a great distance and arrive bright and early at market on the day after Sabbath—all without sinning! Before we smile, we should consider to what lengths we go to enforce our own rules, our own explanations of what God really meant in the Bible.

What are we to conclude regarding Paul's instruction for women to keep silent in the church? Paul was simply restoring order in a disorderly congregation. Perhaps the uneducated, ignorant women were interrupting by asking questions. Paul was telling them to wait and ask their husbands at home. My coauthor, David, will go into this passage in depth in chapters 14 and 15, showing that Paul's intent throughout these verses was to restore order. Paul wasn't silencing all women for all time, everywhere.

Paul didn't confront all of Greek and Roman law and custom headlong. He did as Jesus did. He worked within the culture but laid down principles of truth that would one day completely change that culture. He established principles that would allow women to be educated and step into the pulpit themselves to deliver the Word of God.

WHAT IS GOD'S ABSOLUTE REGARDING GENDER?

Let's step back and look at the issues of gender and ministry, using what we have learned so far to understand scriptures that puzzle us. Knowing God and what He is like gives us understanding, and judging a scripture by lining it up alongside other scriptures helps us to see the truth. David will go into great detail later as he examines verses that have been troubling to women who are in public ministry. But for now, ask yourself: What is God's absolute principle that should guide all of our thinking concerning men and women? It is equality. Absolute equality.

What is modeled for us in the Godhead between God the Father, God the Son, and God the Holy Spirit? Equality. There is no hierarchy in the Trinity, only absolute equality.[34]

What was laid down in the Garden of Eden when God, *Elohim*—a plural unity—created man and woman in His image? Equality.

What absolute is never contradicted in all of Scripture? Equality. Not just equality between men and women but equality between all people of every race, ethnic background, and class, between the haves and the have-nots—everyone.

People contradicted this principle of equal value for all people very early in history. In the book of Genesis, people decided to build a tower. We still have tower builders today, but our towers are more subtle than the Tower of Babel. Our towers are hierarchies, pyramid charts, and structures that appear to give some people more value than others. Our hierarchical structures begin in pride and self-assertion, not in God or His Word, and end in injustice.

Hierarchies are Greek and humanistic in origin. Even Satan's original temptation to the man and woman in Genesis 3—"you will be like God"—suggested that they should assert and elevate themselves. We should refuse this temptation. We all have equal value, even though we have unique personalities and different giftings, callings, and functions. God set up a human judicial system in Exodus 18 out of necessity. He gave certain people control over others based on the need for order in a sinful, imperfect world. He set up authorities on earth, whether parents to lead families or leaders for the church or leaders for government, because we have practical need of them to function. But we should not confuse function with value.

Each of us is equally valuable before God. We should walk in this way, consciously copying the loving, humble pattern given us by the Trinity and backed up by the Word of God. Jesus taught us to wash one another's feet, to serve one another. This is the principle that should rule in the Body of Christ and ultimately in every society and every nation: the absolute equality of male and female.

Men and women were made in the image of God. Jesus paid the supreme price for both with His death on the cross. For God so loved the world—not just the males—that He gave His only begotten Son. Souls are souls. A male soul isn't more valuable than a female soul. A woman has absolute equality with men in God's eyes; therefore, she should be equal in our eyes as well.

This is the only way man and woman can become one in spirit as they become one in flesh in marriage. As we apply this principle in our churches, we will attain the unity Paul spoke of in Ephesians 4, becoming one faith and one body. Then we will see the building up of the saints and the world affected for Christ and His kingdom.

This is God's absolute for all of us.

3.

Your Gifts and Destiny

By Loren Cunningham

Duncan Campbell witnessed one of the most dramatic revivals of history in the Hebrides islands of Scotland during the 1950s. One evening in the long summer twilight of the north, Brother Campbell had just concluded a meeting in a little church. He was watching as the people made their way home across the moors. Suddenly he saw the people begin to crumple under an invisible wave of conviction, crying out to God in repentance. The move of the Holy Spirit begun that night spread throughout the Hebrides. Brother Campbell and his coworkers saw incredible things happen over months of spiritual awakening. Brother Campbell became a dear friend and spoke often at our Youth With A Mission training schools. We traveled together throughout the Hebrides in ministry. He told me about sitting in a building that God shook with a supernatural wind, as on the day of Pentecost.

Brother Campbell was invited to many churches to tell about the revival in the Hebrides. He was invited to one particular church in London known for its legalism. After the meeting, the elders took Brother Campbell aside. They were disappointed. Why hadn't Brother Campbell told about a most dramatic move of God that had just happened on the Isle of Barvas?

Brother Campbell replied, "I didn't think you'd want me to tell that story."

They asked why, since some of the most exciting things of the Hebrides revival had occurred there.

Brother Campbell answered, "I didn't tell about that place because I was not the one God used there. My two colleagues whom God used were women."

"Oh...." The elders grew silent, then the head elder laughed. "Well, if God used a jackass once, then I guess He can use a woman!"[1]

The elder meant it as a joke to break the tension, but the underlying message was truly sad. Unknowingly, he was echoing the Greek teaching by Aristotle, who said that women were subhuman, just above the animals.

Can God use women in public ministry? People who ask this question are actually debating which God-given gifts they will give women permission to use. How presumptuous! Think of the implications! God's Word says we are not to touch His anointed ones or do His prophets any harm.[2] God warns us not to quench the Spirit.[3] Yet people routinely "touch" God's anointed women, harming their ministry and quenching the Spirit's work through them. I believe this is what happens when people deny women the right to minister. I have watched through the years: Those who oppose women in ministry often see their own work wither.

Let's look a little closer at this whole subject of the gifts of God for ministry. There are several meanings of the English word *gift*. We will deal with three kinds of gifts in this chapter: natural gifts, Holy Spirit-imparted gifts, and ministry gifts.

Natural Gifts

One meaning of gift is "a talent someone is born with," as in, "He certainly is gifted musically." Does God have anything to do with that? Is He the source of our native talents and abilities? Or are we the accidental combination of DNA from our parents and other ancestors?

The Bible answers this in Psalm 139, where it shows God at work, creating us during the nine months inside our mothers. As verse 13 puts it, He knits us in our mothers' wombs. Our unique fingerprints, voiceprints, retina prints, DNA, bear witness that God was personally involved in the creation of each one of us. Each of us is handmade by God.

Verse 14 says that we are fearfully and wonderfully made. The text does not say, "Males are fearfully and wonderfully made." Nor does it say, "Males are 100 percent fearfully and wonderfully made, but females are 75 percent fearfully and wonderfully made." No, both male and female are skillfully wrought, created in the image of God.[4]

You are naturally gifted. You were not an accident. It was God's choice for you to be born. Not one of us was a chance collision of a sperm and an egg. God purposefully made you. As He was weaving you inside your mother, He gifted you for a particular destiny, according to verse 16 of that psalm. He designed you uniquely and gave you natural giftings to accomplish your destiny.

The Bible says the gifts and call of God are irrevocable.[5] They are for life. This doesn't mean that God ignores character to use an unrighteous person with the gifts of the Holy Spirit. This refers to the natural gifts that He wove into you during the nine months inside your mother. He doesn't withdraw them if you turn from Him and break His heart. You can choose to use your gifts for sinful purposes. Sin doesn't eradicate the design, but it mars it. You can use your gifts to become a great artist, a talented performer, a record-breaking athlete, a successful entrepreneur, or a charismatic leader yet choose to be dedicated to selfishness, becoming more and more corrupt and corrupting others. Or you can choose to seek God's will, recognize your natural gifts, and allow Him to use them in ways that will amaze you.

Isaiah was a gifted communicator. He said, "*Before I was born* the LORD called me....He made my mouth like a sharpened sword."[6] Isaiah then told how God called him to be a light to other nations. Whether we are Korean, American, or Kenyan, we can read Isaiah's words and they speak to us.

Isaiah wasn't the only one gifted from birth. Jeremiah was also called from the womb to be a prophet to the nations.[7] Esther was said to be put into the kingdom of Persia at that particular time for a special purpose.[8] Paul was called from the womb to be an apostle.[9] John the Baptist was called from his mother's womb and even filled with the Spirit while inside his mother. His calling was to be the man sent from God to announce Jesus' arrival.[10]

God has also called you from your mother's womb. You are a woman or a man sent from God, as John was. But sent where, to do what? How do you find out what God wants you to do? First, make Jesus your Savior and Lord. He will then make your individual calling clear, in His way and in His perfect timing. Make the same choice Paul made. Paul said he was pressing on to lay hold of the calling of God.[11] You must seize your destiny, even though God planned it for you from your mother's womb. You will not receive it passively.

I first began to understand my calling when I was thirteen. I was on my knees telling God I would obey whatever He showed me. That's the starting place: Before you know what it is, tell God you will obey whatever He tells you. You can never honestly call Him Lord unless you're willing to do this. As you obey God, you'll receive more revelation, you'll move in greater freedom, and you'll be on your way to becoming what God destined you to be.

They Will Fit You like a Glove

Your greatest satisfaction will come as you submit to God and fulfill the purpose you were created for. God has gifted you to do what He has called you to do. He's not unjust. He would never ask you to do something without giving you the ability to accomplish it, nor would He give you a gift and then tell you to never use it.

The calling that God has given you is an awesome responsibility. We have learned through more than forty years of leading hundreds of thousands of missionary volunteers that if you try to do what someone else has been gifted and called to do, you'll end up frustrated. If you get out of your area of calling, you end up confused and you confuse others. But when you do what God has called you to do, you feel at home. You are relaxed with yourself and with your calling. This doesn't mean that you won't have to grow. You will. You'll be stretched and challenged, but God's call won't crush you. God will give you grace to fulfill what He has called you to do. And it will certainly never be boring. It will be thrilling.

What if God calls you to do something that others say you cannot do? What if your culture prohibits your doing what He has told you? You must obey God, not people. This isn't being rebellious, it's simply doing what Peter and John did.[12] They recognized that a higher authority was telling them to do something contrary to the orders of earthly authorities. Whom will you obey, God or man? What if world changers like Martin Luther, William Carey, and William Wilberforce had done only what was agreeable to their culture and tradition or to the leaders of their day?

The subject of this book isn't light. It's not merely a recent controversy in the church or the current hot topic. We are talking about releasing millions of people to obey God, to fulfill the destiny He created for them in their mothers' wombs. We are talking about you doing whatever God tells you to do. When you stand before God, He's not going to ask you, "What did your family tell you to do? Did you do what your father or your mother said? What did your culture say was appropriate? Was everyone happy with your career choice?" No. He'll ask you what you did with what He gave you. He'll ask whether you obeyed His call.

GIFTS OF THE SPIRIT

As we stay submitted to God and His call, He allows us to go beyond our natural gifts. He releases Spirit-imparted gifts for specific occasions, for specific individuals, and for specific needs.

Often there's confusion in the church over what are known as the gifts of the Spirit. There are at least four listings of these in the New Testament,[13] but they can be grouped into two categories: the Holy Spirit-imparted gifts (*charismata*) and the ministry gifts.

Holy Spirit-Imparted Gifts

The Holy Spirit-imparted gifts are
— the word of wisdom through the Spirit[14]
— the word of knowledge[15]
— the gift of faith[16]
— gifts of healing[17]
— the ability to work miracles[18]
— prophecy[19]
— the ability to distinguish spirits[20]
— various kinds of tongues[21]
— the ability to interpret an unknown tongue[22]

Sometimes we say someone has the gift of healing. But these gifts aren't owned by any of us. They are gifts imparted by the Holy Spirit, given through yielded individuals to meet the need of an individual or a group.[23] The gifts of the Spirit are received by the one in need of healing or the one in need of a word of wisdom. The Spirit may use you with a particular gift throughout your life or only one time. Sometimes He briefly uses people who aren't yielded to Him, such as when He prophesied through King Saul[24] or when He spoke through the high priest Caiaphas even while Caiaphas was trying to get Jesus sentenced to death.[25] Jesus said that at the judgment there would be people who claimed to prophesy in His name who had never known Him![26] Notice that Jesus will not refute their claims to having done these things, yet these people will be lost for eternity.

Our emphasis should always be on the Giver, not the gifts. We must allow the Lord to continue to be Lord, making ourselves available for whichever gift He wants to use through us to meet the needs of others.

The Gifts of Ministry

The other category of New Testament gifts—the ministry gifts—has to do with function in the Body of Christ. God put these gifts in the Body according to His will also.[27] If we obey God and if we look around us with His discernment, we'll find people with the proper giftings who are already placed to do what God has called our particular group to do. As we carry out these functions in obedience to Him, He will release greater anointing and more of the Spirit-imparted gifts.

The gifts of ministry or function are
— the apostle[28]
— the prophet[29]
— the evangelist[30]
— the pastor[31]
— the teacher[32]
— the one who serves[33]
— the exhorter[34]
— the giver[35]
— the leader[36]
— the one who shows mercy[37]
— the helper[38]
— the administrator[39]
— the preacher[40]
— other giftings[41]

These giftings can overlap. The giver of finances might fulfill the same function as the helper. Many will have more than one of these ministry gifts operating through them. Someone might be gifted both as a prophet and as an evangelist. What's important for us to realize is that all these ministries are for one purpose: to build up the Body of Christ and to carry out Jesus' work on earth.

There is only one Body of Christ, one Spirit, one hope, one Lord, one faith, one baptism, one God and Father of all.[42] How can we read Ephesians 4, then separate the gifts listed there into male and female categories? Wouldn't that make us two bodies? Does God gift a woman just to teach other women in a female Body of Christ? Or is she part of the one Body? Paul said that in Christ there is neither male nor female, Jew nor Greek, slave nor free.[43] We are all one in Christ Jesus— one body, not two or three or more.

NO TOKENISM

The Bible makes it very clear that we don't choose who will be given which gifts. We aren't to survey the membership, find out that it's 60 percent women, then make sure that 60 percent of our leaders are women. Nor are we to invent quotas for other groupings in the church—age, ethnicity, or class. That can be tokenism, and it may bring just as much injustice as the injustice it's trying to correct.

It is God who chooses whom to call and whom to gift in certain ways. It's His design. He sets the quotas. But neither are we to be passive in these matters. We are to be on the cutting edge of changes He is bringing. It's our responsibility to obey Him and, if we're in leadership over others, to champion those whom God has gifted. First Corinthians 12:11 says, "All these [giftings] are the work of one and the same Spirit, and he gives them to each one, just as he determines."

Sometimes God surprises us and shakes up our way of looking at the world. He does what we would never give Him permission to do! That's what happened in Acts 10. God gave the Holy Spirit to Gentiles. This wasn't supposed to happen, according to the apostles, who called Peter in to explain why he had allowed it. But Peter answered, "Who was I to think that I could oppose God?"[44] Some may think God shouldn't use women in certain ways either, but if He chooses to, can we stand in His way?

Which of the gifts—natural, Holy Spirit-imparted, or ministry—can God give to women? Doesn't the question itself sound ridiculous? Is there any gift God has given anyone that He can't use righteously for His glory? Can He do it within the Body of Christ? Can He also use women in the public arena with specific gifts and callings?

GIFTED WOMEN LEADERS IN THE BIBLE

I have heard some claim that leadership is male. However, if leadership is male—some quality in the male genetic makeup—why are there so many men who have no leadership qualities at all? And why are there women who do?

Some say that even if a woman is gifted in leadership, she still shouldn't be allowed to lead. What they're actually saying is, God made a mistake in her case. Maybe there was an accident, a slip-up as He wove her in her mother's womb. Or perhaps God is breaking His own rules, not only gifting certain women to lead but also giving His blessing and anointing on their leadership. Others say that sometimes God allows a woman to lead because a man refused to obey Him. But that would mean that on those occasions God acts unrighteously, setting aside His own laws. This cannot be!

The worst thing is how this reflects on God. We are His people, and we should be very concerned with how He is portrayed to the world. He is a righteous God. He is a just God. A teaching that makes Him look unrighteous or unjust can be an attack on His character. Would God gift a woman to lead and then tell her to never do so? If so, He would be unrighteous and unjust. If God gifts a woman to lead and we tell her to never do so, we are being unrighteous and unjust.

All we need to do to refute this idea—that leadership is male—is to find one woman in the Bible who was a gifted leader. Just one woman, obviously gifted, anointed, and called by God to lead. But as we look at Scripture, we find not one but several, in both the Old and the New Testaments.

Deborah was both a leader and a prophet.[45] She was the head of state, just as Samuel and other prophets were in the days before Israel had a king. Besides that, since the song of praise she authored is the fifth chapter of Judges,[46] she was one of the people moved by the Holy Spirit to speak God's Word, the sacred text of the Bible.[47]

Many years before Deborah, there was another great woman leader. When Israel was being born as a nation during forty years in the wilderness, its three million to four million people were given three leaders: Moses, Aaron, and Miriam. God said, "I sent Moses to lead you, also Aaron and Miriam."[48] One-third of the people's national leadership was female! Not only was this during their critical formative years, but the people were facing uncertainty and hardship as they trekked across harsh, uncharted territory. Miriam's responsibilities, like those of her two brothers, were enormous.

Leadership wasn't the only gift Miriam exercised. Miriam was also a prophet and a worship leader using music and dance.[49]

CHAMPION OF MANY

The New Testament gives several examples of women leaders in the early church. In Romans 16:1, Paul said, "I commend to you our sister Phoebe, a servant of the church in Cenchrea." This is an interesting chapter, for Paul listed many of his close team members and coworkers. In verse one, he demonstrated an important principle as he commended his colleague Phoebe to the church in Rome. If he hadn't done this, an unscrupulous person could have shown up in Rome and said, "I'm with Paul. Trust me. I'm a leader!" There were false prophets then, too, wolves that preyed on the sheep with false doctrine and personal lives that didn't measure up. So Paul sent a letter recommending Phoebe's leadership. He did the same for Titus to the church in Corinth.[50]

Look at the word *servant* in Romans 16:1 describing Phoebe's office. It is *diakonos* in the Greek. Almost everywhere in the New Testament, *diakonos* is translated as "minister." The word was used to describe a minister of the Gospel. Phoebe was a key leader of the church in Cenchrea. Why is the word *diakonos* translated here as "servant" rather than as "minister," as it is elsewhere when describing male leaders? Both translations are correct. However, the inconsistency of the translators reflects their own bias, not biblical realities. There's nothing wrong with calling a pastor a servant. Jesus taught that we should all be servant leaders.[51] But if the word *diakonos* is translated here as "servant," it should be "servant" when describing male leaders, too.

Paul went on to tell the church to receive Phoebe "in a manner worthy of the saints...for she herself has also been a helper of many, and of myself as well."[52] The original Greek word for "helper" was *prostatis*. Again, I question the choice to translate this word as "helper." Leaders do help those they lead. It's part of their role. But

Paul was using this word *prostatis* to describe Phoebe's exceptional leadership.

Josephus was a Jewish historian writing during Paul's lifetime. He used *prostatis* twenty times in his writings.[53] He used it to describe Caesar, the leader respected and feared by all the known world. Josephus said that Caesar was *prostatis* of the universe. Would any translator write, "Caesar is the helper of the universe"? Of course not! "Lord" or "master" would be the natural meaning.

The word *prostatis* has the connotation of someone stronger helping someone who's weaker. A *prostatis* is someone acting with authority. Paul was saying that Phoebe was that kind of leader. Phoebe had been the champion for many, including Paul himself. Paul was letting the church at Rome know this so that they could welcome her in an appropriate way. Phoebe had brought her covering—her leadership and protection—to many.

Junias was another woman leader named by Paul, who said she was an apostle. In Romans 16:7, Paul said, "Greet Andronicus and Junias, my relatives who have been in prison with me. They are *outstanding among the apostles* [emphasis added], and they were in Christ before I was." Longtime family friend Dr. Gordon Fee has written what many Bible scholars consider the definitive work on 1 Corinthians.[54] He's a professor at Regent College in British Columbia, Canada. Dr. Fee and other scholars affirm that Junias was a woman and an apostle, just as Paul was a man and an apostle.

TWELVE MALE DISCIPLES

Some have argued against women leaders in the church because Jesus called twelve men to be His disciples. They say that we should follow His example and appoint only male leaders in the church. If this is a valid argument, why narrow the qualification down to gender? Jesus also selected only Jews, from one nation and one region—Galilee. Each of the ones He chose spoke Aramaic. Therefore, shouldn't we choose only leaders who are Aramaic-speaking male Jews born in Galilee?

Why were there so few women leaders recorded in Scripture? Before the Fall, 50 percent of the leadership was female.[55] But why didn't God elevate at least 50 percent women leaders after that? I don't know. I only know that God is just. It is God who appoints leaders, so the numbers are up to Him. However, humans are able to resist God's appointing and go against His will. Perhaps He wanted more women to be leaders, but the hardness of men's hearts prevented it.

Why didn't Jesus call a woman or two to be among the twelve? I don't know that either. Jesus did have women among the group traveling and ministering with Him.[56] Perhaps He did not choose a woman to be among the twelve because of the many rock-hard cultural beliefs He was already coming up against. By the time of Christ, the Jews had largely abandoned the equality of the sexes God had given them in Genesis 1–3. Instead, they sided with the prevailing culture of the Greeks and Romans, believing women to be inferior.

Jesus set a rather specific agenda for His three years of active ministry. He didn't confront all the other prejudices of His time either. He told His disciples that He had many other things to teach them, but they weren't ready yet.[57] He left the revolutionary step of taking the Gospel to the Gentiles first to Peter but primarily to Paul. And as we learned in the previous chapter, Jesus did not confront slavery. He undercut its roots, but sadly, it would take eighteen centuries before His followers were willing to see that. Throughout time, it seems that prejudices with economic implications take longer and are harder to break culturally. Both slavery and gender issues have economic repercussions in society.

Think about the world Jesus came into. The Greeks and Romans believed that women were inferior, even subhuman. Add to that the belittling of women by the rabbis' teaching, and you can see how daring Jesus was to relate to women in the way that He did. You also have to admire Paul, whose application of Jesus' teaching led him to the release of women leaders such as Phoebe and Junias in the early church.

OTHER GREAT WOMEN LEADERS

Throughout history God has used women leaders, often at critical times. Catherine the Great brought Russia out of feudalism. Joan of Arc united the dispirited troops of France, pulling along a frightened crown prince into battle and victory. In the sixteenth century, Queen Elizabeth I managed to end the bloodbath of religious persecution within England while keeping powerful enemies at bay. Her long reign allowed for a golden age of new ideas and exploration.

In our times we have seen women gifted to lead nations. The most populous democracy on earth, India, was led by Indira Gandhi for fourteen years. Golda Meir took charge in the crucial days following Israel's rebirth as a nation. Margaret Thatcher, along with Ronald Reagan, saw victory in the Cold War. Corazon Aquino won back the trust of Filipinos after the disastrous Marcos years.

Since God can use women as leaders, He can gift them for other critical roles. We will examine this in the next chapter.

4.

WOMEN PROPHETS, EVANGELISTS, AND TEACHERS

By Loren Cunningham

L et us return to Scripture to see which of the other ministry gifts women demonstrated. I won't attempt an exhaustive list, but numerous examples are given of women using their ministry gifts.

ARE WOMEN "NON-PROPHET"?

We've already seen that Miriam and Deborah were prophets. Another who functioned in this ministry was Anna,[1] whom God used to announce the arrival of the Messiah when the baby Jesus was brought to the temple. This wasn't a quiet word behind the scenes but was a public proclamation in the central place of worship. In fact, it was a defining moment in Christian history.

Another prophet was Huldah, who verified that the scroll of the Law found in the temple was God's Word and helped to spark the great religious reform in the days of Josiah.[2] Isaiah described his wife as a prophet.[3] Philip's four daughters were all prophets, according to Acts 21:8–9.

What is a prophet? There are at least two roles in Scripture: A prophet can mean the same thing as preacher—one who speaks on

God's behalf concerning the present—or can mean one who foretells the future. Revelation 19:10 gives a definition: "For the testimony of Jesus is the spirit of prophecy." Let's look at one dramatic day in history when the spirit of prophecy was outpoured.

An Explosive Birth

Do you recall the scene on the day of Pentecost? One hundred twenty men and women were praying in the temple in Jerusalem. Suddenly a violent wind blew into the outer courts. The columnades shook and the pavement shuddered. The believers' eyes flew open, and all those present looked around to see that their neighbor's hair—no, everyone's hair—was on fire! They opened their mouths to gasp and heard themselves saying words. Words of nonsense seemed to pour from somewhere deep inside them. The people's mouths were moving, but their minds couldn't understand. Then, it didn't matter. Warm, liquid joy spread from their heads down through their bodies. In one clap of thunderous praise they began to declare the Good News.

The believers were soon surrounded by thousands of people. Among this multitude were religious pilgrims from every part of the Mediterranean world. The 120 men and women, still bursting with joy, moved out to various parts of the crowd. They were all babbling words they didn't understand. A large group huddled around each of them.

It all looked so strange. Murmurs rippled through the crowd. One onlooker hollered, "You're drunk! You're nothing but a bunch of drunks!" Jeers of agreement spread through the courtyard, but then an outcry was heard near the back.

An Arab in a dusty turban shouted aloud, waving his arms excitedly over the heads of the crowd. "She's speaking Arabic! Come here! Listen! She's talking about God…." He grew silent, then wondered aloud, "How could this Galilean peasant have gone to my country? But she's speaking perfect Arabic!"

Suddenly the people were jostling against one another, pushing their way through the crowd until they found someone speaking the language they had learned from their mother. This is what happened, according to Acts 2. The Holy Spirit didn't just fall on the remaining eleven apostles. He fell on all 120 men and women disciples, and each onlooker in the crowd found someone preaching—in his or her language.

Peter had to get up and quickly explain. After all, besides the strange supernatural signs, many *women* were preaching, declaring the wonders of God![4] This just wasn't done. So Peter reminded them of the words of the prophet Joel: "And afterward, I will pour out my Spirit on all people. Your sons and daughters will prophesy, your old men will dream dreams, your young men will see visions. Even on my servants, both men and women, I will pour out my Spirit in those days."[5]

Every point of Peter's sermon was crucial that day, for the global church was being launched. One of its features would be the absence of nationality, class, and gender barriers. The Holy Spirit was being poured out on sons and daughters and on male and female servants. It was a tremendous birth of freedom, not just for women but for people of all classes, races, and nations.

WOMEN GIFTED TO TEACH

What about Paul's words to Timothy: "I do not permit a woman to teach or to have authority over a man; she must be silent"?[6] What does this mean? I have read one writer who interpreted this scripture to say that no woman should ever teach any man anything, anywhere, at any time.

As we saw in a previous chapter, there are absolute truths stated in Scripture, and there are truths relative to a given time and situation. If 1 Timothy 2:12 is a statement of absolute truth for all time for all people everywhere, we must apply it to every area of life. No woman should ever teach any man. Period. How could we allow women to teach males in high school or at any level of education? They couldn't teach little boys in Sunday school either. If this is an absolute of Scripture, like the Ten Commandments, then breaking it is committing sin. You could even extend this to say that no woman could toilet train her son or teach him how to tie his shoes or brush his teeth.

Again, the thought becomes ridiculous. We could build a logical argument from this word of Paul to Timothy, claiming that no woman should ever teach a man. But would it be true? You can have a logical-sounding argument, but if it's based on a false premise, it's not true.

As we saw in the last chapter concerning the gift of leadership, if we can find one example in the Bible where God uses a woman to teach, blessing the results, then the premise—that God does not want women to teach—is incorrect. Are there women teachers in the Bible?

Yes, certainly! Did you know that at least 886 verses of Scripture came to us through women?[7] One example is Mary's beautiful words glorifying God in Luke 1:46–55. Paul told Timothy that all Scripture was given by God for teaching.[8] If God really did prohibit women from teaching, then men must not read verses that came through women, such as these words from Mary, for then they will be taught by those women! In fact, if we follow this argument to its logical conclusion, to avoid being taught by a woman, those 886 verses should be cut from our Bibles.

One of the most cherished teachings in the Bible—Proverbs chapter 31—was given by King Lemuel. The king acknowledged that it was an oracle his mother had taught him. The chapter outlines the roles and attributes of a godly woman. Not only did King Lemuel's mother teach her son the role of a virtuous woman; she also must have modeled it before the young Lemuel as he grew up.

Priscilla and Aquila took Apollos aside to teach him.[9] Apollos was an emerging star in the early church, but he had some ideas that needed straightening out. The word *enlighten* is used to describe what Priscilla and Aquila did. Some have argued that enlightening is not the same as teaching. But is it possible to enlighten anyone without teaching that person? Is it possible to be taught without being enlightened?

Teaching is also a necessary part of being a prophet, for if you are to speak on God's behalf, you will have to teach those who hear you. Paul named several women who spoke on God's behalf as prophets in the New Testament. In Romans 16, he mentioned Mary, as well as Priscilla and Aquila, whom he called his fellow workers in Christ Jesus. It's interesting to see that here Paul used a nickname for Priscilla: Prisca. He said all the Gentile churches were indebted to Priscilla and Aquila.

Mary and Priscilla weren't the only women colleagues Paul named. Of the thirty-nine coworkers he mentioned by name, more than one fourth were women.[10]

I have seen some try to divide teaching from other public speaking. Years ago, a well-meaning young missionary allowed women on his team to speak briefly in church meetings, but only to report what

God had done through them. He didn't allow them to quote a Bible verse during their report because that would be teaching! This is nothing but playing with words. You can't speak of Jesus without instructing other believers, without enlightening the lost, without teaching them.

ARE WOMEN MORE EASILY FOOLED?

Some have said that women can't be allowed to teach because sin came into the world because of the weakness of women. Be careful! God's Word clearly says that Adam was the one who led humanity into sin.[11]

Others claim that women are more easily deceived. They say that more cults have had female founders. It's possible to hear something so often that it begins to sound right. But is this true? Were more cults started by women? Let's look at the five largest cults in the West: the Mormons, Jehovah's Witnesses, Scientologists, the Unification Church, and Christian Science. Only the latter was started by a woman.[12] You can't even say that of all the cults, large and small, more were started by women than men. For one thing, it's very hard to list all the cults, since new ones are continually emerging.

Two of the most infamous cults of recent times were led into mass suicide by men: People's Temple in Jonestown and Heaven's Gate in San Diego. The Aum Shinri Kyo cult, which planted poisonous gas in a Tokyo subway, killing twelve and injuring thousands of others, is led by a man. So is the Solar Temple in the French-speaking world, which has seen at least seventy-nine commit ritual suicide.

So what did Paul mean when he told Timothy, "I do not permit a woman to teach"? David will deal with this question in depth in chapters 16 and 17. But for me, it's as straightforward as judging one scripture by another. We should never lift one verse out of context and build a doctrine on it, ignoring its historical setting. Nor should we build a teaching around one verse, disregarding biblical statements that contradict our interpretation of an isolated verse.

In the New Testament, Paul reminded Timothy not to abandon the teaching he heard from his mother and his grandmother.[13] God has used His body, including women, to speak to the world throughout history. There isn't one category of ministry in the Word from which He has universally prohibited women to participate.

BY THEIR FRUITS YOU SHALL KNOW THEM

The Bible says we are to judge ministries by their fruit. If you do this, women Bible teachers have had some of the most outstanding fruit in recent history. I have read that Dr. Billy Graham, Dr. Bill Bright, and former Chaplain of the U.S. Senate Dr. Richard Halverson acknowledge the input of one particular godly woman—Henrietta Mears, who founded Gospel Light Press, a leading producer of Christian educational materials. Isn't it ironic that churches that prohibit women from teaching often use teaching materials from a publishing house founded by a woman? Mears's books, such as her classic *What the Bible Is All About,* have taught many hundreds of thousands of people throughout the world. Some of these people have grown in their walk with the Lord as they read her book. But the same people have turned and said that God could not use a woman to teach!

We don't have to reach back years to find outstanding women teachers in the Body of Christ. Today, one of the best-known Roman Catholic teachers on television is a woman—Mother Angelica. And where would the prayer movement be without Vonette Bright or Cindy Jacobs?

Jack Hayford said that Joy Dawson is perhaps the leading teacher of intercessory prayer of our time.[14] In 1967 I had the privilege of staying in Jim and Joy Dawson's home in New Zealand for several weeks. The couple gave me the use of a small apartment in their basement, where I began a time of fasting and prayer that lasted seven days.

During my time with the Dawsons, I became convinced that the Lord wanted Joy released into a worldwide teaching ministry. When I went home to the States, I did for Joy what Paul had done for Phoebe centuries earlier. I sent letters to pastors and talked to leaders, recommending her ministry. Joy left New Zealand for her first trip abroad and taught in seven nations. Since then she has ministered on every continent, with hundreds of thousands more seeing her on television and video, reading her books, and listening to her many cassette tape messages.

While staying in the Dawson home, Joy taught me principles of intercessory prayer and hearing the voice of God that changed my life and shaped Youth With A Mission for decades to come.[15] I can't imagine what YWAM would be like today without the teaching of Joy Dawson during our formative years and until now. It was one of my greatest privileges to open doors for her and for other men and women of God. It's one of the gifts God gave me: an ability to recognize and release others in their giftings. They and others in turn have opened doors for me. That's the way the kingdom of God works.

One warm September day in 1968 in California, a woman named Jean Darnall walked into my office. I had heard of her through her radio ministry. She had never heard of me, but she said that the Lord had given her my name and said to find me and tell me that she was called of God to the United Kingdom and Europe. She had searched for some weeks before finding out who I was. She said with gentle humility, "I don't know why I am to tell you this. I am simply obeying the Lord."

I told her I, too, was called to Europe and would be moving there in a few months. Jean became a great influence and an effective teacher in YWAM. She continues to this day to be used of God in YWAM. At the same time, she has opened key doors in the UK to me and to other YWAM leaders.

In a previous chapter, I told of the effect of the women who taught Watchman Nee. Leaders of that movement in China used to sit behind a curtain to take notes as one woman taught other women from the Bible. Who knows how many other great women teachers laid anonymous foundations behind the scenes?

WOMEN EVANGELISTS IN THE BIBLE

Psalm 68:11 says, "The Lord gives the command; the women who proclaim the good tidings are a great host" (NASB). Whether we look in the Bible or in history books, we find prominent examples of women proclaiming the good tidings. Some women are gifted at persuasion, making them excellent evangelists. We find not a few, but many examples of women evangelists in the Bible.

In the New Testament, the first evangelist to carry the Good News outside Jewish culture was the Samaritan woman whom Jesus met at the well.[16] Jesus overcame incredible cultural barriers that day, breaking taboos of centuries just to talk to her. He spoke to someone from a despised racial minority, someone in a fringe sect, and an immoral woman whom no decent man would be seen with in public.

But most important for our study, Jesus engaged a woman in a theological discussion! Women—Jewish, Samaritan, or otherwise—

weren't taught the Scripture. Many Jewish rabbis refused to speak to women other than their closest relatives. Some even tried to avoid looking at a woman, thereby earning themselves the nickname "The Bleeding Pharisees." When a woman went by, they'd shut their eyes and fall or slam into walls!

You recall from John 4 the story of Jesus' conversation with this woman at the well. Jesus gently led her to repentance. She became an evangelist on the spot, rushing all over town to give the Good News. Notice that Jesus didn't run after her, reminding her that she was a woman, that she shouldn't be doing such things. Maybe she should just tell her male relatives and let them evangelize the town?

If you doubt that women should be allowed to be ministers, I'd like to ask you two questions: First, which truth in the Bible is most basic to our salvation? What one fact separates Jesus from all the other prophets and would-be messiahs? The Resurrection of Jesus Christ. Everything hinges on this, according to Paul.[17] And the second question is, To whom did God first entrust this, the most important truth in the Bible? Women.

Women were the first to proclaim the Good News of the Resurrection. Women went to the tomb, found it empty, and ran to tell the other disciples. Was this a deliberate choice on God's part? Couldn't the angel have just as easily appeared to the men at their lodging? Why didn't Jesus go directly there instead of first appearing to Mary Magdalene? Was He deliberately lingering in the garden so that the men would have to hear this unbelievable tale first from women?

I've noticed that often God tests the pride of men by having them submit in some way to the ministry of a woman before trusting them to work a powerful miracle. Both Elijah and Elisha had to depend on women giving them the ministry of hospitality before God allowed them to raise the dead.[18] Does that sound easy, receiving the ministry of hospitality? Elijah's test wasn't easy. He wasn't answering an invitation to a fancy meal with napkins folded just so. This was hospitality at its most basic—keeping him from starving to death. How easy would you find it to knock on the door of a widow during a famine and ask her for food when she had only enough for herself and her child?

Namaan was the equivalent of a five-star general in the Syrian army of King Aram. Before God healed him of leprosy, Namaan had to submit to the ministry of a little servant girl. He had to be humbled even further, as you see in the story in 2 Kings 5:1–14. But his first step was listening to a young slave girl, who told him about God's power to heal him. The girl did the work of an evangelist.

WOMEN EVANGELISTS IN HISTORY

General William Booth's Salvation Army was one of the most aggressive evangelistic organizations in history. Salvation Army workers went into the worst slums of nineteenth-century England, laboring in neighborhoods ruled by criminals, going where policemen scarcely ventured. The founder of this fearless group said, "Some of my best men are women!" That was a revolutionary statement in his day.

Both General William Booth and his wife, Catherine, were well-known preachers. Contemporaries of the period said that Catherine was better in the pulpit than he. Her husband never held her back, releasing her to use her God-given gifts as a preacher and as a leader of others.

When their daughter Evangeline was only ten, her father heard her preach (to her dolls) on the subject "God Is Love" with such power and earnestness that he took notes. In her teens, Evangeline visited pubs to sing and speak of God's love. She spent a day among the poverty-stricken flower girls, dressing just like them, to get to know their living conditions. While she was still a teenage captain in the Salvation Army, she was called to share her faith with three members of Parliament.

WOMEN WHO ARE MAKING AN IMPACT TODAY

One of the most gifted evangelists of our time is the daughter of Billy Graham, Anne Graham Lotz. She is an itinerant speaker whose growing ministry puts her before auditoriums and stadiums packed with people who have come to hear her anointed preaching. She says that sometimes, "It's like the fire falls, and the Lord just pours out."[19]

Her father and her brother Franklin both say Anne is "the best preacher in the family."[20] But not everyone has accepted Lotz's ministry with open arms. When she spoke at a 1988 pastors' conference, some pointedly turned their chairs around so as not to face a woman preacher! Lotz doesn't try to convince such people. She merely says, "When people have a problem with women in the ministry, they need to take it up with Jesus. He's the one who put us here."

In Youth With A Mission, we have been blessed with many strong women workers. We have seen these women going to some of the hardest places and doing some of the most important works for God.

— Evey Heckman and Reona Peterson Joly risked their lives and freedom to carry the Gospel into Albania when it was the strictest Marxist nation on earth. They were sentenced to die before a firing squad. All through their ordeal, they never flinched. They boldly proclaimed the Gospel to their captors until they were finally deported.

— Nancy Neville is a long-time YWAM leader. God used this tiny giant to launch a Latin American missionary movement on a continent known for its macho culture.

— Eliane Lack led a team over treacherous, steep trails high in the Himalayas to reach the little-known Zanskar people. One of the yaks bearing their supplies stumbled and fell to its death, but Eliane and her team pressed on to the remote valley where they evangelized the Zanskar.

— Marcia Suzuki and Braulia Ribeiro pioneered the YWAM work in the Amazon, braving the spears of hostile Indians as well as jaguars, snakes, and disease in order to translate the Bible for stone-age tribes.

— Liz Baumann Cochrane was imprisoned in Nepal because her team was seeing so many converted to Christ. Her leadership helped open the way for thousands of Nepalese to come into the kingdom of God.

— My wife, Darlene Cunningham, helped me found our mission. Her role has been immeasurable as she has trained thousands of key leaders, ministering and directing training schools on every continent.

There isn't space to name all whom I admire for their courageous work. Disguised in the long black veils of Muslim women, two of our young women recently went to minister to persecuted Christians in a closed country of the Middle East. Another young woman burst into a Latin American police station a few years ago to rescue a young man whom the police were beating to death. One of our women doctors has been kidnapped twice in war zones. Right now we have women serving secretly in countries where the punishment for missionary work is death. Two of the YWAMers who've been killed because of their witness were young mothers—one from New Zealand and one from Florida.

These are just some of our heroic women in YWAM. We have been blessed as a mission to the degree that we have released women to be all that God called them to be. However, we need to release even more.

A SURPRISING SECRET OF THE WORLD'S LARGEST CHURCH

Many have heard of the world's largest church pastored by Dr. Cho Yonggi in Seoul, Korea. Dr. Cho has been a friend for many years. When I first went to Korea thirty years ago, his church was a struggling pioneer work of "only" six thousand. Now Dr. Cho has 763,000 members in his church. Much has been written about the phenomenal growth of this church, but one secret has been overlooked. I have Dr. Cho's permission to tell this story.

Thirty years ago, as we were seated in his office, Dr. Cho said, "Loren, I have a problem. My mother-in-law, Mrs. Choi, is an outstanding Bible teacher and preacher. But in our culture, we can't have her teach or preach. What should I do?"

I said, "Put her in your pulpit!"

He cringed. "Loren, as an American, you don't understand what that means to a Korean!"

"Okay, I have an idea. Get my mom over here to preach for you." Dr. Cho knew my folks. When he first went to the United States as a young, unknown preacher, he stayed in my parents' home. Dr. Cho told how my mom, Jewell Cunningham, taught him from the Word of God at the breakfast table.

"Since my mom is from another culture, they'll accept her preaching," I said. "Then as soon as she finishes, put Mrs. Choi in your pulpit. Your people will see the connection. They'll see it isn't a matter of culture but a matter of ministry."

Dr. Cho did invite my mother to preach in his church. Following Mom's visit, Mrs. Choi emerged as an outstanding leader and preacher. She was the first of thousands of women who became ministers under Dr. Cho's leadership. Several years later I saw him at a large event in the Olympic Stadium in Berlin where we were both speaking. He told me about a certain country he had just visited where the work of God has struggled for many years. He said, "All their churches are so little! And all of them are holding back their women, not allowing them to do what God calls them to do. I've told them to release their women, but they insist that's not the problem. They ask me, 'What's the key to your church?' I tell them again, 'Release your women,' but they just don't hear me!"

God has given this man the largest church on earth to pastor. He has seven hundred senior pastors on his staff, including many women. He also has thirty thousand cell groups; the vast majority of these are led by women.[21] Do you think God might be trying to tell all of us something?

A COURAGEOUS OCTOGENARIAN

Corrie ten Boom was a mighty prophet, teacher, and evangelist. My wife, Darlene, and I were privileged to have her as a friend as well as a frequent minister in YWAM schools. We called her Tante Corrie, which is Dutch for Auntie Corrie. My wife prizes a coffee canister that used to be Tante Corrie's. The canister is still fragrant from Corrie's coffee. She was very dear to us.

Back in the 1970s, when Tante Corrie was living in Holland and we were in Switzerland, she phoned me one day. "Loren, this Saturday's my eightieth birthday. Could you and Darlene come over on Friday and pray for me? I believe God wants to give me a new ministry for my birthday."

I was truly humbled. This was a mighty warrior who had proven God in ways I hadn't, including being imprisoned in the Nazi concentration camp where her father and sister died. She had also known the Lord nearly forty years longer than I had at that time. But it was a thrill as Darlene and I laid hands on her that Friday in Baarn, Holland, praying for God to release Tante Corrie's new ministry.

After that prayer, millions of people all over the world read her testimony, *The Hiding Place*. Then Billy Graham decided to produce a theatrical film based on it. During its first five months, nine million saw the movie. Tante Corrie got a new red suitcase and traveled all over the world, ministering to more people in the next few years of her life than she had in her previous eighty.

Some would say Corrie ten Boom wasn't an evangelist—she was merely sharing her story. If only we could all share so powerfully! In the days before the end of the Iron Curtain, Tante Corrie often went to Russia to minister. Knowing her hotel rooms were probably bugged, she and her assistant deliberately had long conversations in which they preached the Gospel to each other in Dutch, then German, then English. The old Dutch warrior told us about it afterward with a twinkle in her eye: "After all, someone had to listen to those recordings!"

REAL MEN RELEASE WOMEN

What a thrill it has been to have a small role in releasing what God wanted to do through Corrie ten Boom, Joy Dawson, and women leaders in Korea. This is one of the greatest privileges I have known. Am I promoting radical feminism? No, just the opposite. I want to champion the right of women and men to choose the call of God in their lives and to give more and more people the opportunity to serve the Body with all of their gifts. Some women are called to be leaders, some are called to be homemakers. Women must have the freedom to obey God and be fulfilled in the gifts He has given them.

Some worry that women can't be truly feminine if they use the ministry gifts. But God is the giver of their femininity as well as whatever gifts He places within them. He wouldn't contradict one of His gifts with another. Neither will a woman obeying God threaten the masculinity of men who are also surrendered to Christ. A real man is able to release women into public ministry. A man of God doesn't fear man; he fears the Lord. Submission to God is the ultimate strength. I have found that the more people I release into ministry, including women, the more God releases me.

Certain Christians react against the release of women leaders because of what they have seen in the modern feminist movement. It is truly regrettable that so many feminists have become radical in their bitterness and hatred of men. But many have known only pain and degradation from the men closest to them. As men in the church, we should recognize and ask forgiveness for the wounds women have received at the hands of men over the centuries. God never planned for that to happen.

True freedom comes as we submit to Jesus and to one another in humility. Any movement that seeks liberation without such submission will end up forging heavier chains. Only the freedom found in Jesus allows people to be who God created them to be.

The Bible says that the women who proclaim the good tidings are a great host.[22] Is there any gift God can't use in women surrendered to

Him? God is the giver of every good and perfect gift. He was the One who gifted Henrietta, Catherine, Corrie, and Joy. And He has gifted you. Use the gifts He has given you.

Next we will walk into the historical setting of the world of Jesus and Paul—the Greek, Roman, and Jewish societies. My coauthor, David, will also take you into the biblical foundations that were laid for the freedom of all women.

5.

Daughters of Pandora

By David Hamilton

Mention history, and some people's eyes glaze over. But to me history isn't the memorization of dull, dusty dates and hard-to-pronounce names. To me it's more like a fascinating search, going back into the distant past for clues, hunting for pieces of a puzzle to help us see and understand what we're facing today. To understand the pain and uncertainty of our times, the collapse of our homes, the twisting of values, the very unraveling of society, we must reach back into ancient Greece.

So come with me to a very different place and time. You step out of the shade of a portico, and the first thing you feel is the sun blasting on your head and shoulders. Then the smells hit you—the sweet, sickly smell of human sweat, the pungent manure from donkeys and horses, the smoke of distant fires, and, from nearby market stalls, ripe fruit, raw meat and fish, and the subtle perfume of spices heaped in baskets.

You walk into the street and find yourself swept along by the crowd pushing toward the outskirts of the city. You squint into the brightness ahead to discern an arid hill with some kind of temple on top. As you get nearer you see its columns of white fluted marble supporting a massive roof set against an incredibly blue sky. All around you are men, some wearing immaculate, flowing white linen. Others are naked except for a dirty loincloth and a band of leather around their necks. The latter struggle under impossible loads or strain to pull heavy carts.

As you're swept up the incline, you notice a protected hollow under some cypress trees. Beneath their shade, young men sit in the dust at the feet of an old, bowlegged man. The man is speaking to them, and despite the heat, they seem cool and detached, their faces turned to catch his words. You are drawn to the old man, too, straining to hear his speech, which is spoken in easy, patrician accents.

"There is no Hades," the teacher says smoothly. "We have no fear of punishment in some desolate afterplace. Our punishment is with us, here and now. The price for our sinning was exacted at the beginning of time by Zeus himself when he afflicted us with these creatures. He also designed it so that we can neither exist without their aid nor bear their company!"

A ripple of laughter interrupts him.

"We cannot escape this pain, for it lives among us. It is our sisters, our mothers, our betrothed, our wives and daughters, our mistresses and concubines. Furthermore, if we spend our lives in wrongdoing and in cowardice, afterward Zeus will send us back into this life as women."

You pause to take this in, then you turn and ask someone nearby, "Who is that man?"

"Why, don't you know the greatest philosopher alive, the pupil of Socrates himself? That's Plato, of course!"

This little scene may shock or surprise you. Wasn't Plato one of those great philosophers we heard about in school? If our education went very far, we probably studied some of his writings. Plato lived during "the glory that was Greece," and it would be hard to overestimate his influence. One expert said that the history of philosophy could be called "a series of footnotes to Plato."[1]

We scarcely realize it, but Plato and other Greek philosophers, poets, playwrights, physicians, and political thinkers continue to influence us today, in everything from best-selling books to the plots of movies at the local theater to what is taught in our universities, seminaries, and Bible schools. In fact, if we want to understand the typical Western mindset, especially the way we think about women and their roles, we have to go back to the Greeks, for those words we overheard in the scene at the beginning of this chapter were only part of what was believed and taught in ancient Greece. And as we will see in this chapter, those ancient teachings laid the foundations of belief for the Mediterranean world, the conquered lands of the Roman Empire, and, finally, all of Western civilization.

THE STORYTELLERS

Homer laid the foundations of belief for Greek society. He was a poet who wrote eight hundred years before Christ, passing on legends from earlier times. The stories he told in *The Iliad* and *The Odyssey* would be told and retold, studied and interpreted, dramatized and discussed for centuries. They became the foundation for all that the Greeks believed about their gods, themselves, and everything that existed. And most important for us in the study of women and their roles, Homer cast the die for beliefs and customs for thousands of years to come. A current writer says of Homer's works, "The roots of Western misogyny [the fear and hatred of women] go back to...the oldest document in European literature."[2]

In *The Iliad*, women were the cause of all conflict and suffering. Yet they weren't playing active roles; they were merely possessions to be won, pawns in men's power plays. They had no value. One of Homer's characters sneered, "Thou art no better than a woman!"[3]

Homer showed women in the narrow confines in which everyone of his world believed they should be kept—in the home, restricted to certain acceptable tasks, subordinate to men. Nowhere did he tell of a woman with a separate identity. A woman was always "the daughter of," or "the wife of," or "the concubine of...."

A GOD WHO BEAT HIS WIFE

Greek goddesses were shown having more active involvement, but as we look at their character and the way they interacted with the gods, we see the tragic source of Greek beliefs about women. Hera was hateful, and her marriage with Zeus, the supreme god, was filled with deception, manipulation, insults, and fear. Listen to what Zeus told his wife about how he would deal with her:

I shall scourge thee with stripes. Dost thou not remember when thou wast hung from on high, and from thy feet I suspended two anvils, and about thy wrists cast a band of gold that might not be broken? And in the air amid the clouds thou didst hang.[4]

Not only did he beat her, but also Zeus was unfaithful, taunting Hera with his sexual exploits. Besides his children with her, he had offspring with at least seven other goddesses.[5] Is it any wonder the ancients came to accept wife abuse and flagrant adultery as normal, when Zeus was their divine ideal?

WOMAN'S "EVIL" ORIGINS

Hesiod was the next important poet. His epic *The Theogony* painted an even bleaker picture of women's origins. *The Theogony* was like the book of Genesis for the Greeks, and later for the Romans. But unlike Genesis, where the creation of Eve was the loving act of the Creator, the story of Pandora's creation was drastically different.

According to Hesiod, a time existed on earth when men lived blissfully without any women. This paradise was lost when Prometheus stole fire from the Olympian gods and shared it with other men. In a vindictive rage, Zeus conceived the most horrifying punishment possible. Woman was created as man's eternal curse. Zeus "made an evil thing," a woman named Pandora, "a beautiful evil...not to be withstood by men." He said, "From her is the race of women...the deadly race...who live amongst mortal men to their great trouble."[6]

Semonides followed Hesiod. Only portions of his work have been preserved, but in one of the most famous he said, "From the beginning the god made the mind of woman a thing apart."[7] There is no common ground between her and man, no shared origin. It was as if men and women came from different planets. You could read Semonides and conclude that women were not even the same species. Every woman Zeus created came from one of ten sources: a long-haired sow, the evil fox, a dog, the dust of the earth, the sea, the stumbling and obstinate donkey, the weasel, the delicate and long-maned mare, the monkey, or the bee.

Semonides then showed how the first nine were all terrible in some way. Each grouping had grave character defects. Only the tenth, the bee, was commendable. "To her alone no blame is attached," yet such women were rare indeed, for they "are granted to husbands as a special favor from Zeus, for they are the best of all and exceptionally wise."[8] You had only one chance in ten of obtaining a good wife.

Even if a man did claim to have one of the few "bee" wives, Semonides had a quick put-down: "For each man likes to regale others with stories of praise about his own wife, while at the same time finding fault with any other man's wife. We don't realize that we all share the same fate. For Zeus designed this as the greatest of all evils and bound us to it in unbreakable fetters."[9]

I've given only a handful from a multitude of material showing the poets' hateful references to women. But the picture becomes clear and very sad from what Homer wrote eight hundred years before Christ, Hesiod in the seventh century B.C., and Semonides in the sixth. Women were not to be trusted. They were given to men as a curse. They were the greatest of evils, for they were the source of all other evil. It was in their nature, the way their god made them.

Is it any wonder the Greeks held women in such low esteem? And is it any wonder that with these early poets as their most cherished voices of authority they went on to commit even greater outrages when they built upon this foundation?

A DYNASTY OF IDEAS

For most of us, philosophy seems far removed from real life, something a few tweed-clad professors discuss in ivory towers. But in fifth-century B.C. Athens, philosophers were celebrities. And in those days, a dynasty was born that would have far-reaching effects. It wasn't a political or military dynasty. It was a dynasty of ideas, and it still rules today.

Socrates was the first. He discipled Plato, who in turn discipled Aristotle, who became the teacher of Alexander the Great. Alexander's conquests spread Greek thinking over the entire Mediterranean world, shaping the civilization into which Jesus came and in which we still live.[10]

All we know of Socrates is what we are told by his disciples (Plato and Xenophon) or his detractors (Aristophanes). Socrates never wrote anything himself. Even the reason for his execution, when the state forced him to drink a cup of hemlock, is a mystery. It's also unclear what Socrates believed about women. His legacy comes only through his disciples, who made a lasting impact on the world. And one thing becomes more and more clear from the writings of those disciples: a growing hatred of women.

PLATO'S PRAGMATIC AND LEWD PROPOSAL

I've already mentioned the power Plato continues to hold in the world of ideas today. Some call Plato one of the world's first supporters of gender equality. On a few occasions he did argue for the education of women. When you read some of his statements in *The Republic* and in *Laws*, it looks like a ray of hope has finally broken through. However, when you look closer, the picture changes dramatically.

First of all, in both of these works, Plato presented an unattainable ideal, a utopian world. He admitted his concepts would probably never be implemented. Besides, he said women were so contrary that they wouldn't listen.[11]

Second, look at what sort of education Plato had in mind. The Athenians considered education to be in large measure physical education. Plato wasn't talking about teaching girls reading, writing, and arithmetic, but was talking about teaching riding, music, and gymnastics.[12] These activities may sound wholesome. At least the girls would be able to get out of the house. But these activities were usually learned in the nude. Plato said that women should exercise "unclad...together with the men."[13] Plato wasn't arguing for women to develop their intellectual capabilities. He was promoting sensual physical practices that would eliminate their standards of modesty. He called for coed dancing parties, saying,

> The women...must strip, since they will be clothed with virtue as a garment, and must take their part with the men in war and the other duties of civic guardianship and have no other occupation....These women shall all be common to all these men, and that none shall cohabit with any privately; and that the children shall be common, and that no parent shall know its own offspring nor any child its parent.[14]

Third and most important, we must understand that Plato made these recommendations for pragmatic reasons. He wasn't changing the beliefs of centuries, suddenly seeing women as individuals with value before God. He said, "If, then, we are *to use* the women for the same things as the men, we must also teach them the same things."[15] It was strictly a utilitarian proposal to get the maximum service for the state.

If we look more closely at Plato's writings, we see the bias against women. Plato declared, "[F]emales are inferior in goodness to males." He echoed Homer and Hesiod when he spoke of "the female sex, that very section of humanity which, owing to its frailty, is in other respects most secretive and intriguing."[16]

CENTURIES AHEAD OF HITLER

Plato gave yet another version of how women came to be. In *Timaeus* he said, "[A]ll those creatures generated as men who proved themselves cowardly and spent their lives in wrongdoing were transformed, at their second incarnation, into women.... In this fashion, then, women and the whole female sex have come into existence."[17] Hell didn't exist in Plato's teaching. The fear of being reincarnated as a woman was enough to keep any man from sinning! And Plato's utopian proposals for a few women to be trained and "selected to cohabit with"[18] the men who lead the state as a means of state-controlled reproduction foreshadowed what Hitler actually did centuries later with the Nazis' attempt to selectively breed superchildren.

It's hard to imagine, but what Plato said about women paled in comparison to what his disciple Aristotle taught. Aristotle wrote that the female is a "monstrosity,"[19] a "deformed male,"[20] and "a deformity...which occurs in the ordinary course of nature."[21] He also said, "The female sex has a more evil disposition than the male, is more forward and less courageous. Women and the female animals bred by us are evidently so.... The males are in every respect opposite to this; their nature is as a class braver and more honest, that of the female being more cowardly and less honest."[22] He said, "The male is by nature superior and the female inferior, the male ruler and the female subject."[23] That is why, wherever possible, Aristotle advised the males to be "separate from the female, since it is something better and more divine."[24] No wonder homosexuality flourished in ancient Greece.

A SUBTLE POISON

The words of ancient philosophers may seem far removed, but these men's ideas have subtly colored what we think, say, and do. Plato's and Aristotle's influence, including their hostility toward women, permeated the known world and the worlds to be discovered. Space in this book doesn't allow us to show in detail how their ideas were repeated for many generations by Greeks, Romans, Jews, Arabs, and Europeans, shaping politicians, artists, educators, architects, generals, and entrepreneurs, but their influence has been huge.

Periodic revivals of Plato's and Aristotle's ideas made a great impact on the church and pagan societies in the Middle Ages, the Renaissance, the Enlightenment, and on much of today's culture. These ideas have been mass marketed. Many have eaten of these men's fruit, not realizing the roots of what they were taught. The ideas of these men have insidiously clouded the clear understanding of the Bible for many, setting us up to view women as an inferior, subordinate "other."

BOX OFFICE HITS OF ATHENS

What we believe determines the way we live our lives. This is true both of individuals and of whole societies. Our values are reflected in our laws, our political institutions, our works of art, and our entertainment. Whether you're at home stretched out on the couch watching a TV sitcom or at the movies catching the latest action flick, you can discern the values of those who produced the show. If the show is a success, it probably reflects the values of a majority in your culture as well.

The ancient Greeks were no exception. When we look at the plays that they liked to see, we can see the grass-roots expression of what Greek poets and philosophers taught.

A HARSH FATE TO BE A WOMAN

All Greek dramas were either tragedies or comedies. The leading tragic dramatists were Aeschylus, Sophocles, and Euripides. The greatest comedy writers were Aristophanes and Menander.[25] Scholars debate whether these writers were criticizing their society's view of women or simply showing life as it was. Either way, these writers showed the inescapable burdens borne by the daughters of Pandora. It was a very harsh fate to be born a woman.

Even when a rare female character dared to rebel against the status quo in a Greek play, she was invariably crushed. A modern writer notes: "Even when [women] are not essential to the plot, [there is] a background of unremitting female misery. Grotesque marriages or illicit liaisons humiliating or unbearable to women abound…."[26]

"Women Are the Vilest Creatures"

Aristophanes had his chorus of men in *The Lysistrata* claim, "Women ARE a shameless set, the vilest creatures going."[27] Aeschylus' character Eteoles harangued women, whom he considered "intolerable creatures." He said, "I would not choose to live with the female sex either in bad times nor during a welcome peace."[28]

Euripides wrote, "clever women are dangerous,"[29] and "stepmothers are always malicious."[30] Menander agreed, saying women are "an abominable caste, hated of all the gods."[31] Euripides' Hippolytus declared, "My woman-hate shall ne'er be sated."[32] And the chorus in *Orestes* sang, "Women were born to mar the lives of men."[33]

One Man Worth More Than Ten Thousand Women

The playwrights weren't content to have men characters rile against women. They went even further. They showed women to be totally worthless. Sophocles' heroine Tereus said, "But now outside my father's house, I am nothing, yes often I have looked on women's nature in this regard, that we are nothing."[34] Euripides' heroine Iphigeneia volunteered herself as a human sacrifice to secure the safe return of the Achaean troops. After all, she declared, "Worthier than ten thousand women one man is to look on light."[35]

I'm giving only a small portion of the hateful things said against women in Greek tragedies and comedies. If these plays were shown today, substituting slurs against Jews, African-Americans, or any other ethnic group in place of the slurs against women, there would be a huge outcry, and justifiably so! They certainly would not be held up in every institution of higher learning as classics of literature.

So whether their audiences were laughing or crying, these playwrights showed the inferior status of women as normal. And as we'll see next, the attitudes shown by poets, philosophers, and playwrights were reinforced by the scientific community of their time.

THE "WISDOM" OF SCIENTISTS

In its early days, medical science was closely linked to the philosophical schools. The physicians philosophized, and the philosophers prescribed medical treatment. That's why much of what we know of ancient Greece's medical understanding comes from Plato and Aristotle.

Hippocrates is called "The Father of Medicine." He taught, "As a result of visions, many people choke to death, more women than men, for the nature of women is less courageous and is weaker."[36] In fact, much of what Greek physicians considered indisputable truth was ridiculous superstition. For instance, they believed menstruating women could drive away hailstorms and tornadoes. They also believed a menstruating woman could blunt the edge of razors and cause pregnant horses to miscarry![37] Yet Greek physicians were the scientific standard throughout the Western world for nearly two thousand years, and their "scientific" opinions reinforced the idea that women were naturally inferior.

Aristotle said, "A woman is as it were an infertile male; [she] is female [because she] lacks the power to concoct semen." He said this was because of the "coldness of her nature."[38] With his repeated statements of the female's inability to produce semen, Aristotle showed that women were necessary but far less "divine" than men, since only semen carried life. Aristotle, Plato, and generations of scientists believed that semen contained miniature human beings.[39]

WOMEN ARE "DEFECTIVE ACCIDENTS"

The belief that males were the sole begetters of life, providing the "seed," with females providing only the "soil," underscored women's inferior status. After all, it was only a reflection of the created order, the way things were meant to be. Aristotle said that, normally, male insemination produced another male in the image of his father. But sometimes the male form was "subverted" by the female matter and produced a defective human specimen—a female. The female was thus inferior in every way: weaker in body, less capable of reason, and morally less capable of will and self-control.

Greek men yearned for another way to have children, to be free of the bane of women. Euripides' hero Jason said, "Men ought to beget children somewhere else, and there should be no female race."[40] His character Hippolytus proposed that Zeus do away with women and let men beget children by offering a sacrifice in his temple so that men can "dwell free in free homes unvexed of womankind."[41]

THE POLITICIANS

In the meantime, what the philosophers and physicians taught, the politicians enforced through their laws. We often hear of Greece being the birthplace of democracy. But two classes of people—slaves and women—were never free, never counted among the *polis*.

LAWS PROMOTING PROSTITUTION

Athens' first influential political leader was Solon, who lived from 640 to 561 B.C. Solon's contribution to the life of Greek women was to pass laws promoting prostitution. If women were merely possessions, objects to be used by men, why not market them in a way that was profitable to the state? Some say that Solon did this because of his own homosexual practices.[42] We don't have sufficient evidence that his homosexuality caused him to propose such laws, but history has shown us that public policy is seldom unrelated to the private lives of government leaders. Solon's laws definitely degraded women and brought unhappiness to men for generations to come.

One of the ancient Greek writers said:

> You, Solon...seeing that the state was full of randy young men...bought some women and put them in certain places where they were to be public and made available to everyone. They stand there uncovered. Take a good look at them, boy. Don't be deceived. Are you satisfied? Ready? So are they. The door is open; the price one obol. In with you. There is no non-sense, no chitchat or trickery here. You do just what you like and the way you like. You're off: wish her goodbye. She has no further claim on you.[43]

Solon's prostitutes were "civil servants of sex." These official state prostitutes helped bring money into the government.[44] This was praised as "a public-spirited measure," and Solon was called the "savior of the state."[45]

Later the Roman Plutarch praised Solon for prescribing that "a man should consort with his wife not less than three times a month—

not for pleasure surely, but as cities renew their mutual agreements from time to time."[46] The fact that they needed such a recommendation shows the dismal condition of Greek marriages. And how could they be otherwise, since other laws encouraged men to find sexual pleasure outside the home?

Shut Up in Dark, Squalid Homes

In the centuries following Solon, leaders such as Pericles and Thucydides said that women should be shut up indoors, never going out, living in anonymous seclusion.[47] The ideal woman was the unknown woman, for the Greek world was a man's world. While men spent most of their day in public, in ornate marble buildings, in the gymnasium, and in the marketplace, respectable women remained at home. Residential quarters were dark, squalid, and unsanitary.[48] Even at home women were segregated into women's quarters, rarely eating with their male relatives.[49]

Never Free, Never an Adult

The men of Greece cut women off from any significant participation in society. Women had no more legal right than slaves.[50] Greek women never inherited from their fathers and weren't permitted to engage in any business transaction worth "more than a bushel of barley."[51] They were shut out of participation in government, not able to vote or serve on a jury. They rarely received any education, although in later centuries, a few girls were taught reading, writing, and poetry. Mathematics, speech, and logic—necessary for public pursuits—were taught only to boys.[52] A boy's education was an opportunity for discovery, but no one considered developing the gifting of a girl as a human being. A few women, like Phintys,[53] stood out as educated companions of philosophers, but they stood out precisely because they were so few.

Education for women was strictly practical, preparing women for life in the confines of the home. Laws kept them perpetual minors, ruled first by their fathers, then by their husbands, and finally by their sons.[54] Perictione, Plato's mother, said a woman's husband is "her whole universe" and instructed a younger woman to make her mind totally subservient to his, "thinking no private thought of her own."[55]

Mistresses for Pleasure, Wives for Bearing Children

By the time of Demosthenes (384–322 B.C.), considered the finest orator of Athens, the double standard was full-blown. In one speech he said, "Mistresses we keep for the sake of pleasure, concubines for the daily care of our persons, but wives to bear us legitimate children."[56]

Men could have multiple liaisons with no twinge of remorse. To do such was considered normal behavior. Women were strictly forbidden to reciprocate. This double standard touched the morality of society to its very core: What was inexcusably sinful for some was acceptable for others. Women were not persons, not worthy of faithful love and respect. They were objects to be used or, if possible, to be avoided altogether.

All this sprang from the idea that woman was created as a curse from the gods. What the poets sang, the philosophers set out to prove. Playwrights wove those beliefs into tragic dramas and witty comedies. Physicians cemented the beliefs in scientific garb. Political leaders made laws based on the beliefs. A double standard prevented trust and love in marriage. And all of this combined to guarantee that a woman would be born, live, and die on the margins of society, cut off from business and education, excluded from the life and love of her people. It all began with a vindictive god, angry over stolen fire. The story brought generations of pain for Pandora's daughters.

Could anything be further removed from a story that began with a different God, a God who was brokenhearted over the sin committed by both a man and a woman? This God came to them, promising redemption for them both in the midst of a paradise lost. The daughters of Pandora were locked into bondage with no hope, no way out. And their sad heritage was passed on to their Roman sisters.

6.

DAUGHTERS OF VENUS

By David Hamilton

*I*t's important to understand the values and beliefs of the
Romans because that's the world Jesus came into, the ruling culture that defined what was normal for men and women and
what was abnormal. It was also what Paul and the early Christians
confronted, for the *Pax Romana* ruled the Mediterranean world. We
can't see how truly radical Jesus' and Paul's teachings were until we see
them in contrast to what everyone else believed.

Alexander the Great's empire quickly fell, but even as political
power crumbled, the Greeks continued to rule in another way. The
new conquerors, the Romans, were plain, practical men—disciplined,
fair to a large degree, but less elegant, less refined. Though the Romans
came to rule Greek cities and lands, the Greeks ruled Roman hearts
and minds. Like a younger stepbrother, the Romans never felt quite
equal to the Greeks in matters of the intellect and the spirit. So, like a
stepbrother, they tried to trace their ethnic roots as close to the "real
family" as possible. It's not surprising that their first great poet, Virgil,
wrote *The Aeneid* and gave the Romans myths that tied them back to
Troy, back to the tales told by Homer.

GENERATIONS OF UNHAPPY MARRIAGES

The Romans didn't always believe that they came from Troy. It's significant that Virgil began to write during Augustus's rise to power, just before Jesus was born, at the very time the austere republic was changing into a grand empire. Virgil's *Aeneid* gave these new world rulers a little more pedigree.

Unlike the stories of the Greeks, who believed they were the glorious descendants of victorious warriors, Virgil's story traced Roman lineage back to a lesser prince of the defeated Trojans named Aeneas. Virgil also gave the Romans the gods and goddesses of the Greeks, renaming them but offering the same values and similar beliefs, including those regarding the nature of women. Thus, the Greek philosophical dynasty lived on, ruling and shaping the Roman world for centuries to come.

PROSTITUTE OR DOMESTIC NAG

The Greek goddess Hera became the Roman goddess Juno. Juno fought against Aeneas as he fled from the scene of defeat in Troy, going from place to place until he settled in Italy. Along the way his ally was Venus, who came to his aid against Juno time and again. In fact, Virgil reveals in the story that Aeneas was actually the son of Venus and a mortal she had sex with.

So the Romans had a divine origin, too, but it was through Venus (the Greek Aphrodite), goddess of erotic love, the protector of prostitutes. Notice that her enemy was Juno, the goddess of marriage. Venus was beautiful and desirable, known for her many deceptive sexual escapades. We've already seen what Juno (Hera) was like— shrewish, insubordinate, scheming, physically abused by her husband, powerless to prevent his many infidelities. Both Juno and Venus were deceivers, but at least Venus had glamour. However, neither goddess was a good role model for Rome to base her ideals of womanhood on.

The foundations were laid for generations of unhappy marriages. How could a culture that worshiped the goddess of adultery and prostitution and viewed the goddess of marriage as such an unpleasant hag see women as anything but objects of erotic desire on the one hand or unpleasant necessities on the other? It got so bad that Julius Caesar's adopted son Augustus had a difficult job convincing Roman men to marry.[1] This was the natural outcome of their beliefs. You can't love that which you use.

CAN'T LIVE WITH THEM, CAN'T LIVE WITHOUT THEM

There were some genuinely positive attitudes about marriage in the writings of the Romans, but they were definitely in the minority. Most Roman writers held women and marriage in low esteem. One named Aulus Gellius said, "If we could survive without a wife, citizens of Rome, all of us would do without that nuisance; but since nature has so decreed that we cannot manage comfortably with them, nor live any way without them, we must plan for our lasting preservation rather than for our temporary pleasure."[2]

Marriage was reduced to an obligatory duty, one often performed unwillingly.[3] The Romans never hated women quite as much as the Greeks did, but they had a bleak opinion of marriage and believed that women had a precise place—firmly "under their thumbs."[4]

Ovid encouraged men to cheat not only on their wives, but also on their mistresses, saying, "This I do advise, have two mistresses at once; he is yet stronger who can have more." This was only right, because women were considered basically evil. Treating them badly was giving them their just rewards. Ovid said, "If you are wise, cheat women only.... Deceive the deceivers; they are mostly an unrighteous sort; let them fall into the snare they have laid."[5] Men could never trust their women, because they believed they were daughters of Venus, known for her cheating heart.

NOT ENOUGH VALUE TO HAVE A NAME

Because women were inferior, the Romans treated them as if they were not really people. This was shown by the way they named their children. "Roman citizens had three names....Women, however, had only the [clan] name and the family name. They had no individual names."[6]

Imagine being of so little worth that when you were born you weren't even given a first name! Instead of being given her own name, a Roman female was referred to by the feminine form of her father's family name. "Thus, Gaius Julius Caesar's daughter was called Julia; Marcus Tullius Cicero's, Tullia. In fact, so little ingenuity was expended on names for girls that sisters regularly shared the same one, distinguished only as 'the elder' and 'the younger,' or Martia Secunda, and Martia Tertia—Martia the second, Martia the third, and so forth."[7]

MEN ARE FROM MARS, WOMEN ARE FROM VENUS?

Two figures were the most important to the Romans—Aeneas and Romulus. The Roman race traced its origins to Aeneas, the illegitimate son of Venus and a mortal; the city of Rome supposedly came from a descendant of Aeneas, Romulus. A historian named Livy, writing during the time of Jesus, said that Romulus was the son of Mars (god of war, the Greek Ares).[8]

Leaders invoked Romulus' name on every solemn occasion, and around the sacred family hearth, little children heard stories of his valor. The most famous was how young Romulus and his twin brother Remus were nursed by a she-wolf. Surely such an origin was the work of the gods, the Romans reasoned. The gods must have destined them for greatness.

So the Romans were doubly divine: descendants of Mars/Ares, god of war through Romulus; and of Venus/Aphrodite, goddess of erotic love through Aeneas. These two gods made a powerful imprint on the Roman culture, on the way Romans thought of themselves, and on the way Romans believed things should be between a man and a woman. We still have echoes of the importance they placed on these two gods. Since Romans were divinely destined to rule this planet, they named the two closest planets to Earth, Mars and Venus. Even the astronomical symbols for these two planets came to be symbols of what Romans considered truly masculine (♂) or feminine (♀).

As the Romans saw it, the ideal man was like Mars; a perfect woman was like Venus. Men were warriors, women were sexual consorts. Men were strong and conquering; women were beautiful and sexually available.

ALWAYS AN OUTSIDER, ALWAYS A MINOR

Two other things are important to understand regarding women and their role in ancient Rome:

— the worship of ancestors
— the abandonment of children deemed unfit

At first it seems like women had an important role to play in the most widespread religion of Rome. It was their responsibility never to allow the sacred fire of the family hearth to go out. The hearth in every home was the place where ancestors were worshiped, the center of a family's very identity. But when you look closer, you realize that the women's participation was hollow. Women only kept the hearth fires going. The family hearth and its gods belonged to the father. As soon as a girl was given to another family in marriage, she stopped worshiping the gods she had worshiped from the time she was a baby. She had to worship the ancestors of her new family. She learned other rites and said other prayers. She had to forget her ancestors and pay homage to the unknown.[9] She never really belonged to a religion but was passed from that of her father to that of her husband.

What we believe affects everything we do, so naturally this belief made a great impact on a woman's social and legal standing. "Never having a sacred fire which belonged to her, she had nothing of what gave authority in the house. She never commanded; she was never even free, or mistress of herself. She was always near the hearth of another, repeating the prayer of another; for all the acts of religious life she needed a superior, and for all the acts of civil life a guardian."[10]

Since a woman wasn't a real worshiper in her own right, she didn't have other rights. Like Greek women, she never came of age, but rather passed from the guardianship of her father to that of her husband or, if widowed, to another male relative. This was because women were considered mentally inferior. Gaius explained, "Women, even those of full age, should be in guardianship as being scatterbrained."[11]

THE RIGHT TO KILL WIVES

Because the sacred fire of a family was passed from father to son, adultery by one's wife was a grievous sin. It disturbed the order of birth.[12] That's why Roman law gave the husband the right to kill his wife for either adultery or drunkenness, since alcohol made a woman more likely to commit adultery.[13] Therefore, women weren't allowed to drink wine. Plutarch said that this was where the custom of Latin men greeting their female relatives with a kiss began. It wasn't affection— the men just wanted to get close enough to smell the women's breath![14]

Cato said, "If you catch your wife in adultery, you can kill her with impunity; she, however, cannot dare to lay a finger on you if you commit adultery, nor is it the law."[15] Why? Because a man's promiscuity didn't threaten the genetic purity of the family.

KILLING LITTLE GIRLS

It was quite common in the ancient world to allow unwanted babies to die by exposure. This was true for the Romans and the Greeks. Unwanted babies were simply discarded on a hillside, beside a road, or in the woods by a river. According to the Roman historian Livy, Romulus and his twin Remus were abandoned beside the Tiber.[16] After Romulus established the settlement of Rome, he passed laws trying to limit this practice. He didn't want young Roman boys to go through what he had experienced.

Regrettably, he didn't extend equal protection to Roman girls. His laws forced the citizens to raise every male baby unless it was a cripple or a "monster from birth."[17] Females, except for the firstborn female, could be disposed of. The practice was legally and socially accepted.

The very fact that Romulus had to make a law guaranteeing that a family keep at least one daughter alive shows how widespread the practice of killing female babies was. How many female babies were killed is evidenced by such things as burial records that show twice as many male adult burials as female, and by stories of Greek colonies founded by men alone who had to scour the countryside for wives among the natives.[18] From records during the Roman Empire, even after wars that took the lives of many men, there were still far more men than women.[19]

"Ethnic cleansing" thus isn't a new phenomenon. Plato recommended in *The Republic* that the state should determine who lived and who did not, "properly" disposing of "the offspring of the inferior."[20] Although this was never implemented in an efficient, systematic way, the right to terminate the lives of unwanted babies was upheld by Greeks and Romans until Christianity became the state religion under Constantine. The great majority of those doomed babies were female.

Listen to a father-to-be named Hilarion, writing a letter to his wife around the time of Christ: "If—good luck to you!—you bear offspring, if it is a male, let it live; if it is a female, expose it."[21] How casually the father was willing to snuff out the life of his daughter! This horror is all the more ghastly because it was so common.

THE ORIGINAL BOTTOM-LINE GUYS

The daughters of Rome who did survive faced a somber life. Some modern historians argue that Roman women achieved greater freedom, while others strongly disagree. There are reasons for this discrepancy.

First, most scholars who praise the Romans for giving women a few rights are comparing them to the Greeks—one of the most woman-hating civilizations in all of history! It would be hard to find a society that so elevated one sex and subjugated the other as the ancient Greeks. Who wouldn't appear more tolerant when compared to them?

Second, the Romans were always guided by practical results. They had enemies to fend off and a world to conquer. If the old ideals weren't working, they easily traded them for something new, not because of a change in their foundational beliefs but because they were after results. Pragmatism ruled the day in Rome. They were the original "bottom-line" guys.

MODEST GAINS FOR ELITE WOMEN

As time passed, the lot of *some* women improved. Loopholes were found in the laws of guardianship. Some women did quite well in the financial world. When wars arose, most of the men went to battle, and many died. This changed things for a minority of women. But these new opportunities weren't based on a change of belief concerning women's intrinsic value. They were temporary measures taken for expediency.

In any case, when scholars speak of the gains of Roman women, you have to ask *which* Roman women. It certainly wasn't better for the freedwomen, the poor, the concubines, the prostitutes, or the slaves. A very small minority of the women of Rome—the aristocratic free-born—saw an improvement in their lives. And their small gains were because of their newfound wealth and their class, not from an appreciation for their gender.

Listen to Cato in 215 B.C. urging the Romans to return to the old ways, saying that unless they set bounds on "this untamed creature [the females]...what will they not attempt?...If you suffer them to seize these bonds one by one and wrench themselves free...do you think that you will be able to endure them? The moment they begin to be your equals, they will be your superiors."[22]

"SLAVES, WIVES, DOGS, HORSES, AND DONKEYS"

Cicero echoed his concern in the century before Christ, saying, "[T]he slaves come to behave with unseemly freedom, wives have the same rights as their husbands, and in the abundance of liberty even the dogs, the horses, and the asses are so free in their running about that men must make way for them in the streets."[23]

Notice the ones listed by Cicero—slaves, wives, dogs, horses, and donkeys. These are all *possessions*. A few women might have gotten new privileges, but underlying beliefs hadn't changed—women were counted as possessions, just as slaves were.

Female slaves had the worst lives of all. Like male slaves and women of other classes, they were "objects" of the law, not "subjects." But female slaves also had to do the heaviest work, cleaning, grinding grain, and cultivating the fields. And they had one more duty—they had to be available to the male members of the household should the men want sexual relations at home rather than outside the home with prostitutes.[24]

No, the world of Rome remained a dismal place for women. It was into this world that the Gospel came, a tiny seed for the mightiest social revolution of all.

7.

DAUGHTERS OF EVE

By David Hamilton

You couldn't have a greater contrast than the creation of man and woman in Genesis and the story that Hesiod told the ancient Greeks. Whereas Zeus created Pandora as an "evil thing," an eternal curse for men, the God of the Bible used His creative talent to form Eve as a beautiful gift to man. He set the couple in the Garden as friends and lovers. Instead of the brutal battles of gods and goddesses in Greek and Roman myths, we see mutuality, partnership, and love.

In the first three chapters of the Bible, man and woman are shown to have

— a shared origin
— a shared destiny
— a shared tragedy
— a shared hope

Genesis 1:1–2 begins by emphasizing **who** the Creator was. Then Genesis 1:3 through 2:3 gives us a broad panorama of **what** was created, starting with the nonanimate world, continuing with the animal world, and concluding with humanity. Then Genesis 2:4–25 gives a closer look, going back into the story to show **how** God created man and woman.

When you view the art of a great master like Rembrandt, first you stand back and take in the beauty of the whole. Then you bring your face within inches of the canvas to scrutinize the individual brush strokes. This is similar to the way the story of Creation is told in these two chapters. Genesis 1 gives the big picture of God's Creation, then Genesis 2 takes us closer for a more precise inspection of the Master Artist's brush strokes.

Before we look at how God created us, there's something special to notice. When God was ready for the crowning touch of His Creation—humanity—Scripture breaks into poetry for the first time:

> So God created man in his own image,
> In the image of God he created him;
> Male and female he created them.[1]

Hebrew poetry is based not on rhyme or the rhythm of sounds but on the rhythm of parallel ideas. One thought echoes the preceding, enriching it from a different perspective, embellishing it with synonyms. In this poem about God's work, the first line emphasizes the image of God; the second line builds on that, saying this image was true for all of humanity;[2] then the third line crescendos, saying that humanity was created as male and female.

In Ephesians 2:10, Paul said, "We are God's workmanship." The Greek word for *workmanship* Paul used was the source of the English word *poem*. Humanity—man and woman together—was God's master poem!

It Wasn't Paradise Yet

For the details of how God created us, Genesis 2:4 flashes back to the middle of the story, what happened on day six. God created the first man "from the dust of the ground,"[3] just as He made all the animals.[4]

To see the drama, we must read chapter 2 in light of the sequence of events of chapter 1. Throughout the process of Creation, God had paused to give His opinion of what He had just made. Six times during the process of Creation He had said, "It is good."[5] Then, in the middle of day six, He paused and looked at His handiwork and said, "It is not good." What brought out that only negative reaction?

How could anything in Eden not be good? After all, God lavished the Garden with tall shade trees, sparkling brooks, green meadows dotted with red, blue, and yellow flowers, delicious fruit, even gold and precious stones. Yet God looked at man standing there in the midst of this abundance and said, "It is not good for the man to be alone."[6] So He created woman to be with man. Her arrival transformed Eden into paradise. Then God gave His final approval, declaring that "it was very good."[7]

A SHARED ORIGIN

Next, look how God created woman. To make sure that we would understand that man and woman were equally made in the divine image, God did not create Eve from the dust of the ground as He had Adam. If He had, someone would have claimed females had a different origin, for perhaps the pile of dirt God used for her was inferior to the dirt He used to make Adam! You would have ended up with a different origin for woman than for man—something like Semonides did with his story of long-haired sows, weasels, and monkeys![8] This would have made Eve somehow less than Adam, with her bearing less of the image of God.

No, God wanted to emphasize that both were made of the same substance. Eve would not be a separate creation but a separate expression of the same creation. You might say Eve was the first human clone, but with a significant twist! God made Eve from "the rib he had taken out of the man."[9] He reached down into the man's very core, took some of his DNA, adjusted it slightly, and made the first woman.

First Doesn't Mean Best

Some say that because Adam was made first, he is superior. By the same thinking, pigs and dogs would be superior to man, since they were created earlier! As the rabbis said, "If a man's mind becomes [too] proud, he may be reminded that the gnats preceded him in the order of creation."[10] God's design for each of His created beings, not the sequence of their arrival, is what gives them value.

Serving Alongside, Not Underneath

The Bible says God designed woman as "a helper suitable for him."[11] Some use this to say that man was greater and woman was just his "helper." But take a look at the Hebrew phrase translated "a helper suitable"—*'ezer k͏eneged*. Let's examine the first word in this phrase, *'ezer,* a powerful word in the Hebrew. Think about when you were a kid and needed help with a math problem. Did you go to someone smarter than you, or someone not so smart? What if you were having trouble with a bully at school? Did you seek help from someone bigger and stronger or someone smaller and weaker?

That is exactly what this Hebrew word *'ezer* means. A helper is not a subservient peon but a more capable, more powerful, more intelligent ally. It's the same word used throughout the Old Testament when talking about God.[12] The psalmist used this word when he declared, "I lift up my eyes to the hills—where does my help come from? My help comes from the LORD, the Maker of heaven and earth."[13] "The one who helps is the one who has something to offer the one who is helpless or needs help. Adam needed help. He had no partner. God created a partner—a helper."[14]

The second word of that phrase, *k*e*neged*, shows what kind of partner God gave Adam. God qualified the powerful word *'ezer* with the adjective *k*e*neged*, which means "equal." He made for Adam an equal helper. In Genesis 2:18, God gave man "a help corresponding to him… equal and adequate to himself."[15] "Woman was created not to serve Adam, but to *serve with* Adam."[16] If God hadn't added that word *equal* to the word *'ezer*, we might have been writing this book trying to prove that men could be leaders, too!

How did Adam react when he first laid eyes on woman? He broke into song with

> This is now bone of my bones
> and flesh of my flesh;
> she shall be called 'woman,'
> for she was taken out of man.[17]

So the first human words we hear in the Bible are a love song. You could say Adam looked at what God had given him and said a big primeval "Wow!"

Man Leaves All for Woman

Every time you've attended a wedding you've probably heard the phrase "For this reason a man will leave his father and mother and be united to his wife."[18] The constant repetition of this scripture has rendered it meaningless to most of us. We fail to realize how radically revolutionary it was in its original context. In no culture of antiquity did a man give up anything to be married to a woman. Women were not considered worthy of such a sacrifice. On the other hand, a woman had to give up everything on the day of her marriage.

God's statement in Genesis 2 totally reverses the world's value system. God's perspective is that a man should consider a woman to be of such high value that he would be willing to give up anything—even those who gave him his most treasured possession, his life—to be forever united to her!

A Shared Destiny

God had a great destiny for men and women. When He first laid out His plans He said, "...and let *them* rule over...all the earth."[19] That's shared leadership with global implications. As if to underline this, God then "blessed *them* and said to *them*, 'Be fruitful and increase in number; fill the earth and subdue it. Rule over the fish of the sea and the birds of the air and over every living creature that moves on the ground.'"[20] God's mandate was for both of them to rule.

Notice that God didn't give man dominion over the earth until woman was standing beside him. Adam realized that Eve was serving with him. After their sin, Adam said, "The woman whom Thou gavest to be with me."[21] Adam did *not* say, "The woman Thou gavest me," but said the one "to be *with* me." Lee Anna Starr says, "Eve was not his property....[but] his associate in government as well as his companion in the home."[22]

Recall how the Romans clumped together women, slaves, and horses, seeing them as possessions. What a different viewpoint the Bible has! We'll see a little later how Jewish scholars watered down that revelation before Jesus came. But if we look only at the Word of God, we learn in its first chapters that leadership was given by God and had nothing to do with gender. God created man and woman and then shared some of His authority with them. Man and woman were going to join Him in ruling the world. What a heartbreak that they threw that away, surrendering their authority to an enemy of God.

A Shared Tragedy

The beauty of Genesis 1 and 2 was followed by the shared tragedy of Genesis 3. The telling and retelling of this story, with popular culture

adding fairy-tale elements, have inoculated us against its horror. We
need to read it afresh. All the calamities that have broken God's heart
and devastated people for thousands of years were bound up in those
bites of fruit. Pain, torment, the twisting of nature, the perversion of
humanity's gifts—incalculable loss came when Adam and Eve turned
their backs on God. They were enticed by the empty promise that they
would "be like God."[23] The irony was, they had already been created in
the image of God and given the opportunity to rule with Him!

Something often overlooked is their apparent unity at the moment
of their sin. When the serpent spoke to the woman, he asked, "Did God
really say, 'You must not…'?"[24] In English, *you* can refer to one or more
than one. But Hebrew has two different words; the *you* used here is
plural. Eve also responded in plural, saying, "We may…."[25] The serpent's next words again used the plural *you* when he said, "You will not
surely die."[26] Even though we only hear the words of the serpent and
Eve, the text suggests that Adam was standing there, too, a silent
accomplice in the crime.[27] This becomes plain when, after taking a
bite, Eve turned and "gave some to her husband, *who was with her*, and
he ate it."[28]

Once again the Bible story stands in sharp contrast to the Greek
myths. Evil didn't enter the world through one woman, Pandora. It
entered through a human couple. Both were present. Both participated.
Both were guilty before God, and both would suffer the consequences.[29]

The Beginning of the Battle of the Sexes

Those consequences included the destruction of male-female relationships. Immediately, shame and blame, manipulation and control
began.[30] Both had thrown away their destiny, and both were responsible. And they couldn't undo the tragedy they had unleashed. For that
they would need a Redeemer.

People often call God's words in Genesis 3 "the curse." But God
cursed only the serpent and the ground—the spiritual and natural
worlds. God's words to Adam and Eve only told of the inevitable consequences of their decision. God wasn't putting anything on them. He
was describing a future filled with sin. His words didn't declare His
will for humanity. They merely described the inevitable results of sin
in the lives of those who violate His will.

A SHARED HOPE

Then in a heartbeat, right after their sin was revealed, God promised the guilty pair that He would fight the invader who tricked them. He gave the first Messianic prophecy: A Redeemer would come! Jesus—the seed of woman—would restore hope to all their descendants. Speaking to the serpent, God said: "And I will put enmity between you and the woman, and between your offspring and hers; he will crush your head, and you will strike his heel."[31]

Look how He described Eve's offspring: The Hebrew for *offspring* is literally *seed*. What an extraordinary statement in light of Greek medical thought[32] as well as that of the other ancients! They thought man sowed his "seed" in woman's "soil." Scientists didn't discover that women had anything but a passive role in the creation of life until the 1800s. Then science finally caught up with the accuracy of God's Word. As Starr points out:

> *"Her seed"* was something uninspired man would never have allowed. Prior to the time of Francis I, of France, dissection of the human body was regarded as sacrilege. Not until this prejudice was overcome was it known that the ovum was the mother's contribution to life. In 1872, Nov Baer discovered the ovule.[33]

If only God's people had held on to the purposes revealed in God's Word! Next, we will see how some Jewish teachers abandoned the shared origin, destiny, tragedy, and hope for men and women found in the first three chapters of Genesis and instead added teachings that God never intended, darkening and distorting the image of God.

8.

DISTORTING THE IMAGE

By David Hamilton

The Old Testament tells the story of how God prepared the way for the woman's Seed, the coming Messiah. In its pages we see a few people holding on to God's promise while most are wandering farther and farther away from God's original design. We see respected women such as Deborah and Huldah rising to their destiny in God.[1] We also see women who weren't respected, such as Tamar and the Levite's concubine.[2]

As centuries passed, many Jews strayed from God's original call. Instead of the Jews spreading God's revelation and affecting their world, the world left its mark on them. The Jews were shaped more and more by the values of their pagan neighbors. Some Jews swallowed the ruling Greek philosophy whole. Later in this chapter, we'll look at what one Jew—Philo of Alexandria—did to mix the writings of Aristotle and Moses.

WALLS ENCIRCLING WALLS

At the same time, other Jews built "walls" to protect their religious beliefs. They put the oral traditions of the rabbis in the Mishnah. Soon those walls weren't enough, so walls were built around the walls, outer defenses to protect inner defenses: the Tosefta, the Jerusalem Talmud, and the Babylonian Talmud—these teachings of rabbis were added to the Word of God. The rabbis insisted that these "ramparts of ritual [contained in the Mishnah and the Talmud] could preserve [the Jew] from the Gentiles more securely than any frontiers guarded by troops."[3] Regrettably for many, the traditions of man became what Jesus called "burdens hard to bear."[4]

A sea of differences separated Philo and the rabbis, but neither offered women a safe haven. Instead, God's revealed role for women was lost by both—by those who had compromised with the dominant pagan culture and by those who tried to avoid the influence of the Greeks and the Romans. Let's begin by looking at those who thought they were keeping God's revelation untainted.

The first "wall"—the Mishnah—was obviously a document written by men for men. Men's "interpretations [of scriptures] regarding women seem so forced that one must assume these scholars first held a bias against women and then imposed that attitude upon the words of Scripture."[5] For instance, the Mishnah contained a long section with rules for women, Seder Nashim, but included nothing equal for men. It has been noted that "the absence of a corresponding [section for men shows]…that in the patriarchies men make rules about women, but women do not make rules about men….Women…occupy a marginal position."[6]

The rabbis didn't always agree with one another in either the Mishnah or the opinions that made up the Talmud. Their writings were filled with heated arguments that continued for generations. Some of these debates were about women. At times, the arguments were based on the account in Genesis, and the value of women was upheld. More often, though, the rabbis strayed from the values shown in Genesis. They heaped scorn upon Eve, claiming that the serpent had sex with her, and this had "infused her with lust."[7] Although Genesis showed the essential unity between men and women, the rabbis preferred to point out the differences.[8]

DEVALUING WOMEN

It's easy to read our own cultural values into Scripture rather than look at God's Word and form cultural values from it. The rabbis seemed to have done the former, saying, "Compared with Adam, Eve was like a monkey to a human being."[9] Their belief in male superiority shaped their teaching, as shown by the following examples:

— "A man must be saved alive sooner than a woman, and his lost property must be restored sooner than hers."[10]

— "Though a man has the *exclusive* right to his wife's sexuality, the wife's right to the husband's sexual function is never *exclusive*. She cannot legally preclude her husband from taking additional wives or having sexual relations with unmarried women."[11]

— "Ten *kabs* of gossip descended to the world: nine were taken by women."[12]

— "Women are gluttonous."[13]

— "Women are of unstable temperament."[14]

— "Woe to him who has female children! A daughter is like a trap for her father.... When she is small he fears that she might be seduced; when she is a maiden—that she become promiscuous; when she matures—that she might not marry; when she marries—that she might not produce children; when she grows old—that she would practice witchcraft."[15]

WOMEN MORE SINFUL THAN MEN

Contrary to the teaching of Scripture, the rabbis said that woman is more prone to sin than man.[16] "For evil are women, my children... the angel of the Lord told me, and taught me, that women are overcome by the spirit of fornication more than men."[17] That's why so many of the rabbis' laws concentrated on controlling women's supposed natural bent to lust.

THE "BLEEDING PHARISEES"

Everything about the female body was considered sexual. The rabbis said, "[I]f one gazes at the little finger of a woman, it is as if he gazed at her secret place!"[18] Women were held accountable not only for their own sins, but also for the lust they awakened in men.

Like the Greeks, the rabbis believed that women were possessions to be used or, better yet, avoided altogether. If possible, one should not look at or talk to a woman. One class of Pharisees was called the "Bleeding Pharisees" because they often ran into things while walking with their eyes shut to keep from seeing a woman. They praised one

man who locked his wife inside every time he went out.[19] They went so
far as to compare a man's wife to a piece of meat: "A man may do whatever he pleases with his wife [at intercourse].... Meat which comes from
the slaughterhouse may be eaten salted, roasted, cooked or seethed."[20]

RARE PRAISE

It would be unfair to say that all the rabbis' teaching about women
was negative. Some occasionally said positive things. One who supported the value of women was Gamaliel, Paul's mentor, who likened
women to a "golden pitcher."[21] Another rabbi praised his mother
beautifully. Whenever he heard his mother's footsteps, he said, "I will
arise before the approaching *Shechinah*" (a Hebrew word for the glory
of God).[22] The reason a rabbi praising a woman stands out is that it
was so rare! Sometimes even their attempt at praise showed that rabbis
thought of women as possessions—heart-warming possessions, but
possessions nonetheless. Many of their laws categorized wives together
with slaves, cattle, and other "possessions."[23]

This is why it was easy for a man to divorce his wife, but not the
other way around. As one writer said, "Whereas an owner can give up
his property, property cannot abandon its owner."[24] Even if her husband became insane, a woman was chained to him for life.

The rabbis disagreed as to what constituted "righteous" grounds for
a man to discard his wife.[25] They tried to draw Jesus into this argument,
but He refused to take sides. Instead, He pointed them back to Genesis,
quoting God's original purpose for marriage: "For this reason a man
will leave his father and mother and be united to his wife, and the two
will become one flesh."[26] He said, "So they are no longer two, but one.
Therefore what God has joined together, let man not separate."[27]

CULTURAL BLINDERS

Jesus' words did far more than discourage divorce. They elevated
woman to God's original intention—equality with man. His words
stood in stark contrast to those of the rabbis who had so distorted
God's simple revelation. But the religious teachers had cultural blinders on that kept them from seeing the truth: that women were created
in the image of God, just as men had been. Because they denied that
simple truth, they had to erect elaborate explanations, applying different laws to men and women through a complex grid.

We may marvel that the Jews had the Word of God and yet were so blind to the truth. But have we done any differently in the church? Haven't we made categories of whom God could use and how? We can only wonder what Jesus would say if He were to come today and confront our cultural prejudices.

BUILDING WALLS GOD NEVER INTENDED

What an irony that in their zeal to protect Judaism from the pollution around them, the rabbis ended up with such unscriptural teaching. Their opinion of women was more similar to that of their pagan neighbors than to that which God had revealed in Genesis.

Jewish women were marginalized from the worship of God. They couldn't participate in many of the most important rituals. They were segregated into a separate court in Herod's temple, even though this was not part of God's original design for the tabernacle, nor was it the case in Solomon's temple, nor in the temple rebuilt by the exiles returning from Babylon.

As is so often the case, art followed belief. The rabbis had built walls of teaching that divided people. Now the architects of Herod's temple made those walls literal, with separate courts dividing Gentiles from Jews, then Jewish women from Jewish men. The architecture underlined what the architects believed: Some were allowed closer access to God than others. The rabbis of the Mishnah had compromised so much that they actually praised the design of the godless king instead of seeing how radically Herod had distorted God's design.[28]

WOMEN DON'T COUNT

Most Jews could come to the temple only a few times a year for special celebrations. Weekly worship took place in the synagogue. By the second century after Christ, archaeology suggests that the synagogues kept women in screened second-floor galleries that they entered by a back door.[29] The rabbis decreed that a synagogue could be established wherever there was a quorum of ten *men*.[30] Even though there was no basis in Scripture for this, they were sending a clear message to their women: "You (quite literally!) do not count."[31]

An important public celebration of Judaism was the public reading of the Torah (the first five books of the Old Testament). Even in this, a woman was usually excluded. The rabbis said that the reading of the Torah by a woman would dishonor the community.[32] Women were also discouraged from private study of the Torah, despite the fact that this was their closest tie to God, their highest form of worship.[33] The rabbis said, "Happy [is] he who was brought up in the Torah and whose labour was in the Torah."[34] If that's true, then the flip side is also true: Unhappy is she who was not brought up in the study of the Torah!

Most rabbis would not think of teaching the Torah to a woman. Rabbis such as Gamaliel, Paul's mentor, who taught his daughter, were the rare exception.[35] Every young boy was required to study the Law. It was a primary way to gain merit before God, but the Tosefta said that women were "not obligated."[36] This clearly communicated to women that they had no real value. The rabbis taught that to be in right relationship with God, you had to observe the Law He gave Moses at Sinai. Yet that law was binding only on free adult males. Therefore, no children, no slaves, and no women could serve God fully.[37]

Boys grew up to be men. Even a male slave had the possibility of becoming a free man. But women could never have the same relationship with God as men had. The rabbis told women to earn God's favor by making sure their children and their husbands went to the "house of study," the rabbinic academy.[38] A woman had to reach her spiritual destiny through others. She was always one step removed from God, even in the privacy of her home.

Though some rabbis believed that God endowed women with more understanding than men,[39] they did nothing to encourage women's spiritual or intellectual development. When they said that women were "not obligated" to study the Law, they made women "peripheral Jews."[40] In the words of Hillel, "An ignoramous cannot be a saint."[41] Teaching a girl the laws of God was considered a waste of time—or even worse. Rabbi Eliezer said, "If any man gives his daughter a knowledge of the Law it is as though he taught her lechery."[42] Similarly, the Jerusalem Talmud states, "Let the words of *Torah* be burned up, but let them not be delivered to women."[43]

THE DEEPENING DARKNESS

Someone has said that you can't hear the good news until you've really heard the bad news. Put in another way, a candle never seems brighter than when held up in pitch darkness. So before we turn to

Jesus and His message of hope and freedom, we must look at still one more arena of the darkness He came to penetrate.

While the rabbis were trying to build walls around Judaism, others were enthusiastically building bridges, linking their Jewish heritage with that of the Greeks and the Romans. One of the best known of these was Philo of Alexandria, who lived during the time of Jesus.

Philo was one of the first persons in the Judeo-Christian tradition who tried to marry revealed Truth (with a capital "T") to the "truth" that arose out of the reasoning of man. Regrettably, Philo was fabulously successful. He not only built a bridge to Greek and Roman philosophy, but also served as a bridge to the future. Many times church leaders and theologians would follow his lead and embrace these philosophies, too.

The deadly virus of Greek thinking would spread and infect religious teaching throughout Western civilization. For instance, today we are led to believe that revealed truth from God must be irrational. If we are "educated" and want to have faith, we must "take a leap of faith" into irrationality. This was an idea that began with Philo and his attempts to combine the rational thought of the Greeks with the revealed truth of the Bible. This is absolutely wrong. Revealed truth *is* reasonable, but it is built upon a radically different foundational idea.

Greek philosophies were built on the idea that man is the measure of all things. Using only his reason, man can figure out anything. The Bible's foundational idea is that an immeasurable God created humanity and everything else that can be measured. How can the finite begin to fully comprehend the infinite? Truth comes as God reveals it to His creation, man.

These two ideas—rationalism and revelation—are ideas violently opposed to each other. Anyone who tries to mix them as Philo did ends up with something like water and oil. When you mix what cannot be mixed together, one will rise to the top. When Philo tried to reinterpret revealed truth to accommodate the Greeks' presuppositions, man's ideas came out on top. The oil of Greek teaching rose to the surface in Philo's mixture, clouding the truth. It was a devilish brew.

PHILO JOINED GREEKS IN HATING WOMEN

Philo loved Greek culture, so it shouldn't surprise us that he joined the Greeks in their hatred of women. Using Greek philosophy in one hand and his reinterpretation of Scripture in the other, he poured contempt on all women. He said woman "was the beginning of evil."[44] The female sex wasn't just weaker, it was more wicked, more easily deceived, and more prone to deceive.[45]

According to Philo, it was the way women were created. He said, "The judgments of women as a rule are weaker" than those of men[46] for they "want of sense."[47] Echoing Aristotle, he stated firmly that "the male is more perfect than the female."[48] Therefore, "it was fitting that man should rule over immortality and everything good, but woman over death and everything vile."[49]

BENDING GOD'S WORD

To support this unbiblical view, Philo pulled scripture out of context. Instead of allowing the Word to shine light on his cultural beliefs, Philo bent the Word to serve his beliefs. Instead of presenting Genesis 3:16 as the sorrowful description of the outcome of Adam and Eve's sin in the Garden of Eden, he distorted the verse to try to prove that God's will was that women be subservient to men. But the fruit of sin is never the will of God. Nowhere in the Old Testament was there any divine command for wives to be in servitude to their husbands.

Since by his foundational ideas woman couldn't be anything but evil, how did Philo account for women of virtue in the Old Testament? He did so with a stretch of logic that would be comical if it weren't so tragic. For to Philo, the idea of "virtuous female" was a contradiction in terms! The very word *virtue* comes from the word *manly* in both Latin and Greek. To prove his point, Philo quoted a phrase in Genesis 18:11: "Sarah was past the age of childbearing." The original Hebrew literally said, "There ceased to be to Sarah the ways of women." Philo used this euphemism for menopause to explain the impossible. Sarah was virtuous because after menopause *she had inwardly become a man!* No other explanation was possible, for Philo said the female nature was "irrational and akin to bestial passions, fear, sorrow, pleasure and desire, from which ensue incurable weaknesses and indescribable diseases."[50]

There is nothing so foolish as an intelligent man using his mental gifts to explain away the simplicity of truth.

Philo wasn't the only one who tried to combine Judaism with the prevailing philosophies of the day. Josephus, a Jewish historian, did so, as did a writer of the Apocrypha named Sirach. Sirach abandoned the biblical concept of shared responsibility for the Fall and placed all the blame on Eve: "From a woman did sin originate, and because of her we all must die."[51] He also said, "Do not...sit in the midst of women; for from garments comes the moth, and from a woman comes woman's wickedness. Better is the wickedness of a man than a woman who does good; and it is a woman who brings shame and disgrace."[52]

This last verse is shocking indeed! No wonder the Apocrypha isn't universally accepted by Christians as part of the Word of God. Sirach's words contradict the scriptures that teach, "The soul who sins is the one who will die."[53] No mention was made of gender, for this is equally true for both men and women. The soul of whoever does the sinning will die.

Paul affirmed God's revealed truth, saying, "There is no difference, for all have sinned and fall short of the glory of God, and are justified freely by his grace through the redemption that came by Christ Jesus."[54] Standing against what nearly everyone in his time believed, Paul declared the truth with echoes from the first three chapters of Genesis: Men and women have a shared origin, a shared destiny, a shared tragedy, and a shared hope.

9.

JESUS BROKE DOWN
THE WALLS

By David Hamilton

There's a danger when we approach well-known, beloved passages of Scripture. The danger is that we will not really *hear* the words. We have become so used to Jesus' words in the Gospels that we have a hard time not skipping over them. Or we read the familiar words and screen them through our childhood memories, unconsciously coloring them with all the cultural tones in which we grew up.

When it comes to the subject of this book, however, there's no more important time to hear clearly Jesus' words in Scripture. We must imagine their impact on His first audience, who lived in a culture entirely different from our own. When it comes to what was considered normal in the ways that male and female related to each other in first-century Israel, Jesus' words and actions were controversial, provocative, even revolutionary.

Jesus came to set in motion the healing God had promised when Adam and Eve shared the great tragedy of the Garden. He came to end the painful consequences of a broken and sinful world, including the rift between men and women. Jesus came to set men *and* women free. But because of the terrible exclusion that women had suffered, His open welcome meant even more to them. Women had been offered so little in a hostile world. In the words of one author, "Jesus did not start a movement for women, but a movement for humans. It is not surprising, however, that women were especially responsive to his ideas. Trapped in the isolation of a sometimes hostile family, women knew how insecure, unjust, and lonely the world was."[1]

Jesus' mission wasn't gender biased; it was gender inclusive. Jesus said, "All that the Father gives me will come to me, and whoever comes to me I will never drive away."[2]

FIRST AT THE CRADLE, LAST AT THE CROSS

Dorothy Sayers put it very well when she wrote:

> Perhaps it is no wonder that the women were first at the Cradle and last at the Cross. They had never known a man like this Man—there never has been such another. A prophet and teacher who never nagged at them, never flattered or coaxed or patronized; who never made arch jokes about them, never treated them as "The women, God help us!" or "The ladies, God bless them!"; who rebuked without querulousness and praised without condescension; who took their questions and arguments seriously; who never mapped out their sphere for them, never urged them to be feminine or jeered at them for being female; who had no axe to grind and no uneasy male dignity to defend; who took them as he found them and was completely unselfconscious. There is no act, no sermon, no parable in the whole Gospel that borrows its pungency from female perversity; nobody could possibly guess from the words and deeds of Jesus that there was anything "funny" about woman's nature.[3]

Let's look at the way Jesus' ministry revolutionized the lives of women. We'll see that what He offered was totally different from their usual treatment in a male-centered world. For Jesus, there was

— *no* double standard
— *no* exclusion
— *no* limits on their God-given destiny

It Takes Two to Tango

They dragged her against her will, kicking and screaming. It was obvious from her tangled hair and disheveled clothing that she had been given little time to put her clothes on. Her face was smeared with tears and dirt. She twisted and squirmed, trying to escape the men's viselike grip on her arms. But she was small and helpless, surrounded not only by angry men but also by the disgust reserved for loose, immoral women.

They flung her into the dirt of the street, right at the feet of the popular rabbi from Nazareth. They didn't need a judge or a jury. Hadn't she been caught in the very act of adultery by the teachers of the Law and the Pharisees? They stood back from her with sneers and folded arms and waited to see what Jesus would do.

Have you ever wondered about this story? Why do we call it the story of the *woman* caught in adultery?[4] Can a woman commit adultery by herself? It's impossible! She couldn't have been "caught in the very act" alone. And what about the biblical law the men were supposed to be so zealously upholding? It stipulated that in the case of adultery, *both* man and woman were to be put to death.[5] Why did these "teachers of the Law" forget to arrest the other guilty party? Why was he allowed to grab his clothes and scurry away? The truth was, their actions were governed more by the double standards of their culture than by the Word of God.

Jesus didn't point that out to them. It was too obvious, almost ludicrous. Perhaps a sad smile crossed His lips as He squatted down to write silently in the dust with His finger.

I wonder what He wrote? We aren't told, but we are shown that Jesus refused to be pulled into their biased judgment. Jesus wouldn't support a culture that favored one gender over the other. As Starr puts it, "He refused to approve a double standard. He rebuked the cry of His own and of subsequent ages: 'Stone the woman and let the man go free.'"[6]

Finally He spoke. His words were quiet and few, but they stripped His audience bare. "If any one of you is without sin, let him be the first to throw a stone at her."[7] As He bent down again and continued to write His message in the dirt, silence and guilt settled over the mob. Shame replaced anger. One by one they stole away.

Jesus' words were few, but they spoke volumes. Sin was sin—whether it was committed by a man or a woman. Every one of us will stand before God in judgment. No one will be able to hide or slip away. No one will be able to point to another.

The woman's sin wasn't worse than the man's—nor was it better. When equity is the standard, stones are rarely thrown.

LOVE BETWEEN EQUALS

This wasn't the only time Jesus cut across everyone's beliefs. In fact, His teaching on marriage and divorce was downright shocking. Jesus "presupposed that women had rights and responsibilities equal to men's."[8] Ironically, it was His enemies who gave Jesus the opportunity to teach on marriage and divorce. The Pharisees hoped to trap Him by bringing up the controversial subject of divorce. It's very important to listen to Jesus' reply, for it did more than show God's broken heart over divorce. Jesus also directed their eyes back to what everyone had forgotten: the equality of men and women that God established in the Garden of Eden.

Jesus referred to Genesis 1:27: "But at the beginning of creation God made them male and female."[9] This laid the foundations for the rest of His argument: Because man and woman had the same origin, they should have equal rights and obligations.[10] Then He reminded them of the first marriage counselor, God Himself, who advised, "For this reason a man will leave his father and mother and be united to his wife."[11] What was Jesus implying as He took them back to Genesis 2? By this time, the Jews' ideas of marriage and gender roles were far from God's plan. Their thinking was more like that of the nations surrounding them, which were ruled by Greek thought and reinforced by Roman custom. For a young Roman girl, marriage meant a complete break with everything she had known. As we saw in chapter 6, even her gods were taken from her when she moved into her husband's family compound.

Jesus' words were radically different. He was saying that woman wasn't inferior in any way. The man was told to take the initiative in relinquishing rights to *his* family in order to enter into marriage with *her*. It was simply unheard of!

Jesus also highlighted the unity and equality of husband and wife, quoting further from Genesis, "…and the two will become one flesh."[12] They are still two individuals, but one in love. The Hebrew *one* is a compound singular word, like a *cluster* of grapes or a *pair* of shoes. It's the same word used in the most important proclamation of Judaism:

"Hear, O Israel: The LORD our God, the LORD is *one*."[13] So the unity God intended between a husband and wife is like the unity that God the Father, God the Son, and God the Holy Spirit have enjoyed for eternity. This is part of the significance of that statement, "Let *us* make…in *our* image…male and female."[14] As there is no hierarchy in the Trinity, no inferior or superior in the unity of the Trinity, so there cannot be any between a husband and his wife.

JESUS DID AWAY WITH THE DOUBLE STANDARD

Then Jesus added a direct command: "What God has joined together, let man not separate."[15] He was doing more than condemning divorce here. He was also commanding us not to separate people according to human systems of value. We can't have one standard for men and another for women. A double standard is another way of separating what God has joined together.

Even His disciples were amazed when they heard these words. Jesus was holding men and women to the same standard! They sputtered, "If this is the situation between a husband and wife, it is better not to marry."[16] Why, if men had to play by the same rules as women, they'd have to think twice about marrying. Jesus had leveled the playing field.

What if divorce is unavoidable? Jesus said that this tragedy comes as a result of the hardness of our hearts.[17] But even if the unthinkable happens and there is a divorce, the woman has equal rights and responsibilities with the man. Jesus taught, "Anyone who divorces his wife and marries another woman commits adultery against her. And if she divorces her husband and marries another man, she commits adultery."[18]

Now Jesus had really gone too far! He was coming against hundreds of years of rabbinical teaching. Everyone knew that both the right of betrothal and the right of divorce belonged exclusively to men.[19]

Jesus' words didn't weaken marriage. On the contrary, they strengthened it by pointing back to God's initial plan for marriage: a lifelong discovery of love and intimacy between equal partners.

STANDING STRAIGHT AND TALL

Another story reveals how radically Jesus challenged the rabbis' double standards. In Luke 13:10–17, we read about the day Jesus was teaching in a synagogue when he spotted a crippled woman, bent over

double. Jesus called her forward. When He laid hands on her, she immediately stood up straight, completely healed.

Just another healing? Hardly. By Jesus' day, women had been completely marginalized in places of worship. As we saw in chapter 8,
women were relegated to the back of the synagogue,[20] separated from
the men. Jesus' invitation to the crippled woman struck out against the
male monopoly of public worship. When Jesus put her in the spotlight, right down in front of the whole synagogue, He shattered the
men's worldview. There must have been a collective gasp from digni-
fied rows of men that day. Didn't Jesus know what He was doing?
Women were supposed to be kept in their place, hidden behind the
dividing screens![21]

The leader of the synagogue put words to everyone's disapproval
that day. However, he shifted the focus from Jesus' deliberate snubbing
of social convention onto safer territory—the importance of honoring
the Sabbath. What followed next compounded their outrage. Jesus
defended Himself by saying that this "daughter of Abraham"[22]
deserved to be released from her affliction, even on the Sabbath.

There was no precedent for Jesus' use of the phrase "daughter of
Abraham." Nowhere in rabbinical teaching was an individual woman
called "a daughter of Abraham." Jewish men were often referred to as
"sons of Abraham,"[23] but never women.[24] Everyone knew that women
weren't heirs of Abraham in the way that men were. But Jesus lavished
this term on a woman, and an old, used-to-be crippled woman at that.

I think there was another reason the woman stood straight and tall
that day in the synagogue. Jesus had done more than heal her back. He
had restored her dignity as a person, showing her that she was valued
by God. She was an equal heir with her male counterparts to all that
God had promised Abraham.

NO EXCLUSION

Jesus didn't exclude women either by word or by action. He deliberately chose words that emphasized His common standing with
women and men.

Words are important. Wars have been fought over language. Today,
nations are threatening to divide over this issue. Elections are lost by the
careless slip of a politician's tongue. Mighty corporations see their stock
values plummet when prejudiced words of executives are reported.

Words are important because they show what we believe—the roots of our values. So it's important to see the words Jesus used—especially the ones He used to describe Himself. The most common term He used for Himself was "Son of Man."[25] Because of our limitations to our own language, this sounds like He was emphasizing His maleness, but He wasn't. The Greek word *anthropos* used in the phrase "Son of Man" is a gender-inclusive word. It is better translated as "human" or "person" than it is as "man."[26] Jesus was affirming the amazing reality of the Incarnation. He was simply saying, "I am human."

It is interesting that all the writers of the New Testament followed His lead. When referring to Jesus, they always carefully used the gender-inclusive Greek term *anthropos*, which means "human being or person," instead of the gender-specific Greek term *aner*, which means "male or man."

We know, of course, that Jesus was a male human being. But the Bible never dwells on His maleness. Jesus was also a Jew, but that wasn't the priority either. The important thing was that He was truly *human*, fully identified with us in every way,[27] while being totally God at the same time. As God and as a human, He came to lay His life down for every person, not just for Jews and not just for males. His choice of words and the choice of every New Testament writer underscore that.

WHY DID JESUS CALL GOD "FATHER"?

The words Jesus used to describe the others in the Trinity are also important. Of all the words He used for the first person of the Godhead, the most common was "Father."[28] This might sound normal to the majority of us today because we grew up in a Christian context. But it sounded quite foreign to first-century Jewish ears, for such terminology was very rare in the Old Testament.

Why, then, did Jesus call God "Father"? Was He saying God was masculine, like human fathers? No. He was trying to give an image that His listeners could grasp, a term that showed just how intimate God wanted to be with them. This was drastically different from the comfortably distant, theoretical God that non-Jews and many Jews had.

A common Jewish term for God was "the God of Abraham, Isaac, and Jacob." When these words were first used hundreds of years earlier, they sounded immediate and personal. They referred to the God whom those men had met personally. But as generations passed that reality slipped away. He became the God of long-dead fathers. Tradition replaced personal experience. It became more important to be a descendant of Abraham, Isaac, and Jacob than to know the God these men knew.

Jesus shook up everything when He constantly referred to God as "our Father." However, He wasn't saying God was male. In fact, by using "God our Father" instead of "Father God," He was putting distance between His ideas and those of centuries of fertility cults in that part of the world. The ancient religions of the land had always worshiped a "father god" (Baal in earliest times) and his female counterpart, the "mother goddess" (Asherah). These cults had been absorbed into the popular Gentile religions of Jesus' time. Such finite ideas of God and His nature had always threatened to seduce the Jews. That's why the Lord specifically commanded them not to make male and female images of God.[29] He didn't want them, or us, to make the mistake of attributing gender—a quality He built into His creatures—to Him, the Creator. So Jesus avoided the cultic "Father God" and called Him, "God our Father."

God was referred to as "Father" nineteen times in the Old Testament,[30] but God was also described in feminine terms in the Hebrew scriptures.[31] One dramatic instance was in Isaiah 42:13–14, where God is likened first to a mighty man marching into battle and then to a woman in childbirth.

On at least two occasions Jesus spoke of God using feminine terminology—in the parable of a woman searching for a coin and in the parable of a woman hiding yeast in a loaf.[32] He wasn't saying that God was both male and female, nor were others in the Bible who used both masculine and feminine metaphors for the Lord. God is neither male nor female. He is greater than what He has created, including gender distinctions. Indeed, Jesus' words suggest that our human gender distinctions may not be as enduring as we might think. When asked about the Resurrection, Jesus said we wouldn't marry or be given in marriage in heaven because we would become "like the angels."[33] His words mean that in eternity, gender distinctions will either be nonexistent or be irrelevant. Therefore, if we are living in light of that eternity, we cannot discriminate according to gender.

A New Initiation Rite

Jesus brought the dawn of a new day. Before ascending into heaven, He gave final instructions to His disciples.[34] He established a sacrament designed to include persons of both genders in the church, the new people of faith. The old sacrament, circumcision, was only for males. But the new initiation rite Jesus gave was baptism. It was an opportunity for both men and women to make a public declaration that they had joined the people of God.

As recorded by the Gospel writers, women were an integral part of Jesus' life and ministry. The record of their presence stands in stark contrast with the literature of the ancient world. Except for the works of the playwrights, most Greek and Roman literature gave little voice to women. Women are talked about, but they rarely talk. Women are even more silent through the centuries of Jewish literature—the Mishnah and the Talmud. But the Gospels were markedly different. Matthew, Mark, and Luke wrote of women in 112 distinct passages.[35]

It has been noted that the most striking thing about the role of women in Jesus' life and teaching is the simple fact that women were there. It was nothing short of revolutionary. Jesus saw women as persons He came to reach and to serve. He treated them as individuals of worth and dignity, unlike Jewish society, which often viewed women as property.[36]

Not only were women present, they were participating. Jesus taught them the Gospel, the meaning of the Scriptures, and religious truths in general. Most Jews considered it improper, even obscene, to teach women the Scriptures. Jesus' actions were deliberate decisions to break this discrimination against women.[37]

Jesus included women when He taught in public. It's interesting that He didn't choose the temple of Jerusalem as His usual place to give public teaching. Instead, most of His teaching ministry took place in the towns and countryside around the Sea of Galilee, where no dividing walls segregated women from men.[38] Jesus could teach both men *and* women. Matthew, writing for a Jewish audience, faithfully records the presence of women at these public teaching sessions. It was something novel and therefore noteworthy.[39] Even when Jesus did teach in the temple, He picked the more public areas, the outer courts where women were allowed,[40] so that they also could hear Him speak.

THE FOUNDATION STONE OF TRUTH, LAID BY A WOMAN

Jesus also taught women in private settings. One such incident took place in the home of Mary and Martha, the sisters of Lazarus.[41] The writer tells us that Mary "sat at the Lord's feet listening to what he said." To "sit at the feet" of a teacher was a common expression used to show the formal mentoring relationship between a rabbi and his disciple. "Luke is indirectly telling his readers that Mary was taking a position typical of a rabbinic pupil."[42] It's the same expression Paul used to describe his education under Gamaliel.[43]

The collection of rabbinical teaching—the Mishnah—exhorted its readers, "Let thy house be a meeting-house for the Sages and sit amid the dust of their feet and drink in their words with thirst."[44] In the very next paragraph, however, the Mishnah states, "Talk not much with womankind…. He that talks much with womankind brings evil upon himself and neglects the study of the Law and at the last will inherit [hell]."[45] Though the house was to be a forum for training, women weren't allowed to participate. Jesus defied the rabbinical exclusion of women from education. He defended Mary's right to learn as His disciple, saying, "Mary has chosen what is better, and it will not be taken away from her."[46]

Mary wasn't the only one who benefited from Jesus' private instruction. Jesus also taught Martha at the time of Lazarus' death. "When Martha heard that Jesus was coming, she went out to meet him."[47] Over the next few verses, Jesus privately engaged Martha in one of the most significant dialogues in the Gospels. The two of them grappled with theological truth in the midst of their shared pain over the loss of Lazarus.

Jesus said to Martha, "I am the resurrection and the life. He who believes in me will live, even though he dies; and whoever lives and believes in me will never die."[48]

Jesus didn't give this central tenet of our faith, this intimate self-revelation, to any of the twelve apostles. These words are some of our most treasured in the church. They're often repeated during the times of our greatest pain, at deathbeds and at funerals. But we might not have these words if Jesus hadn't taken time to teach crucial theological issues to a woman. Nor would we have them if that woman hadn't chosen to pass on her private lesson to the rest of us.[49]

Jesus didn't just declare truth to Martha. Like any good teacher, He actively engaged her mind, prompting her to think through the implications. He asked, "Do you believe this?"[50] Martha's answer revealed the depth of her spiritual insight: "'Yes, Lord,' she told him, 'I believe that you are the Christ, the Son of God, who was to come into the world.'"[51]

Martha's statement in John is virtually identical to Peter's confession reported in the other three Gospels.[52] On that occasion, Jesus replied to Peter by saying he was *petros*, meaning "little rock," and upon this *petra*, or "big rock," He would build His church.[53] Jesus wasn't saying that Peter was going to be the foundation stone for the church. He was saying that *upon this confession*—that Jesus is the Christ, the Son of God come into the world—His entire church would be built!

Thus we see that the foundation stone of our faith was declared by Martha as well as by Peter. Both understood who Jesus was. Both equally declared truth revealed to them by the Holy Spirit. If we accept this foundational teaching from Peter, a man, we must also accept it from Martha, a woman. If we consider that Peter's spiritual insight was a significant qualification for his spiritual leadership, should we think any differently in the case of Martha?

THREE TIMES AN OUTCAST

Another woman Jesus took time to instruct was the Samaritan woman at the well.[54] In fact, this is the longest recorded private conversation Jesus had with *any* individual. This woman was well acquainted with being an outcast. As a Samaritan, she was rejected by Jews. As a woman, she had been marginalized by men, except when they wanted her sexual services. And as an immoral woman, she was even shunned by other Samaritan women.[55] She was among the least valued of her day. However, Jesus didn't add to her rejection. He looked past her hardened features and gaudy clothing and took her seriously, speaking to her as an equal.

The woman reacted with surprise to Jesus' openness, asking a question about the racial tension of the day. Jesus didn't brush her aside. He didn't say, "Don't worry your pretty little head about that. Leave those questions to the menfolk!" Instead, He gave this "bimbo" an invitation to a serious theological discussion. And the woman responded, asking a question that showed that she, too, had serious questions about her faith.

Jesus listened to her. He answered her questions. He spent time with her. He included her. Not only that, He gave her one of the most

122 Why Not Women?

significant statements about God in the whole of Scripture: "God is spirit, and his worshipers must worship in spirit and in truth."[56] To her Jesus stated for the first time—even before Peter and Martha came to understand this truth—that He was the Messiah.[57] Indeed, this is the first of the "I am" statements that form the theological backbone of the Gospel of John.[58]

For Jesus, this encounter with a person outcast in three ways was just as significant as the one He had with Nicodemus,[59] a distinguished Jewish leader. In fact, as you compare these two encounters, Jesus spent more time explaining the ways of God to the woman than to Nicodemus.[60] Jesus directed His full attention to instructing a rejected woman in the ways of God. The Master Rabbi modeled excellent teaching skills in that encounter, and He did it for someone everyone else thought was a most unworthy, unpromising pupil.

What happened when the disciples returned from their grocery shopping and found Jesus immersed in this theological discussion at the well? John said they were "surprised to find him talking with a woman."[61] It wasn't her race so much as her gender that alarmed them! The situation brought out the disciples' male-centered view of the world.

Because He was such a gifted teacher, Jesus seized this teachable moment to enlighten the disciples. He gave them two commands in John 4:35 (NASB): (a) *lift up your eyes* and (b) *look*. If He had merely said, "Look," it might have sounded like a common opening to any declaration. But when He said, "Lift up your eyes, and look," He was telling His disciples: "Look at this situation in a new way. Your worldview's too small! Take off your cultural blinders that keep you from seeing. I want to stretch your mind. I want you to see people in a new way." That included seeing women in a new way. Women were to be included; they were part of the harvest Jesus had come to reap.

The Samaritan woman rushed off immediately to become an evangelist. She went into the city, saying, "Come, see a man who told me everything I ever did. Could this be the Christ?"[62] Her ministry was very successful. Indeed, many in her hometown "believed in him because of the woman's testimony."[63]

The epilogue to this story of "the wellside classroom" is given by John, the eyewitness, in verse 42. After the woman had led them to Jesus, her converts declared, "We no longer believe just because of what you said; now we have heard for ourselves, and we know that this man really is the Savior of the world." This declaration is one of the climactic moments of John's Gospel account[64]—all because Jesus had treated a despised and alienated woman as He would have treated any other person hungry for truth.

A SNEAKY WOMAN GETS WHAT SHE NEEDS

There's another story of a woman excluded by society.[65] It happened this way.

Jesus was hurrying through the streets in response to the request of the synagogue official Jairus, who had begged Jesus to go home with him to heal his precious little girl. A crowd was following Jesus along the street on the way to Jairus's house. In fact, they were crushing in on him, trying to get His attention.

All of a sudden Jesus stopped dead in His tracks. He had felt one touch in particular. It was brief and tentative—just the lightest tug on the back of His robe. But He had felt the familiar warm surge of power going out of Him into another. He whirled about. "Who touched My garments?"

His words were a great joke to the disciples. "You see the people crowding against you, and yet you can ask, 'Who touched me?'"[66]

Jesus ignored this. His eyes searched the crowd for one person. Several seconds passed. The woman who had committed the deed held her breath, hoping He wouldn't notice her in the crowd. Maybe she could still slip away undetected.

What was the big deal here? To understand the woman's "transgression," we need to remember the law of Moses. This woman had been suffering from incessant vaginal hemorrhaging for twelve years. According to Jewish ceremonial law,[67] she and everything she touched were considered "unclean." The woman was painfully aware of this. For twelve years, she had been required to keep away from people to avoid defiling them. Mark tells us, "She had suffered a great deal under the care of many doctors and had spent all she had, yet instead of getting better she grew worse."[68]

When she heard of Jesus, she knew He was her only hope. But how could she approach Him? In her condition of impurity, she would defile the great rabbi! He would have to go through the ritual bathing of Himself and His clothing. He would be contaminated until evening.

Certainly, no other religious leader had allowed her anywhere near him. She had known twelve long years of isolation and shame.

She saw the crowds that day, jostling and pushing around Jesus, and she thought, "Here's my chance! I'll just reach through the crowd and barely touch Him…. No, I mustn't even do that. I'll just touch His clothes. That's all. No one will ever know!"

Sneaking through the crowd, she reached through and did it. Immediately, Jesus' power flowed into her and she was healed. But then to her horror, He stopped and asked, "Who touched my clothes?"[69]

The woman froze, holding her breath. She knew what was coming. How well she remembered hundreds of reprimands over the past twelve years given by religious leaders afraid of contamination by her menstrual impurity. And now, here in this very public place, in front of this great man… It was just too terrible! Maybe He'd give up and go His way. But no, she wasn't going to be able to escape. He was standing there, waiting.

Finally she came forward and threw herself at His feet, confessing what she had done. "In the presence of all the people, she told why she had touched him and how she had been instantly healed."[70] Then the most extraordinary thing happened. Instead of the expected rebuke, she heard Jesus commending her. His words poured like balm over the wounds inside her: "Daughter, your faith has healed you. Go in peace and be freed from your suffering."[71]

In this brief encounter on a crowded street, Jesus showed that menstruation was no longer an occasion for impurity. No longer would the flow of menstrual blood exclude women from full participation among the people of God. The flow of His blood on the cross would see to that. He had truly inaugurated "the year of the Lord's favor."[72] The Age of Messiah had come. The Son of Hope promised to Eve had come to redeem and restore.

No Limits on a God-Given Destiny

Some may see exclusion in the fact that Jesus chose twelve men to be His apostles. But as Loren mentions in chapter 3, this shouldn't give us the idea that Jesus was setting maleness as a requirement for ministry in His church. If we limit leadership to men, we must also limit leadership to people who are Galilean Jews by birth. In fact, our leaders must also speak Aramaic. Further, only eyewitnesses to His ministry for three years can qualify.

This standard was applied once and only once.[73] Even then, only two people met the criteria: Joseph Barsabbas and Matthias. Later as the church grew, it discovered that such requirements for leadership were inappropriate and inadequate. It quickly abandoned them for other criteria as the church spread through the nations.

The question remains, though. Did Jesus allow women to minister? Yes. The Gospel evidence is clear. Women ministered both *to* and *with* Jesus. The verb *diakoneo* is associated with seven women in the Gospel narratives.[74] This is the same verb that describes the ministry of seven men appointed to leadership in the early church.[75] Though the ministry of the seven men "deacons"[76] is well known, the ministry of the lesser-known women "deacons" to Jesus and His followers was equally important. These women were

— Peter's mother-in-law[77]
— Mary Magdalene[78]
— Mary, the mother of James and Joses[79]
— Salome, the mother of Zebedee's sons[80]
— Joanna, the wife of Cuza[81]
— Susanna[82]
— Martha, sister of Mary and Lazarus[83]

These women are held up as examples of those whose servant ministry blessed Jesus and His followers.

"AND ALSO SOME WOMEN"

Luke says something interesting:

After this, Jesus traveled about from one town and village to another, proclaiming the good news of the kingdom of God. The Twelve were with him, *and also some women* who had been cured of evil spirits and diseases: Mary (called Magdalene) from whom seven demons had come out; Joanna the wife of Cuza, the manager of Herod's household; Susanna; and many others. These women were helping to support them out of their own means.[84]

This unique phrase "the Twelve were with him, and also some women" makes us wonder: Did these women have a special, publicly recognized role similar to the twelve? At least one scholar believes that they did:

Did this group of women constitute a parallel to the Twelve? There is a mosaic in the *Titulus* Church of Saint Praxedis that suggests it. There is a double circle around the doorway of the chapel of Saint Zeno consisting of the busts of eight women together with Our Lady in the center and two deacons on either side of her. It certainly gives the impression of a tradition of a collateral group of apostles, of men and women.[85]

No matter what we think about this archaeological finding, the Gospels tell of women who were constantly part of Jesus' ministerial entourage. Luke speaks of "*the* women who had come with Jesus from Galilee"[86] as a definite and recognized part of His ministerial team. We don't know all they did as they traveled with Jesus. But come to think of it, we have very little evidence of how the twelve spent their days. Too many pieces of the puzzle are missing.

The purpose of the Gospels is to bear testimony to the person and work of Jesus, not to give us a daily journal of the original disciples. Even so, there was a definite group called either "the women" or "our women" by those close to Jesus.[87] The significant thing is, "the women" were regularly with Jesus—just like the twelve. And wasn't this the primary reason Jesus called people to Himself? Mark 3:14 states, "He appointed twelve—designating them apostles—that they might be with him…." We have seen that the women, like the twelve, spent regular time with Jesus. But what of the second part of Jesus' call? What about the words "that he might send them out to preach and to have authority to drive out demons"?[88]

Perhaps women were included among the seventy-two whom Jesus sent out to preach.[89] It's a distinct possibility, although we can't be positive one way or another.

What we can be sure of is that Jesus commissioned a woman to carry the first proclamation of His Resurrection. He commanded Mary Magdalene, "Go instead to my brothers and tell them, 'I am returning to my Father and your Father, to my God and your God.'"[90] Lee Anna Starr says, "No higher commission to preach the Gospel was ever given. There is little wisdom in inquiring—shall women preach?—when the Head of the church Himself sent a woman out to preach the Resurrection before the sluggish male disciples had yet had apprehension of the fact."[91]

Mary Magdalene wasn't the only one. To the women who came to Him, clasped His feet, and worshiped Him on that first Easter morning, Jesus said, "Do not be afraid. Go and tell my brothers to go to Galilee; there they will see me."[92] How on earth can we question whether to trust women to faithfully preach the Good News today when Jesus trusted them with the first proclamation of the Resurrection? Are we more wise and careful than Jesus? Jesus didn't merely give them permission to preach the Gospel; He commanded them to proclaim the Good News.

In closing, we'll look at one more significant encounter Jesus had with a woman. It's sort of a strange story, but it demonstrates how Jesus challenged the traditional gender roles of that culture. In their place He created a heavenly standard by which all women and all men can discover their God-given destiny.

Jesus was teaching. Suddenly, "a woman in the crowd called out, 'Blessed is the mother who gave you birth and nursed you!'"[93] I guess her excitement got the best of her that day. But her words reflected the traditional rabbinic position: Women receive God's blessing indirectly through their menfolk, their sons or husbands. A woman couldn't serve God in her own right. The rabbis had taught: "Whereby do women earn merit? By making their children go to the synagogue to learn Scripture and their husbands to the [rabbinical school] to learn *Mishnah*, and waiting for their husbands till they return."[94] According to this restrictive worldview, the woman who called out these words was right. Mary was indeed blessed above all women, for no woman had ever had a Son who served God as Jesus had.

But Jesus rejected her words. "He replied, 'Blessed rather are those who hear the word of God and obey it.'"[95] What was He doing? Was He showing ill will toward Mary, His mother? Certainly not. All His life Jesus loved her, respectfully calling her "dear woman."[96] Even when He was suffering physical and spiritual torment, dying on the cross, He was concerned for His mother.[97] Nor was Jesus belittling the role of motherhood.

Jesus was rejecting the system of thought that for centuries had cut women off from active participation in the things of God. Jesus would have no part in religious values that relegated, exempted, excluded, and limited a person's walk with God or her ministry for God. It would be different in His kingdom. No more would women have to rely on what their men did to receive God's blessing. The new standard was personal obedience to the Word of God.

Why do we restore limitations that Jesus swept away? Instead of making gender one of the qualifications for ministry, we should ask a candidate: Have you been faithful to the call of God upon your life? Are you hearing the Word of God and obeying it? If the answer is yes, there is no God-given limit on your destiny.

10.

PAUL TURNED HIS WORLD UPSIDE DOWN

By David Hamilton

Everywhere Paul went things were shaken up. Some rejoiced as their lives were transformed. Others reacted in hatred and fear as Paul threatened their standing. Everywhere he went, churches were planted and riots erupted. Paul was no maintainer of the status quo. He threatened the world's systems. This was evident in the words of the Thessalonians who cried out, "These men who have turned the world upside down have come here also."[1] Wherever Paul ministered, the Gospel disrupted centuries of tradition among pagans and Jews alike.

It was especially dramatic in Ephesus where once again the enraged mob gathered against Paul and his team. The Jewish leaders were jealous of Paul, whose preaching was endangering their status within the Jewish enclave of this powerful, multicultural city. The pagans also hated Paul. A good part of the economy of their city was built on the tourist trade of pilgrims to the famous temple of Artemis. Paul's converts were turning away from the worship of Artemis and taking their money with them. Since the pagans could not refute Paul's ideas, they incited the mob to kill him and his team.[2]

However, something even deeper and darker was at work in Ephesus. Paul hadn't just angered human opponents. He had also stirred up a demonic hornet's nest. His preaching had assaulted the devil's stronghold—the Ephesians' intellectual pride entangled with supernatural, occult power and the perverse sensuality of their temple rituals. We don't have a parallel to Ephesus today. Nothing quite compares with Ephesus of old. But try to imagine a city with the intellectual fame of Oxford, the economic power of Tokyo, the artistic splendor of Florence, the spectacle of Las Vegas, the sex trade of Bangkok, and the dark, occult powers of Kathmandu. No wonder Paul barely escaped with his life!

SOMETIMES THE ENEMY'S WORDS ARE TRUE

Years later, Paul would not be so fortunate. While worshiping in the temple in Jerusalem, some Ephesian Jews stirred up another riot against Paul. A Roman centurion saved Paul from a sure lynching and enabled him to have his day in court.[3] When they brought Paul to trial, the Ephesian Jews claimed that he had defiled the temple in Jerusalem by bringing a Gentile past Herod's dividing walls into the sacred area reserved for Jewish males. This specific charge wasn't true, but Paul was guilty in another way. In fact, his real "crime" was even bigger. He wasn't bringing Gentiles past dividing walls. He was declaring to Gentiles *and* to slaves *and* to women that Jesus had torn down the walls. In the twilight of his life, Paul wrote the Ephesian believers from his prison cell:

> But now in Christ Jesus you who once were far away have been brought near through the blood of Christ. For he himself is our peace, who has made the two one and has destroyed the barrier, the dividing wall of hostility, by abolishing in his flesh the law with its commandments and regulations. His purpose was to create in himself one new man out of the two, thus making peace, and in this one body to reconcile both of them to God through the cross, by which he put to death their hostility.[4]

As we saw in chapter 8, Herod's walls in the temple were never God's idea. They were the invention of man—an architectural expression of the social barriers erected by man's ungodly traditions.

Have you ever visited a farm and seen an electrical fence? Long after the power is turned off, the animals remain meekly inside the pasture. After a few times of being jolted, they never try to escape again. That's the way it was with the early church. Jesus had already torn down the walls. But now believers had to be taught to walk into their new freedom. We'll see how Paul did this in the heart of his letter to the Ephesians.

A Most Unlikely Revolutionary

There couldn't have been a less likely person to challenge the status quo than Paul. As Saul of Tarsus, he was born into privilege as a Roman citizen. He also received the best education available to a Jewish youngster. He was the star pupil of an esteemed master, educated at the feet of Gamaliel,[5] one of the most influential rabbis of the first century A.D. Saul was gifted with a razor-sharp mind and was wholly devoted to everything he had been taught—the Torah of Moses as well as the writings of centuries of accumulated wisdom from the great rabbis.

Saul not only was educated according to the best rabbinic tradition but also was well acquainted with the Greek and Roman ideas of his day.[6] He had impeccable credentials, and he was well traveled.[7] If it hadn't been for an unexpected turn of events on the road to Damascus,[8] we might well have been reading the thoughts of Rabbi Saul in the Mishnah today. Everything did change, though, on that day when Saul fell to the ground and was blinded by the light. Much of what he had previously been taught had to be radically altered.

When Paul began teaching others, his ideas couldn't have been more different from the teaching he had received from the rabbis. His thoughts weren't some rehash of Greek and Roman philosophy, as were Philo's. Paul's ideas were new because they were revelation from God. They were ideas intended to transform every part of people's everyday lives. For instance, an underlying concept throughout the ancient world was that of the "household code." This concept permeated all ancient literature, including the Jewish writings known as the Talmud. Everything in ancient society was built upon the household code, which was the the basis for law.[9] The household code was defined by three pairs of relationships:

- ─ husband and wife
- ─ father and child
- ─ master and slave

Everyone's role in society was defined by the household code—no one was excluded. For Greeks, Romans, and Jews, the world was strictly a patriarchy. One person, the husband/father/master, was in complete control of wife, children, and slaves. No one questioned what he did in his household. Individual laws and court rulings upheld his privilege. Submission was a one-way street from wife to husband, from child to father, and from slave to master.

When Paul wrote to the Ephesians from his prison cell in Rome, however, he took the household code and stood it on its ear. He did something unheard of: He commanded *mutual submission*. No longer should men rule like despots in their homes. Submission should be a two-way street. Paul said that God's purpose was to bring all things together in unity in Christ.[10] He told believers they had the shared tragedy of sin,[11] but now they were heirs together.[12] There was equality at the foot of the Cross. Equality of forgiveness. Equality of hope. Equality of purpose. Believers were all being built together into God's future dwelling.[13]

PAUL DIDN'T DO SOUND BITES

Many use Ephesians 5:22 to show something other than equality before Christ. Like many modern translations, the NIV puts verse 22 as a separate sentence, saying, "Wives, submit to your husbands as to the Lord." Was Paul singling out women, telling them to submit to their husbands? To give a fair answer to this question we have to carefully consider the precise language of Paul's intricate writing. Paul was certainly no sound-bite communicator. In fact, if we try to divide his long, complex sentences into good sound bites, we can distort his ideas.

Ephesians 5:15–23 is an excellent example of Paul's transforming ideas. These verses form only one sentence in the Greek. However, to make it easier for modern readers, translators have made sentences and paragraphs where there were none. While they've done this to make it easier for the modern reader, they have separated ideas that were meant to be fused together. If you separate these ideas, it appears that Paul is saying something opposite to what the original Greek conveys. Verse 22 of Ephesians 5 isn't a separate sentence at all! It's a continuation of one very long one. To go even further and put a paragraph break and a subtitle between verses 21 and 22 is both unfair and incorrect.[14]

This long sentence is built around two imperative verbs (that is, two commands) and five subordinate clauses. Here is a clear translation of Paul's sentence that accurately reflects its original form. I've used correct verb tenses and highlighting to emphasize the structure of the sentence.

Do not be filled with wine which leads to debauchery,
but be filled with the Spirit,
    speaking to one another with psalms, hymns and spiritual songs,
    singing and
    making music in your heart to the Lord,
    always giving thanks to God the Father for everything, in the
        name of our Lord Jesus Christ,
    submitting to one another out of reverence for Christ, wives, [ ]
        to your husbands as to the Lord, for the husband is the head
        of the wife as Christ is the head of the church, his body, of
        which he is the Savior.[15]

Paul's long sentence hinges on the command "Be filled with the Spirit." What does it mean to be filled with the Holy Spirit? Some have used speaking in tongues as a sign of being filled with the Spirit. But Paul gave another measuring stick: Are we living a life characterized by mutual submission? The Holy Spirit doesn't know any other way to live. He has lived throughout eternity in mutual submission with the Father and the Son. If the Holy Spirit is active in our lives, we'll have the same attitude.

Paul was definitely not urging women to submit to men while allowing men to go scot-free, as all other ancient cultures had done. Because of a grammatical feature called an ellipsis,[16] the verb *submit* doesn't even appear in the original of verse 22. It really says, "…wives [ ] to your own husbands…." To fill in the blank, the ancient Greek reader knew to go to the previous phrase of the sentence to find the verb *submit*. Yes, wives were to submit to their husbands but in the context of the mutual submission of verse 21. Yes, they were to submit to their husbands in the same way that their husbands were to submit to their wives and all were to submit to one another in the Body of Christ.

Unprecedented, Unheard Of, Extraordinary

Paul went on to describe what being filled with the Holy Spirit would mean in our everyday relationships: between wife and husband, child and father, and master and slave. We could call Ephesians 5:18–6:9 Paul's household code. And Paul made it extremely practical. The results of being filled with the Holy Spirit shouldn't just be experienced in church or in a prayer meeting ("speaking to one another with psalms, hymns and spiritual songs, singing and making music in your heart to the Lord"). They should also be obvious as we relate to one another at home and on the job. After all, anyone can put on a smile and sing hymns on Sunday, but can we treat each other with love, respect, and mutual submission Monday through Saturday? This is where the rubber meets the road, isn't it?

As we've said before, it's hard for us to imagine the impact of Paul's teaching on his original audience. Paul took phrases of the household code familiar to them and said something radically fresh, something born in the heart of God, revealed in the Garden of Eden, and made possible through the Cross. In the next 328 words in Greek,[17] Paul spelled out the responsibilities of the traditionally "greater" (husband/father/master) of the household code to the "lesser" (wife/child/slave). This was new, even shocking. No culture's household code had ever made the "greater" responsible to the "lesser" for anything.

It is especially shocking when we consider the specific commands Paul gave the Ephesian believers. Of eight direct commands…

— five are directed to the male head of the household
— two are directed to children
— one to slaves
— none to wives[18]

Some may point to Ephesians 5:33. Didn't Paul give an imperative to women when he said, "The wife must respect her husband"? No, not in the Greek. In the original, this verb is in the subjunctive mood, which is used to express a desire, a wish, or a hope. Furthermore, this phrase is introduced by the Greek word that means "in order that." This is a dependent clause, built upon the first half of verse 33. Paul tells the husband to love his wife in order that she may respect him. You cannot command true respect—it must be earned.

Within Paul's description of the Spirit-filled life in Ephesians 5:22–6:9…

— He gave 40 words in the Greek to describe what being filled with the Spirit would look like for the wife responding righteously to her husband. But then Paul gave 150 words to describe the husband's responsibilities to his wife. Unprecedented!

— Paul gave 35 words to children, showing how they were to behave toward their fathers, but he gave 16 words of instruction to fathers. Unheard of!

— He gave slaves 59 words to illustrate what being filled with the Spirit meant for them while giving masters 28 words. Extraordinary!

If these latter two categories seem unfair, keep this in mind: Fathers and masters of slaves had ruled without *any* restraints up till now. A man's control over his household was nearly total. In ancient times, the patriarch could even put his children or slaves to death if he chose to. When Paul commanded fathers, "Do not exasperate your children,"[19] he was doing something no one had done before—placing gracious constraints on fathers. For the first time, the need for a loving, nurturing environment for growing children was highlighted.

Similarly, Paul didn't directly confront the institution of slavery. Instead, he told slaves to work for their masters as if they were working for Christ, then told the masters to treat their slaves "in the same way"[20] because they were equal in the eyes of God. Clearly, Paul intended his words to undermine slavery, eventually causing it to crumble worldwide. He sowed the seeds of social change. But change would not come through rebellion and violent revolution. It would come through repentance and recognition of human equality before God.

When we see the boldness of Paul's proposals, we see a pattern for ourselves. How should we approach issues in a changing culture or questions of conduct when we enter new cultures? We shouldn't keep our cultural blinders on and say, "This is right because it's what I've always been taught." No, like Paul, we should hold individual questions of conduct up to the Word of God and allow the Holy Spirit to give us entirely new behavior patterns and social structures wherever necessary. Or the Holy Spirit may show us that a particular behavior is not wrong but is an expression of the wonderful variety He has put into the families of human culture. In such cases, we should redeem cultural expressions, using them to declare God's glory.

WHAT PAUL *DIDN'T* SAY

It is important to see what Paul *didn't* say in his household code. He didn't say wives were to obey their husbands. This is striking, because he told children and slaves to obey. He wasn't merely breaking the tradition of other household codes of the ancient world. He was altering his normal literary symmetry to startle his readers. The effect on his readers was like hearing one shoe drop and waiting but never hearing the other one drop. Paul seemed to spotlight this issue by leaving it out.

Notice how Paul told husbands to love their wives. He used two ideas, each of which he repeated, to underline their importance in the strongest way possible:

— Husbands were to love their wives "as Christ loved the church."[21]

— They were to love them "as their own bodies."[22]

— Husbands were to love their wives "as Christ does the church."[23]

— The husband was to love his wife "as he loves himself."[24]

Could anything be further removed from the abusive, heavy-handed machoism of the ancient world? Paul infused the traditional household code with the transforming power of the Gospel. Or perhaps we should say, he "filled it with the Spirit." Paul didn't mindlessly mimic his culture. He presented a radical alternative. What he wrote was so extraordinary that it must have left the Ephesian believers with their mouths hanging open.

The High Value of Women

When Paul told husbands to love their wives *as Christ loved us*, think what that meant. It's one thing to love someone *as much* as you love yourself. But to love someone *as much as Christ loved us* is setting the highest standard of love possible. Christ laid His life down for us. When Jesus died for us, He showed what a high value God placed on us. The Cross was God's most tangible expression of how much He loves people. Human beings are extremely precious because the Son of God gave His life for each one of us. Therefore, women are to be highly valued. God tells husbands that they should love their wives so much that they'd be willing to lay down their lives for them. Could there be any higher value placed on one's wife—or one's sisters, mother, or daughters?

A Partner, Not a Piece of Property

Paul went on to explain more about the sacrificial love a husband should have for his wife. He did that by recalling Genesis 2:24, when God first created woman: "For this reason a man will leave his father and mother and be united to his wife, and the two will become one flesh."[25] At first glance, these words may mean nothing to us. We've heard them at every wedding we've ever attended. What was Paul saying by repeating them to the Ephesians? Was he saying, "You married her. Now you have to love her"?

Look how Paul underscored what Jesus had already said. Paul reminded the men of Ephesus of God's original design for marriage: *The man leaves all behind for his wife.* This wasn't how marriage took place in antiquity. In fact, it was the exact opposite of what the Greeks and Romans did. We have already seen how the Greeks and Romans required the woman to leave all to be wed to her husband. Marriage didn't mean any sacrifice for the man. All the sacrificing, all the relinquishing of rights was done by the woman who came to be joined to a new hearth fire.

Even the Jews, who rejected the pagan hearth cult, failed to hold on to the values laid out for women in Genesis. Right from the beginning, God had clearly established that a woman was to be treated not as property that a man may *take* for himself but as a partner to whom a man must *give* himself. Men began to stray from this almost immediately. Frequently, the Old Testament records how men "took wives" to themselves.[26] That had never been God's intention. As centuries passed, Jewish customs strayed even further from God's revelation.

Paul said in Ephesians that God was restoring His intent in Jesus, who took the initiative of self-renunciation, coming to earth and giving Himself for the church.[27] This self-sacrificing, rights-relinquishing, first-in-humility kind of love was to characterize a husband's treatment of his wife. Not since Eden had such a high concept of marriage been portrayed. Not since Eden had woman's value been so recognized, her worth so esteemed. Mutuality was to be the hallmark of the kingdom of God. Where Christ ruled, respect was something each partner in marriage could give to the other. Because Jesus came, women could give of themselves in submission to their husbands, and men could give of themselves to their wives, taking the initiative of self-renunciation. In Christ, the one-way lane had become a two-way road. Jesus, who had come as Eden's Hope, had begun to correct Eden's tragedy.

THE RADICAL EQUALITY OF THE GOSPEL

Paul closed his household code by stating the underlying principle for these radical new proposals: We are equal before God for "there is no favoritism with him."[28] That is the underlying principle beneath the mutual submission of Ephesians 5:21. God simply does not put human beings into hierarchies. The reason we can submit to one another is that God sees us all as one. This is a central tenet of the Gospel. Equality isn't based on a humanistic premise; it is rooted in God's impartiality. Because He treats all humans equally, so should we. Our view of others is to be shaped by His view of us.

Equality before God is a frequent theme of Paul's writing. One of the clearest examples of Paul attacking the hierarchical status quo is Galatians 3:28: "There is neither Jew nor Greek, slave nor free, male nor female, for you are all one in Christ Jesus." Why would Paul say this? Notice that he gave three pairs of relationships. But these weren't the three pairs of traditional household code. Instead, Paul was using another grouping, just as familiar to his audience. In Galatians 3, the father/child pair is replaced with the Jew/Gentile pair. What was Paul stirring in the minds of his original audience with the three pairs, Jew/Greek, slave/free, and male/female?

I believe this was a deliberate choice on Paul's part. Before his dramatic conversion, Paul was a good, strict Pharisee. More than this, he was their golden boy, well on his way up the rabbi's ladder of success. So, like all devout Jewish males of his day and his persuasion, he probably recited this prayer as soon as he awoke every morning while still in bed:

> Blessed be He who did not make me a Gentile;
> Blessed be He who did not make me a woman;
> Blessed be He who did not make me an uneducated man
> (or a slave).[29]

Because every pious Jew said this prayer, the *beraka*, as soon as he woke up and before he got out of bed, it was the first thing his wife heard as she lay beside him. Can you put yourself in her position? These cruel words were the first thing you heard upon awakening every day of your married life. You lay in bed listening as your husband thanked God that he wasn't you! And then the bleak realization would settle over you: A slave could become free, Gentiles could convert, but you could never stop being a woman.

Several versions of this prayer are recorded in rabbinic literature.[30] The fact that men fervently prayed the *beraka* every morning shows how far they had strayed from the equality of the sexes God set forth in Genesis. These words clearly show the prideful heart of rabbinic Judaism, where only free Jewish males could fully participate as the people of God.

Other writings of the rabbis backed up this view. Gentiles were worthy of less consideration than a beast of burden. "As for an ass, you are under an obligation that it should rest; but as for a Gentile, you are under no obligation [to ensure] that he should rest."[31] Slaves were equated with animals when they are called "people who are like the ass."[32] Similarly, a woman was valued at two percent of the value of a man when the Talmud stated that a "hundred women are no better then two men."[33]

It seems that Paul deliberately chose the three pairs of the traditional morning prayer (Gentile/Jew, slave/free, male/female) to declare in Galatians 3:28 that these distinctions no longer existed. He passionately begged men not to cast aside this wonderful new freedom. Why would they want to throw away such a great salvation and return to the legalism of men?

Paul called out to his listeners, "It is for freedom that Christ has set us free. Stand firm, then, and do not let yourselves be burdened again by a yoke of slavery."[34] Part of that legalistic yoke was people ranking others according to their own prejudices. But no more! In Jesus Christ, Paul declared, all these distinctions and categories are swept away. All are one. "Galatians 3:28 does not say, 'God loves each of you, but stay in your places'; it says there are no longer places, no longer categories, no longer differences in rights and privileges, codes and values."[35]

If we're preoccupied with maintaining our status, if we're trying to protect the privileges of some hierarchy taught by our particular culture, we are acting in a non-Christian way. These reactions are the opposite of the Gospel message. Gentiles, slaves, and women are not inferior; they are not less human; they are not less valuable to God.

Jesus came into a darkened world of oppression, where walls separated people, where the chains of thousands of years bound so many. Jesus tore down the walls and broke the chains. In Christ there are no Jews or Gentiles, no slave or free, no males or females. All are equal at the foot of the Cross.

Jesus became like the least of us to redeem all of us—no one is excluded; no one is left on the margins looking through the lattice of a balcony or through the cloth of a veil. Jesus' death challenged all the established cultural views. No more walls are left standing. We are no longer to be either prisoners or perpetrators of discrimination in any form. Jesus is our one shared hope. His birth as a human reminds us of our shared origins. His death on the cross forever heals our shared tragedy. His Resurrection restores us to our shared destiny. We are called to sit with Christ in heavenly places, to go out into the world filled with the Spirit, to walk out the Gospel in all of our relationships, to stand tall because each of us is valuable in the sight of God.

11.

Bringing the Gospel
to Sin City, a.d. 50

By David Hamilton

Any serious student of Paul's view of women should
concentrate on 1 Corinthians, for Paul devoted more
space to gender issues in this Epistle than in any other.

When we read what Paul has to say, we must keep in mind that his
words are only half of a dialogue. It's like overhearing someone speaking on the phone. We have to re-create what the other person is saying. Paul's Epistles were written in response to communication—oral
reports and letters that he received from the fledgling churches. Since
we don't have the other half of the communication, to gain greater
understanding of this letter we must find out everything we can about
the situation in Corinth.

First, let's look at the city itself.

Sordidly Rich, Miserably Poor

Corinth straddled a narrow neck of land four miles (six kilome-
ters) wide connecting the two main parts of Greece. All traffic from
northern Greece to the south had to pass through Corinth. Also, to
avoid the dangerous waters off the southern tip of Greece, most sea
merchants from the eastern Mediterranean chose to have their goods

carried overland through Corinth before continuing their sea passage westward. This made Corinth a major crossroads, wealthy because of her ability to dominate commerce and trade. Soon she rivaled Athens as the center of Greek culture. During Roman occupation, Corinth also attracted many freedmen of the empire, including veteran Roman soldiers whose faithful service had won them citizenship.[1]

By the first century A.D., Corinth had grown from a small colony of perhaps 3,000 to become the greatest city of Greece. Although we have no census records, it's estimated that "the total population of the city and its territory approached 100,000 by the second century."[2] Corinth became very wealthy, "a kind of marketplace...everywhere full of wealth and an abundance of goods."[3] However, though Corinth was "a town charming indeed to look upon and abounding in luxuries," the "sordidness of the rich" was contrasted with the "misery of the poor."[4]

DON'T EVER TRUST A CORINTHIAN!

The city was both a center of the arts and culture—filled with beautiful statues, paintings, and highly prized craftsmanship—and host to important athletic events. But Corinth became famous for something else: It was so filled with promiscuous activity that the verb *korinthiazesthai*, "to live like a Corinthian," meant to live a life of sexual immorality. Likewise, Corinth was so filled with drunkenness that in many Greek plays Corinthians were depicted on stage as drunk.[5] That's why Paul warned Corinthian believers against drunkenness.[6] And that's why the Greek poet Menander wrote, "Trust [not] a Corinthian, and make him not thy friend."[7]

A GREAT ARMY OF HARLOTS

Like many port cities, Corinth became famous for its sex trade. A writer not long after Paul's time wrote that Corinth's "beauties, her passions, and her erotic pleasures attract many...for clearly this is Aphrodite's city."[8] Aphrodite was the Greek goddess of erotic love (known to the Romans as Venus). She was worshiped throughout the Mediterranean world, but especially in Corinth. Because of the city's reputation for immorality, Plato used the term *korinthia kore*, "a Corinthian girl," to mean a prostitute.[9] One author spoke of Corinth's "great army of harlots,"[10] while Strabo, writing at the time of Christ, said:

The temple of Aphrodite [in Corinth] was so rich that it owned more than a thousand temple-slaves, prostitutes, whom both men and women had dedicated to the goddess. And, therefore, it was also on account of these women that the city was crowded with people and grew rich. For instance, the ship captains freely squandered their money, and hence the proverb, "Not for every man is the voyage to Corinth."[11]

Besides Corinth's "sacred" prostitutes who gave their earnings to the temple, there were thousands more "secular" prostitutes. These prostitutes—sacred and secular—were central to Corinth's economy. They were also an honored part of the city's spiritual life. The ancients noted:

It is an ancient custom in Corinth…whenever the city prays to Aphrodite in matters of grave importance, to invite as many prostitutes as possible to join in their petitions, and these women add their supplications to the goddess and later are present at the sacrifices.[12]

A Smorgasbord of Cults

Though the patroness of the city, Aphrodite, reigned supreme, other gods and goddesses were also worshiped. Corinth was a veritable smorgasbord of religious cults. Most of the religions barred women. The exceptions were the mystery cults, which became very important to women. For example, in the secretive cult of Dionysus, women spent several days on the mountains dancing, drinking, and engaging in sexual immorality.[13]

Female worshipers of Dionysus were known as *maenads*, meaning "mad ones." It is significant that the term did not apply to men and that it was usually women who were smitten by the god's *mania*. The maenads boasted of this altered state of consciousness as a gift from Dionysus, who was the god of wine and madness. These women, who seldom saw the world that lay outside their own front door, hailed him as their liberator, Lusios. Biennially his god-given *mania* "set them free from shuttle and from loom" and drove them to the mountains to dance and rave and celebrate his revels, free from all restraint.[14]

Before Paul came, the religions open to Gentile women in Corinth were ones that often celebrated immorality or insanity. This was the corrupt, deceived city at which Paul arrived preaching the righteousness of Jesus Christ and His death on the cross.[15]

THE CHURCH PAUL FOUNDED

When Paul came to Corinth, about the year A.D. 50, he met two Jewish exiles from Rome named Aquila and Priscilla.[16] Since the couple also were tentmakers, Paul moved in with them to practice his trade while together they began the church. Paul was also joined by Silas and Timothy.[17] He and his team stayed about two years, preaching the kingdom of God.

The church founded by Paul and his team reflected the highs and lows of Corinth society:[18]

— Some of the new believers came from lifestyles of idolatry, immoral behavior, and financial corruption.
— Some were rich, but most were poor.
— Some were educated, but most were not.
— The church had both Jews and Gentiles.
— The church had slaves and free.
— The church included men and women.

This group of people crossed all demographic lines, probably showing far greater diversity than the church you or I attend every Sunday. This is important to understand when we look at Paul's admonitions to the people.

PRISCILLA, PAUL'S ESTEEMED COLLEAGUE

Paul didn't work in isolation. He usually worked with a team, relying on his coworkers to help him proclaim the Gospel and plant the churches. We've already seen that a married couple, Priscilla and Aquila, were on his team in Corinth. These two colleagues also helped plant the church in Ephesus and Rome. Paul expressed great confidence in their leadership skills and considered them among his most trusted coworkers.[19]

Sometimes God calls men to be ministry leaders. Other times, He calls women. And sometimes He calls a couple to serve together.

Priscilla and Aquila are an example of this. In the seven times these two are named in the New Testament, they are always mentioned together, inseparably linked in ministry. Not only that, but of those seven references, in five of them Priscilla's name comes first. This is contrary to the Roman custom of naming the man first when referring to a couple. In fact, this was so rarely done in antiquity that it seems to indicate that Priscilla was the more prominent member of this ministry couple.

So when Acts 18:26 says that together Priscilla and Aquila "invited [Apollos] to their home and explained to him the way of God more adequately," Priscilla probably took the lead in teaching Apollos the Gospel. Like Henrietta Mears in our time, who influenced Billy Graham and Bill Bright, Priscilla's pupil went on to have a prominent public ministry. Apollos was a powerfully anointed preacher in Corinth and elsewhere.[20] This understanding of Priscilla's contribution was given by John Chrysostom, a church father writing in the fourth century A.D.:

> This too is worthy of inquiry, why, as he addressed them, Paul has placed Priscilla before her husband. For he did not say, "Greet Aquila and Priscilla," but *"Priscilla and Aquila."* He does not do this without a reason, but he seems to me to acknowledge a greater godliness for her than for her husband. What I said is not guess-work, because it is possible to learn this from the Book of Acts. [Priscilla] took Apollos, an eloquent man and powerful in the Scriptures, but knowing only the baptism of John; and she instructed him in the way of the Lord and made him a teacher brought to completion (Acts 18:24–25).[21]

These words by John Chrysostom are all the more remarkable because he was known for making many statements against women.

NOTHING UNUSUAL

What seemed so obvious to Chrysostom in the fourth century is not clear at all to some Bible teachers today who argue that the word *explain* (*ektitheimi*) in Acts 18:26 is entirely different from *teach* (*didasko*) in 1 Timothy 2:12, where Paul seems to prohibit women from having the same ministry Priscilla had. But what is teaching if it's not explaining the truth to someone? The only reason for splitting semantic hairs is if you start with a bias against women teaching, then try to support that position while excusing obvious Bible examples that contradict it.

No, Luke clearly said that Priscilla, with her husband's help, taught Apollos the ways of God. What's astounding is the very natural, almost casual way Luke mentions this. If Paul actually did teach against women ministers, how can we account for his close companion and colleague reporting Priscilla's contribution in such a matter-of-fact way? For Luke, there was nothing unusual about the fact that Priscilla was teaching.

Another writer said:

> It is crucial to notice the subtle yet astounding information Luke provided when he recorded a woman guiding one of the most noted teachers in the early church. One must not overlook the key fact that Apollos accepted Priscilla's instruction without reservation. Moreover, neither Luke nor Paul criticize Priscilla for having taught a man. If Priscilla had violated Paul's alleged prohibition against the teaching ministry of women it seems likely that either Luke or Paul would have criticized her for having taught a man.[22]

Even Tertullian, the early church father so often quoted for his accusatory statements against women,[23] recognized that "[b]y the holy Prisca [or Priscilla] the Gospel is preached."[24]

DID PRISCILLA WRITE THE BOOK OF HEBREWS?

In recent times, several scholars have advanced the possibility that Priscilla was the author of the letter to the Hebrews, the nineteenth book of the New Testament.[25]

The following are some of the indications that Priscilla may have written Hebrews:
— The fact that the letter is anonymous may point to its having a female author, since a woman's byline might have discredited it.
— Priscilla was known to be an excellent teacher—much of what's said in Hebrews could have been taught to Apollos.
— The author of Hebrews obviously was a close associate of Paul's, as Priscilla was.

— Paul seems to be dead at the time of the book's writing, and Paul specifically mentioned Timothy, Priscilla, and Aquila in his last known letter.

— Several women are listed as heroes of the faith in Hebrews chapter 11.

— The writer of Hebrews includes a number of practical examples of childhood and parenthood.

— Four nautical terms are mentioned in the Greek (not apparent in English translations), and Priscilla made at least four sea voyages.

— The author's great interest in the tabernacle could indicate the author was a tentmaker.

— Sometimes the author uses a plural voice, which might indicate she was including Aquila.[26]

Did Priscilla write the book of Hebrews? I don't know. But she was undoubtedly a gifted teacher. Apollos and Paul respected her. This anointed woman played a crucial role, helping to establish churches in Corinth, Ephesus, and Rome.

OTHER WOMEN LEADERS IN CORINTH

Other women were significant in the life of the Corinthian church. Chloe was mentioned in 1 Corinthians 1:11: "My brothers, some from Chloe's household have informed me that there are quarrels among you." The word *household* does not appear in the Greek because Paul used an ellipsis.[27] The Greek literally says, "those...of Chloe." This phrase grammatically parallels two phrases in Romans 16. In the second half of Romans 16:10, Paul said, "Greet those...of Aristobulus." Again, *household* is understood but not stated in the Greek. This also occurs in the second half of Romans 16:11, where Paul said, "Greet those...of Narcissus who are in the Lord." Once again Paul used an ellipsis, leaving out *of the household.*

These two greetings are commonly understood as greetings to house churches led by Aristobulus and Narcissus. How interesting that Paul used the exact same phrase to describe the household of Chloe. It seems that Chloe was more than a homeowner; she was a leader of one of the Corinthian house churches.[28]

If Chloe was a leader in the Corinthian church, Paul's words in 1 Corinthians 1:11 take on new urgency. Paul wasn't responding to some idle gossip that somehow made its way to him. He was responding to the report of an official delegation sent by one of the church's leaders. Paul took Chloe's report seriously. This was in clear contrast to another Jew of Paul's upbringing who said, "How could a woman possibly evaluate spiritual matters and rightly assess the condition of the people of God?"[29]

Paul considered Chloe's evaluation to be trustworthy. Because he believed her assessment of the condition of God's people, we have the book of 1 Corinthians.[30] If the words of a woman leader in the church of Corinth led to Paul's writing this Epistle, how can we believe that Paul would categorically silence women in the church?

SUBMITTING, LABORING TOGETHER

It's possible that Paul named another woman church leader in Corinth. Stephana is mentioned in 1 Corinthians 16:15. Stephana was a woman's name. In rare instances it was also used as a diminutive for a man's name, Stephanos. Since Stephana in this instance was clearly someone in authority, commentators and translators have assumed that Stephana was a man, even though the most natural sense of the Greek would appear to point to a woman.[31] Apparently translators have assumed this because Paul urged the Corinthians to submit to Stephana's authority: "I urge you, brothers, to submit to such as these and to everyone who joins in the work, and labors at it."[32] Could Paul ask "brothers"[33] to submit to a person in leadership if that person were a woman?

If you view submission in a hierarchical way, with "lesser" individuals submitting to those who are "greater," and if you believe that women are lesser than men, Paul's words in 1 Corinthians 16:15–16 could pose a real problem. On the other hand, if you understand the mutual submission commanded of all believers, and if you believe in the equality of men and women, there is no problem at all.[34] Submitting to one another in the Body of Christ is a normal part of life in the Spirit.

I don't think it really matters whether Stephana was a man or a woman. What is important in 1 Corinthians 16:15–16 is that Paul urged everyone to *submit*,[35] to *join in the work*, and to *labor* at it. These latter two words are forms of Greek words Paul used to describe women whom he considered his peers and partners in ministry:

— *sunergos*, or coworkers—Euodia, Syntyche, and Priscilla[36]

— *kopiao*, or laborer—Mary, Persis, Tryphena, and Tryphosa[37]

In fact, if you check out the thirty-nine people whom Paul specifically mentioned as colleagues in ministry, you discover that he spoke of the ten women and the twenty-nine men in identical ways.[38] F. F. Bruce states:

> [Paul] seems to make no distinction between men and women among his fellow workers. Men receive praise, and women receive praise for the collaboration with him in the Gospel ministry, without any suggestion that there is a subtle distinction between the one and the other in respect of status or function.[39]

VIP TREATMENT FOR A VERY IMPORTANT WOMAN

Last but certainly not least was Phoebe, also associated with the church at Corinth. Phoebe was from Cenchrea, a suburb of greater metropolitan Corinth. Paul's words about her in the closing lines of his letter to the Romans tell us much about the status of women in the Corinthian church:

> I commend to you our sister Phoebe, a servant of the church in Cenchrea. I ask you to receive her in the Lord in a way worthy of the saints and to give her any help she may need from you, for she has been a great help to many people, including me.[40]

Evidently, Paul entrusted Phoebe with the important job of carrying his letter to the Roman believers. Let's look carefully at his words about her and how he expected the Roman church to receive her.

Standing with Phoebe

Paul started off by saying he "commended" Phoebe. The Greek word for *commend* literally means "to stand with." Paul was saying that he would stand with Phoebe and unreservedly endorsed her. Given the Corinthian context, this commendation was extremely significant.[41]

The Corinthians were obsessed with status. Today we say of such people, "He believes his own press releases!" Paul refused to play their prideful games. He rebuked those "who commend themselves."[42] He said, "It is not the one who commends himself who is approved, but the one whom the Lord commends."[43] Paul wouldn't seek for himself letters of recommendation[44] so coveted by those who aspired to spiritual leadership in the church. This makes it all the more important that Paul wholeheartedly commended Phoebe. Paul said that the Corinthian believers should have commended him and didn't.[45] He wanted to make sure this didn't happen to Phoebe. So he stood with her, giving her the commendation she merited. In the status-conscious Corinthian church, this was a clear sign of recognized spiritual authority.

No Gender Distinction

After declaring his endorsement of her, Paul used two key words to describe Phoebe. He called her a sister in the same way that he often called his male coworkers brothers. Then he called her a *diakonos*. Many translations render this Greek word as "servant." This is not incorrect, although it might be better to translate it "deacon" or "minister" as is done in other New Testament passages.[46]

However you translate it, the important thing to note is that Paul used the same word here that he often used for his male coworkers.[47] The King James translation inserted a feminine form, *deaconess*, in Romans 16:1. But there was no feminine form of *diakonos* in the New Testament or in any church literature until about three hundred years later.[48] There was no gender distinction in this term for ministers of the Gospel. Both men and women were simply called "deacons."[49]

We should also realize that over the centuries the church has come to define *deacon* as something different from a full-time minister. In most Protestant churches, a deacon is a layperson serving on a board with others, helping the pastor run the business of the local church. However, no such distinction between *minister* and *deacon* existed in the New Testament.

Double Honor

It is especially significant that Paul said that Phoebe was "a servant/deacon/minister" of the church in Cenchrea. This is the only place in the New Testament that the noun *diakonos* is modified by the phrase "of the church." Paul wanted his readers to understand that

Phoebe was not just a servant girl. She was a minister of the Gospel who served the church in a publicly recognizable way.

Then Paul got to the point. Because Phoebe was who Paul said she was, the Romans were supposed to "receive her." This was the same word Paul used on one other occasion. When he wrote to the Philippians, he praised a highly esteemed coworker named Epaphroditus, telling them to receive him in the Lord because of his great service.[50]

Interestingly, Paul tells the Romans to receive Phoebe "in a way worthy of the saints." This is similar to his teaching in 1 Timothy 5:17, where he said that elders who directed the affairs of the church well were worthy of double honor, especially those whose work was preaching and teaching. This shows how strongly Paul was commending Phoebe: He asked his readers to receive her with the same attitude universally due godly church leaders.

Give Her a Blank Check

Paul also told the Roman believers to help Phoebe. This word is related to the verb *commend,* meaning literally "to stand with." Just as he *stood with* Phoebe, Paul wanted them to *stand with* Phoebe. Plus, he asked them to give her the equivalent of a blank check, saying they were to stand with her in "whatever she may need."

At this point, the Roman church might have been wondering, "Just who *is* this Phoebe, anyway, for Paul to ask all this?" Paul told them why she deserved special treatment, saying she was a *prostatis.* The Greek word *prostatis* is rich with meaning, but it appears only this one time in the New Testament. Most translators have used *helper* in this passage, but that is far weaker sounding than the word in Greek.[51] *Servant-leader* comes a little closer because it describes a leader who champions the cause of others rather than pursuing self-interest. We don't have a strong enough equivalent in our language, yet there is no word in the Greek to better describe the godly leadership modeled by Jesus, who said that anyone aspiring to leadership must be the servant of all.[52]

In other ancient literature, *prostatis* was used to describe the noblest, most gracious, and beneficial rulers. Emperors, kings, governors, nobles, patriarchs, captains, and numerous other authoritative officials were referred to by this word. Only one person was so described in the New Testament: Phoebe. Paul couldn't have honored her more.[53]

As if this weren't enough, Paul went on to say that "many people" had benefited from Phoebe's role as servant-leader. Her role wasn't insignificant. Her authority had served a great number of people.

Then he added the final salvo. The last phrase of Romans 16:2 can be translated two ways: either "and *of* me myself," indicating that Paul himself had personally benefited from her servant-leadership, recognizing her authority over him in certain areas, or "and *by* me myself," which would mean that he had appointed her to this role of church leadership.[54] Whichever the case, since Paul gave her such an extraordinary commendation, Phoebe was obviously an extraordinary sister, deacon, and *prostatis*.

Thus we see that the idea of women in leadership was anything but foreign to the Corinthian believers. Capable women had closely collaborated with Paul in his missionary endeavors in Corinth. Phoebe, Priscilla, Chloe, and perhaps Stephana were significant to the life and leadership of the church in Corinth. This lay in stark contrast to the role of women in other religions of Corinth, where women either were not allowed at all or participated as objects of lust or as drunken madwomen.

PAUL'S TEACHING ON GENDER ROLES

Paul spent more time in 1 Corinthians on the sexes and how they relate to each other than he did in any other letter. Take the Greek word for *man/husband*.[55] Paul used it sixty times in his Epistles, with thirty-two of those in 1 Corinthians. He used the Greek word for *woman/wife*[56] sixty-four times, forty-one of which are in this Epistle. Therefore, it would be unwise of us to gloss over all Paul had to say on the genders in this Epistle and jump straight into the "problem verses" for women.

Right at the beginning of his letter, Paul said he was going to preach the Gospel, but not with words of human wisdom.[57] He knew well the competing versions of human wisdom in Corinth, and he didn't mince words in dealing with them. He said the unconverted Jews who sought miraculous signs and the Greeks who looked for wisdom were both wrong. He declared these two views to be weak and foolish. Only the power of the Cross could transform people.[58]

Paul confronted the prevailing philosophies of Greeks, Romans, and Jews and showed how men and women were to relate to each other in light of the Cross and its transforming influence. We've already seen in earlier chapters of this book how human wisdom had relegated women to secondary status. Greek philosophers said that women were a separate creation, that they were less than human. The results of this belief were disastrous for society. This philosophy paved the way for a city where they not only had an army of harlots but also took pride in it! After all, women were only objects—either for men to use for self-gratification or objects of sin to be avoided by men who wanted to be righteous. Either way, women were objects, not real people.

In his letter to the Corinthians, Paul showed women as persons. Women were neither to be objects of lust nor to be avoided as inherently sinful. They were to be fully included as equals in the Body of Christ.

CONFRONTING THE FOULEST ACTS

Paul's first instructions to the Corinthians in the area of gender are in chapters 5 and 6, where he squared off against those who were using women as objects of pleasure. Paul pointed out that a man in the church was having an open, incestuous affair with his father's wife.[59]

The ancient pagans considered mother-son incest one of the foulest acts. Paul said that "such fornication…is not so much as named among the Gentiles."[60] Even in sensuous Corinth, this was shocking. So how on earth did such a situation come to be tolerated? And how could such an individual be proud of what he was doing?[61]

It was the result of Greek philosophy, specifically an idea called "dualism," combined with a distorted view of God's grace. Dualism was the belief that spirit/soul were separate from body/matter. Because the dualist believed that the physical world was separate from the spiritual world, and since grace had redeemed the soul, it didn't matter what a man did with his body. In fact, the more sin he committed, the more it showed that he was trusting in the grace of God instead of his own righteousness! The more you sinned with your body, the more "holy" you were in the spirit.

Paul came down on this devilish lie, and he came down hard. He used some of the strongest language in the New Testament to correct this and told the Corinthian believers to "hand this man over to Satan."[62]

Coming Against Culturally Acceptable Acts

Unlike incest, prostitution was considered normal and beneficial in Corinth. Some in the church were using women as objects of lust in this way. Again, the culprit was that theological mixture of dualism and distorted grace. Because their bodies were separate from their souls, which Jesus had died for, everything was permissible with their bodies.[63]

Again Paul countered with a resounding, "No!" He told the Corinthians that despite what their culture taught, despite what they had been raised to believe, "The body is not meant for sexual immorality, but for the Lord, and the Lord for the body.... Shall I then take the members of Christ and unite them with a prostitute? Never!...Flee from sexual immorality...honor God with your body."[64]

The Opposite Extreme

After he dealt so forcefully with those who used women, Paul then turned in 1 Corinthians 7 to those who avoided women. Men often react to gross immorality by going to the other extreme, advocating celibacy. Instead of receiving God's gift of sex in marriage, they believe sexual behavior itself is evil and degrading.

So in Corinth, while some said, "Anything goes," others answered, "No, nothing goes!" It wasn't enough to flee sexual immorality; they wanted to flee all sexuality. To them, sin was not bound up in the choices of their heart; it resided in matter itself, particularly in the bodies of women. Therefore, they taught, "It is good for a man not to marry."[65] They had a wrong view of creation in general and of women in particular. These Christians thought they could be closer to God if they could stay away from women entirely.

Paul's response in 1 Corinthians 7 was nothing short of revolutionary. It presented a picture of marriage and of singleness that was startling in its simplicity. No longer was gender the great divide. Paul swept away the double standards. Instead, he spoke to men and women equally, sometimes addressing the men first, sometimes addressing the women first, sometimes speaking to both together, giving a seamless symmetry of obligations and expectations. To see how evenly he did this, I have put his instructions on marriage in two columns.

1 CORINTHIANS 7

²ᵃ …each man should have his own wife,	²ᵇ and each woman her own husband.
³ᵃ The husband should fulfill his marital duty to his wife,	³ᵇ and likewise the wife to her husband.
⁴ᵃ The wife's body does not belong to her alone but also to her husband.	⁴ᵇ In the same way, the husband's body does not belong to him alone but also to his wife.

⁵ Do not deprive each other except by **mutual** consent and for a time, so that you may devote yourselves to prayer. Then come together again so that Satan will not tempt you because of your lack of self-control…

¹¹ᵇ And a husband must not divorce his wife.	¹⁰ᵇ A wife must not separate from her husband. ¹¹ᵃ But if she does, she must remain unmarried or else be reconciled to her husband.
¹² …If any brother has a wife who is not a believer and she is willing to live with him, he must not divorce her.	¹³ And if a woman has a husband who is not a believer and he is willing to live with her, she must not divorce him.
¹⁴ᵃ For the unbelieving husband has been sanctified through his wife,	¹⁴ᵇ and the unbelieving wife has been sanctified through her believing husband…

¹⁵ But if the unbeliever leaves, let him do so. A believing man **or** woman is not bound in such circumstances; God has called us to live in peace.

¹⁶ᵇ Or, how do you know, husband, whether you will save your wife?	¹⁶ᵃ How do you know, wife, whether you will save your husband?
³²ᵇ …An unmarried man is concerned about the Lord's affairs—how he can please the Lord. ³³ But a married man is concerned about the affairs of this world—how he can please his wife—³⁴ᵃ and his interests are divided.	³⁴ᵇ An unmarried woman or virgin is concerned about the Lord's affairs: Her aim is to be devoted to the Lord in both body and spirit. But a married woman is concerned about the affairs of this world—how she can please her husband.

WHO HAS THE AUTHORITY IN MARRIAGE?

Notice a couple of points in these pairs of teaching. First, Paul said that marriage was between *one* man and *one* woman. It was an exclusive commitment: Each was to be absolutely faithful to the other.

Next we see that Paul told them they shouldn't refuse their spouse's desire for sex. Unlike the rabbis, who gave men the right to withhold themselves from their wives but never the other way around, Paul forbade either to do this. In fact, Paul did something even more remarkable. The only place where the word *authority*[66] appears in the New Testament regarding the relationship between a husband and wife is here, and it's used twice. It literally says that the husband has *authority* over his wife's body and that she has *authority* over his body! So, the only time the New Testament mentions *authority* in relation to marriage, it is made mutual. Incredible!

We could go through every one of the points on Paul's list, but we can already see how radically different Paul's view of marriage was. Only equality and mutuality were acceptable at the foot of the Cross. No longer could one sex look down on the other or demand subjugation. No longer were women to be avoided. They were to be valued as partners and treated as peers.

You may notice a gap in Paul's teaching on marriage in this chapter from verses 17 to 31. That's because he turned to discuss Jew/Gentile issues and slave/free issues before returning to the subject of marriage and singleness. In a sense, chapter 7 of 1 Corinthians was Paul's expanded version of Galatians 3:28: "There is neither Jew nor Greek, slave nor free, male nor female, for you are all one in Christ Jesus." In his letter to the Galatians, Paul was dealing with the Galatians' big issue: racial conflicts. Here, in his letter to the Corinthians, he is dealing with another big issue: gender problems. Paul knew the power the Gospel had to transform the way men and women related to each other.

VALUE FOR SINGLE WOMEN

It all came down to mutuality and equality because of Jesus Christ. Whether we are married or single, Paul's overall principle was given in 1 Corinthians 7:17: "Nevertheless, each one should retain the place in life that the Lord assigned to him [or her] and to which God has called him [or her]. This is the rule I lay down in all the churches."[67]

Paul repeated this in 1 Corinthians 7:20 and 24. It sounded simple, but it was profound in its implications. In their world, women were not valued for themselves. A woman was valued only because of her reproductive potential. If she was married and producing children, she was worth something. Otherwise, she was not only a nuisance but also a drain on society's resources.

Paul contradicted this thinking in 1 Corinthians 7 when he encouraged women (and men) to consider singleness as a lifestyle. It wasn't that Paul didn't value marriage. It was because he fully valued human beings. Because men and women were intrinsically valuable, marriage was no longer the all-encompassing goal of life for women. Life's goal wasn't wrapped up in sexual affairs; it was being "concerned about the Lord's affairs"[68] and living "in a right way in undivided devotion to the Lord."[69] That's why Paul personally relinquished the right of marriage.[70] When he affirmed a woman's intrinsic value, regardless of whether she was single, married, or widowed, he gave her the same lifestyle options that he gave to men.

There is one more thing to see in this passage: When Paul said both men and women can be "concerned about the Lord's affairs,"[71] he was doing away with the rabbis' teaching to the contrary. The rabbis had excluded women from the spiritual life of the people of God, relegating them to an exclusively domestic role. But with this one phrase, "concerned about the Lord's affairs," Paul opened myriads of ministry opportunities for both men and women. You cannot find a ministry restriction based on gender within the framework Paul developed in 1 Corinthians 7.

RESTORING THE CREATION STORY

Paul effectively corrected those who saw women as objects to be used or avoided. He made it clear that women were peers in the church when he turned to the subject of resurrection. In 1 Corinthians 15:39, Paul began his explanation of resurrection by reminding the church at Corinth that humans—men and women—were different from the animals. "Not all flesh is alike; but there is one flesh for human beings, another for animals, another for birds, and another for fish."[72]

In this verse, Paul recounted the order of creation in reverse:

— human beings[73]

— animals[74]
— birds[75]
— fish[76]

By doing this, Paul reminded the Corinthian believers that both men and women were created in the image of God: "[T]here is one flesh for human beings." It's easy for us to miss the impact of Paul's words on his original audience. They grew up hearing the creation stories of Hesiod and Semonides,[77] who made elaborate divisions, separating the origin of men from women, saying that women were a divine curse, originating from a sow, a donkey, or some other despised animal.

Paul swept those deceptions aside, affirming our shared origin, that men and women have "one flesh,"[78] telling of the shared tragedy of sin, and proclaiming our shared hope of redemption in Jesus. "For since death came through a human being, the resurrection of the dead has also come through a person; for as all die in Adam, so all will be made alive in Christ."[79]

We have seen how committed Paul was to the equal standing of every man and woman before God and each other. With this firm foundation under our feet, let us turn to Paul's more difficult passages concerning women.

12.

THE QUESTION OF HEADSHIP

(Part One of 1 Corinthians 11:2–16)

By David Hamilton

*P*eople who love Jesus want to be obedient to His call upon their lives. The hearts of both men and women who follow Jesus stir with the desire to use their God-given gifts and talents to see the kingdom of God extended and the Great Commission fulfilled. However, three statements of Paul's pose a problem for women who are committed to obeying the Word of God yet feel called to public ministry.

1. "The head of a woman is the man."[1]
2. "Women should remain silent in the churches."[2]
3. "I do not permit a woman to teach."[3]

How can a woman read these passages and be both faithful to the Word of God and faithful to the gifts and callings God has given her?

We will look squarely at these passages in the next several chapters and answer the questions that they have raised. Many look at these passages, such as the one in 1 Corinthians 11, and wonder. It appears that Paul is contradicting the equality he has been promoting. What happened to the great egalitarian whom we saw moments ago, overturning patriarchal societies, flying in the face of the second-class status given to women? Is he backing down, soft-pedaling, retreating from his previous statements? Is Paul contradicting himself? Does the Bible contradict itself?

God Welcomes Our Questions

Though some passages may at first appear contradictory, we can be sure that God does not contradict Himself. God is truthful, unchanging, the absolute source of all knowledge and wisdom. Not only that, but He reveals truth to us and invites us to question Him when we don't understand. God doesn't ask us to abandon our minds. The God of the Bible created our minds, and He will help us as we wrestle with things we find difficult to comprehend. He said that if we lack wisdom and we come to Him, He will give it.[4] There are answers, and He will help us find them.

Look at the Context

We need to look at any troubling verse in its context to discern its true meaning. So let's back up and take a look at the big picture of this section of 1 Corinthians. Starting with 1 Corinthians 11:2, Paul addressed pressing concerns in the corporate life of the Corinthian church. In the following four chapters, he dealt with

— 1 Corinthians 11:2–16   gender issues in public ministry
— 1 Corinthians 11:17–34   instructions regarding the Lord's Supper
— 1 Corinthians 12:1–11   the diversity of God's gifts
— 1 Corinthians 12:12–31a   unity in the Body of Christ
— 1 Corinthians 12:31b–13:13   love as the motive of ministry
— 1 Corinthians 14:1–25   the gifts of prophecy and tongues
— 1 Corinthians 14:26–40   how corporate worship should take place

Leading with Gender Issues

Paul began with gender issues because, evidently, it was one of the leading issues in Corinth. Earlier in this Epistle, he had given teaching that placed men and women as equals and showed each individual's value. Now Paul has turned to how men and women should relate in public ministry.

For this discussion in 1 Corinthians 11:2–16, Paul used a method of teaching common in the Bible called "interchange." He alternated between two sets of ideas, different but related. Scholars call it the A-B-A-B structure. On one hand ("A"), Paul discussed right attitudes—bedrock principles that guide all behavior for all Christians everywhere. On the other hand ("B"), he showed the practical outworking of those attitudes in the right attire for their society, for first-century Corinth.

Let's look at 1 Corinthians 11 with the A-B-A-B structure in mind:

1 CORINTHIANS 11:2–16 [5]

[INTRODUCTION]

²I praise you for remembering me in everything and for holding to the teachings, just as I passed them on to you.

"A"

³Now I want you to realize that the head of every man is Christ, and the head of a woman is the man, and the head of Christ is God.

"B"

⁴Every man who prays or prophesies with his head covered dishonors his head. ⁵And every woman who prays or prophesies with her head uncovered dishonors her head—it is just as though her head were shaved. ⁶If a woman does not cover her head, she should have her hair cut off; and if it is a disgrace for a woman to have her hair cut or shaved off, she should cover her head. ⁷A man ought not to cover his head, since he is the image and glory of God; but the woman is the glory of man.

["A" RIGHT ATTITUDE "B" RIGHT ATTIRE]

"A"

⁸For man did not come from woman, but woman from man; ⁹neither was man created for woman, but woman for man. ¹⁰For this reason, and because of the angels, the woman ought to have authority over her head. ¹¹In the Lord, however, woman is not independent of man, nor is man independent of woman. ¹²For as woman came from man, so also man is born of woman. But everything comes from God.

["A" RIGHT ATTITUDE "B" RIGHT ATTIRE]

"B"

¹³Judge for yourselves: Is it proper for a woman to pray to God with her head uncovered? ¹⁴Does not the very nature of things teach you that if a man has long hair, it is a disgrace to him, ¹⁵but that if a woman has long hair, it is her glory? For long hair is given to her as a covering.

[CONCLUSION]

¹⁶If anyone wants to be contentious about this, we have no other practice—nor do the churches of God.

WHAT DID HE MEAN BY "HEAD"?

Read Paul's words carefully: "Now I want you to realize that the head of every man is Christ, and the head of a woman is the man, and the head of Christ is God."[6] Was Paul contradicting the equality he had already promoted? Much hinges on our interpretation of the word *head*.

What comes to your mind when you hear the word *head*? Probably something like boss, leader, authority, ruler, top dog, the big cheese, or head honcho. Right? To be honest, it doesn't matter what you or I think. What matters is what Paul's original readers thought. What image did the word *head* bring to the mind of first-century Corinthians?

In Greek, the word is *kephale*. Like its English equivalent, it is used to refer to the part of our body that sits above our shoulders and is also used in several metaphorical meanings. When it comes to these various meanings, we enter a real battleground between Greek experts. Some of these word warriors believe it could mean "authority over," as it does in English when we say "the *head* of a department." Others think this Greek word was primarily used to convey the idea of "source" or "origin,"[7] as it does in English when we speak of the *head*waters of a river. On the one hand, Liddell and Scott list forty-eight English meanings for *kephale* in their dictionary, and not one of them means "leader," "authority," "first," or "supreme."[8] On the other hand, Bauer's lexicon gives "superior rank" as one of its meanings.[9] How could experts disagree over the meaning of a word?

"Waiter, Could You Please Bring Me a Diaper?"

Several reasons exist for disagreement between the experts. For one, any language is a living thing. Meanings for words change dramatically over time.

Sometimes this happens very quickly. Consider the word *gay* and what it meant to our grandparents versus what it means to us today. To our grandparents, *gay* meant "happy" or "carefree." It was first used to mean "homosexual" in the late 1960s. That happened in a few years, but scholars of ancient Greek are attempting to define words that evolved over many centuries. Imagine how hard to pinpoint the precise meaning for a word during a limited period of time, such as the few decades of Paul's ministry.

Added to that are the differences within a language as it is spoken in various parts of the world. Americans discover this when they visit

England. A tourist in a restaurant might drop his "napkin" and ask the waiter for another, not realizing he has just asked the waiter to bring him a "diaper"! Such differences existed in Paul's day, too, as educated people from every part of the vast Roman Empire spoke the Greek language.

Ancient Clues

Where does that leave us? Can we discover what the word *kephale* meant to Paul when he said that man was the *kephale* of woman? We have several sources that will aid us. For one, we need to look at the ancient Greek translation of the Hebrew Scriptures. This translation, called the Septuagint, would have been what Paul would have used when ministering among Greek-speaking people. This gets a little complicated, but it's worth our time to search carefully for the clues to solve this puzzle.

The word for "head" in Hebrew is *ro'sh*. As in English, *ro'sh* can mean part of the body, or it can mean "leader" or "ruler." When *ro'sh* meant a physical head in a passage of the Old Testament, the Septuagint translators chose *kephale* (the word Paul used in 1 Corinthians 11:3) to translate it 226 out of the 239 times, or about 95 percent of the time. However, when *ro'sh* clearly meant "ruler" or "leader," the Septuagint translators used some other word 171 times out of 180. They used *kephale* for "ruler" or "leader" only 5 percent of the time.[10]

To put it simply, it is possible that Paul used *kephale* in 1 Corinthians 11:3 to mean that man should be the "leader" or "ruler" over woman, but that would be a rare usage of the word, as seen by the evidence of the Septuagint. On the other hand, we find many, many times in ancient literature where *head/kephale* meant "source" or "origin." This came from the ancients' idea that semen, the *source* of life, was produced in the male brain, which is, of course, located in the *head*. Aristotle believed this and influenced generations after him.[11] Therefore, the head represented the source of life for them. Because of this, the Romans occasionally referred to sexual intercourse as "diminishing one's head."[12]

Likewise, *kephale* was the word used for the source of a river. This is why the Greeks and Romans often set up the bearded head of a man or a bull at a fountain or at the source of a river. This meaning was carried over into Latin and later into English, so that we still refer to the source of a river as its *head*waters.

Erich Lessing/Art Resource, NY

Which Is It?

Back to our question for 1 Corinthians 11:3: If *kephale* could be either "ruler" or "life source," how was Paul using it here? If we were to substitute these meanings for *head/kephale* in the text, we could come up with two alternatives:

1. "Now I want you to realize that the *authority/leader* of every man is Christ, and the *authority/leader* of a woman is the man, and the *authority/leader* of Christ is God."

2. "Now I want you to realize that the *source/origin* of every man is Christ, and the *source/origin* of a woman is the man, and the *source/origin* of Christ is God."

Which meaning for *kephale* best fits the context of 1 Corinthians 11? Four things about this passage give us clues.

Clue #1: What's Missing?

If Paul was talking about man being the authority/leader over woman, if he was teaching that women should submit to men's "God-given" leadership, we could expect to see that theme woven throughout these verses. But when we look at the passage, two things are striking because of their absence:

1. The word *submission* is never used once in this passage.
2. *Authority*[13] appears only once, and there it speaks of "the authority a woman has over her own head."[14]

What about the other meaning for *head/kephale* as "source/origin"? The idea of "origins" is found throughout the passage. First of all, the language of verse 7 is reminiscent of the Genesis account. Then, verses 8 and 9 talk about how the first woman originated from man. Next, verse 12 brings that idea full circle to say that since then every man has originated from a woman. Paul finally sums it all up by saying that everything originated from God. It is all about origins. Remember the A-B-A-B structure we said Paul used here? It fits perfectly. The first "A" is verse 3. After "B" (verses 4–7, where Paul discussed what to wear on their heads), verses 8–12 go back to "A" to further explain verse 3. It is precisely these verses that address at length the subject of origins. So if you translate *kephale* as "source/origin," it's a perfect flow within the structure of the passage. But if you try to fit "authority/leader" into verse 3, it doesn't fit the rest of the passage.

Clue #2: Who Is "The Man"?

Look again at verse 3. See the first two pairs of relationship (every man/Christ, and a woman/the man)? The first pair is a universal statement—*every man...Christ.* The second pair is specific, about *a woman...the man.*[15] Why does Paul shift from the universal to the specific? Who is this "woman," and who is "the man"?

If Paul is talking about "authority/leader" in verse 3, you get into some real difficulty here. *Which* man is the authority/leader over *which* woman? If Paul is talking about husbands being the authority over their wives, why does he switch from "every man" to the singular, specific "the man"? Or, since marriage isn't specifically mentioned, is Paul saying *any* man has authority over *any* woman? Or if this is about marriage, though not mentioned, where would this leave single women? What about widows? If a man has authority over any woman, does a mother need to submit to her son?

Some Messy Questions

If you translate *head/kephale* in verse 3 as "authority/leader," you inherit some very messy questions. Also, it seems inaccurate to say that Christ is presently the "authority/leader" of every man.[16] Is this true? Is Jesus Christ presently the "authority/leader" of everyone on earth? Look around you. Read the headlines. Check out what's on TV. No, Jesus is not the "authority/leader" of every person, not yet. The Bible says that someday He will be. Someday, every knee will bow and every tongue will confess that Jesus Christ is Lord.[17] But it's not that way right now.

On the other hand, if we look at 1 Corinthians 11:3 with *head/kephale* meaning "source/origin," everything falls into place in the entire passage. Jesus is the "source/origin" of everyone and everything, even though not everyone yet acknowledges Him as his or her "authority/leader."

Paul told the pagan philosophers in Athens that Jesus "gives all men life and breath and everything else.... For in him we live and move and have our being. As some of your own poets have said, 'We are his off-spring.'"[18] Jesus *is* the "source/origin" of life for "every man." In fact, Paul established this point earlier in the Corinthian letter, declaring, "[Y]et for us there is but one God, the Father, from whom all things came and for whom we live; and there is but one Lord, Jesus Christ, through whom all things came and through whom we live."[19]

Translating *head/kephale* as "origin/source" also answers the question, Who is "the man" in 1 Corinthians 11:3? Paul started by saying that Christ was the origin/source of every man, then went on to say "the man" was the origin/source of woman. Who else could that man be but Adam? Adam was the origin/source for Eve. Once again, Paul was denying the teaching of Greek philosophers, who claimed that women had a separate and inferior origin. No, Paul said, woman came from man, making her fully human and fully equal to man. This also fits the A-B-A-B structure, for when Paul explains in verses 8 and 9 what he meant in verse 3, he refers to Adam when he wrote, "For man did not come from woman, but woman from man; neither was man created for woman, but woman for man."

Clue #3: A Question of Who Came First

Another indication of what Paul meant can be found in the order in which he listed the three pairs: "every man/Christ," "a woman/the man," and "Christ/God." If Paul were giving us a divinely established hierarchy, we'd expect him to begin at the top and work his way down. The usual way to present a chain of command would look like this:

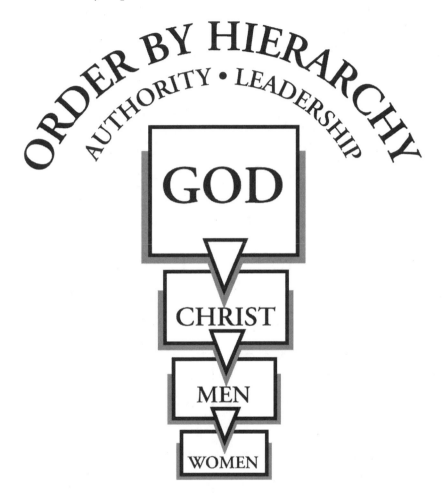

However, Paul did *not* list the pairs in a normal flowchart. Instead, he began with "every man/Christ," then, "a woman/the man," and finally, "Christ/God." If Paul meant *head/kephale* to be "authority/ leader," he was arranging this supposed hierarchy in a strange order, starting with the second pair, then moving to the third, and then jumping back to the first pair.[20] Paul was a very orderly writer. His linear logic was always precise and clear, line upon line and precept upon precept. This haphazard listing would be very odd unless he had something entirely different in mind.

If you read "origin/source" instead of "authority/leader" for *kephale*, Paul's list in 1 Corinthians 11:3 makes perfect sense.[21] In the order of creation, Adam was created first, from whom "every man" descended. Then God created Eve, "a woman" from "the man." Finally, "When the time had fully come, God sent his Son, born of a woman, born under law, to redeem those under law, that we might receive the full rights of sons."[22]

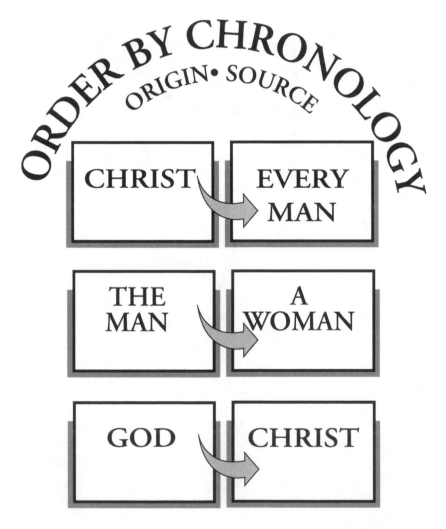

Of course, the only begotten Son existed throughout eternity with the Father.[23] In space and time, however, "the Word became flesh and made his dwelling among us"[24] many generations after the creation of

Adam and Eve, thus following them chronologically. Paul returned to this chronology again in 1 Corinthians 15:47 when he compared Adam—"the first man"—with Christ—"the second man." So Paul didn't give a hierarchy or flowchart in 1 Corinthians 11:3. He gave a clear timeline.

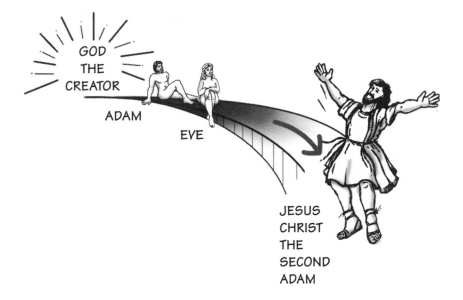

It Doesn't Fit

By now we see that it's highly unlikely that Paul meant to convey that man was "authority/leader" over woman. It simply doesn't fit. However, if he meant "source/origin," there's a harmonious flow to his argument.

The church fathers agreed with this interpretation. Cyril of Alexandria in the fifth century A.D. said, "Thus we say that the *kephale* of every man is Christ, because he was made through Him and brought forward to birth.... And the *kephale* of woman is man, because she was taken from his flesh and has him as her source. Likewise, the *kephale* of Christ is God, because He is from Him according to nature."[25]

It's important to see that the only other time Christ was spoken of as "head" in context of gender issues was in Paul's Ephesian household code.[26] Paul said in Ephesians 5:23, "For the husband is the head of the wife *as* Christ is the head of the church, his body, of which he is the Savior." If authority had been on Paul's mind, you'd expect him to conclude with the phrase, "of which he is the Lord," but he didn't. Instead, he chose the far less usual "Savior" over the more usual "Lord"[27] in this passage. By not using "Lord," he deliberately steered away from the concept of authority when speaking of Jesus as head of the church. Instead, Paul portrayed Him as "Savior," the one who redeemed us from death and is the *source* of new life. Once again, when Paul discussed gender issues he showed the concept of *head/kephale* as "source/origin" of life.

Clue #4: Christ Is Equal to God the Father

The fourth reason we believe that *head/kephale* in 1 Corinthians 11:3 should be understood as "source/origin" rather than "authority/ leader" is based on the theological implications for the third pair in the series, Christ/God. We know that Jesus voluntarily yielded to His Father's will throughout His earthly ministry. But this doesn't mean that within the Trinity the Son is in some sort of permanent, one-sided submission to the Father. In fact, the mutual submission we're supposed to have in the Body of Christ[28] flows out of the mutual submission of members of the Trinity to one another.

In the Bible we see each member of the Trinity lovingly bestowing honor on the others. The Father always commends the Son[29] and works through the Spirit;[30] the Son always yields to the Father[31] and promotes the Spirit,[32] and the Spirit always points to the Son[33] and does what the Father says.[34] The Trinity is the ultimate model of servanthood, preferring one another in love and honor, always submitting to one another in perfect unity.

Distorting the Trinity

Whatever else it may mean, the phrase "the head of Christ is God" cannot mean that there is inequality between the Son and the Father. Jesus is "very God of very God," fully equal to the Father in every respect. There is no hierarchy within the Trinity. This is why Athanasius, the fourth-century church father, said regarding 1 Corinthians 11:3 that "'head' must be understood as 'source' rather than 'boss' lest one arrive at a faulty understanding of the Trinity."[35]

We cannot say that Paul meant *kephale* as "authority/leader" without giving a distorted image of the Trinity. Nor can we divide the parallelism of Paul's sentence to say that he meant the word one way in one phrase and another entirely different way when speaking of man and woman in the same sentence. However, if we use "source/origin" to interpret *kephale,* 1 Corinthians 11:3 is a straightforward affirmation of the incarnation of Christ. The self-sacrificing love of the Trinity is made even clearer. It was sacrificial love that led the Father to allow His dearest Son to leave heaven, to be born on earth, and to give His life to redeem us.

Now recall Paul's use of the A-B-A-B interchange. We've been looking at the first "A": dealing with the right attitude (verse 3). Paul was a complex thinker. He expected his reader to hold on to what he had said in verse 3 when he picked up the subject later in verses 8–12. So, to make it easier to understand his train of thought, we're going to jump ahead to the second "A" section, dealing with more of his thoughts on right attitude.

WE NEED EACH OTHER

> For man did not come from woman, but woman from man; neither was man created for woman, but woman for man. For this reason, and because of the angels, the woman ought *to have authority over* her head. In the Lord, however, woman is not independent of man, nor is man independent of woman. For as woman came from man, so also man is born of woman. But everything comes from God.[36]

Paul used the Genesis account of Creation to remind men and women of their shared origins. In 1 Corinthians 11:8–9, he emphasized that both men and women should live in interdependence. Paul didn't leave room for either sex to despise the other. Women can't be independent from men because woman was created from man.[37] But neither can men adopt an attitude of prideful disdain for women, since woman was created because of man's need for her.[38]

Those who see in verse 8 a foundation for male-only leadership because the male was created first have, regrettably, completely missed the point. Do you recall our discussion in chapter 7?[39] You don't have to read many chapters in 1 Corinthians before you see that chronological sequence doesn't qualify anyone for ministry or a particular level of leadership. If it did, Paul, to whom Christ appeared "last of all," shouldn't have ministered as he did.[40]

The point such readers miss is that Paul was reminding men in 1 Corinthians 11:9 that Adam stood in need of an *'ezer k^eneged,* a strong partner.[41] God designed Eve for full partnership with Adam because Adam couldn't do the job without her help. In the same way, Paul showed male believers in Corinth their need for women to be ministering alongside them. Men couldn't accomplish the task alone, because God designed men and women to work together in interdependence.

WORDS NOT IN THE ORIGINAL

Because women are full and equal partners in ministry, Paul said, "For this reason...the woman ought to have authority over her head."[42] The NIV translation of this verse is unacceptable. It adds the phrase "sign of," which does not appear in the original Greek. The phrase translated "authority over" is *exousia epi.* This phrase occurs fifteen times in the New Testament,[43] and in every instance it is an active description of authority possessed by someone over someone else or over something. The word *exousia* means "the right, authority, freedom, and decision-making ability."[44]

Paul was simply saying that women have the right to wear whatever they want to on their heads—just as men do. Of course, in the context of the rest of Paul's words throughout 1 Corinthians, women *and* men must be guided by love. Right attitudes of heart will dictate what styles will best serve the purposes of the Gospel.

RELINQUISHING AND CHALLENGING

Rights are never ours to be grasped. We should hold our rights loosely, relinquishing them whenever necessary to extend the kingdom of God or to protect a weaker member of the Body of Christ. The overriding principle Paul gave in 1 Corinthians—equal rights for men and women, but surrendering personal rights whenever necessary—can be applied wherever we find ourselves in ministry.

You might find yourself ministering in a culture vastly different from first-century Corinth. If you were to go to Samoa, instead of worrying about covering or uncovering your head, you would need to sit quickly when an older person walks into the room. If you were to go to India or the Arab world, you'd use Paul's principles and avoid touching someone with your left hand.

PAUL ADDS SOME CURIOUS WORDS

Paul inserted a very curious phrase in this declaration of women's authority. He said, "For this reason, and *because of the angels*, the woman ought to have authority over her head."[45] If you look up this phrase "because of the angels" in a dozen commentaries, you will find a dozen different suggestions as to its meaning. This is because no one knows for sure why Paul used it. Some of the suggested interpretations are quite ridiculous; others are more reasonable. Because Paul mentioned angels three other places in this Epistle, these references can serve as clues in helping us try to understand this odd phrase. Even so, we lack sufficient information to make a definite affirmation of Paul's intent. Though we can't be sure, the following possibilities may get us thinking in the right direction.

Possibility 1

In 1 Corinthians 4:9 and 13:1, angels are mentioned alongside *anthropos,* the gender-inclusive word for human beings. It seems that in both verses Paul was summing up the totality of the moral beings in God's Creation, contrasting humans, who have gender distinctions, and angels, who seemingly do not.

This brings to mind Jesus' teaching. Jesus compared humans and angels when questioned by the Sadducees. He taught that after the Resurrection, we will not marry because we will be "like the angels in heaven."[46] Either we will no longer have gender or our gender will be irrelevant. Perhaps Paul had Jesus' words in mind when he wrote the curious words in 1 Corinthians 11:10. Perhaps he was reminding the Corinthian believers that gender distinctions would not be important in eternity. For that reason, we should not make such a big deal about them now.

Possibility 2

The other passage where Paul referred to angels is 1 Corinthians 6:3, where he said, "Do you not know that we will judge angels? How much more the things of this life!" Maybe this was what Paul had in mind in 1 Corinthians 11:10, for three verses later he commanded the Corinthians, "Judge for yourselves: Is it proper for a woman to pray to God with her head uncovered?"[47] Perhaps Paul was simply saying,

"You're going to judge angels someday. Surely you can make responsible choices now about what to wear on your head!"[48]

AUTHORITY, NOT INDEPENDENCE

Whereas Paul said in verse 10 that women had *exousia* (the right, authority, freedom, decision-making ability) over their heads, he went on in verse 11 to remind both men and women that for them, all God-given rights and authority had to be exercised in cooperation, not in autonomous independence: "In the Lord, however, woman is not independent of man, nor is man independent of woman."[49] Keep in mind that "Paul was writing this in the context of discussing public worship. His words opposed the pagan practice of excluding women in worship and the synagogue practice of relegating women to a side chamber or a balcony as silent observers of the men at worship."[50] Exclusion based on gender was to be unheard of among the redeemed of Christ. Neither gender could rightly function without the other. Ministry was to be shared.

Rabbi Akiba wrote an interesting parallel to this in Genesis Rabbah, a Jewish text from the early second century A.D. Akiba said, "Neither man without woman nor woman without man, and neither without the *Shekinah*,"[51] that is, the "glorious presence of God." When men and women minister together in interdependent partnership, the *Shekinah* glory of God is manifested.

Another important thing to notice is that in verse 11, when Paul said "in the Lord," he wasn't limiting equality between the sexes to church or worship. The idea of separating the sacred from the secular is not a biblical idea. Everything we do—throughout the week, in our homes, in the workplace, as well as in our places of worship—is "in the Lord."

Nor was Paul limiting this new equality of women to Christians. Believers were simply to be the first to live it out. Freedom from centuries of oppression was to begin with the house of God, then permeate society. Jesus inaugurated and Paul promoted a whole new order of equality in the world not known since Genesis 3. The aim was to restore God's original plan—the partnership for which He created men and women.

The change has begun. Not a change of violent revolution or one of angry demonstrations and bitterness between the sexes. God does not employ bombs to usher in His kingdom and bring about change. He uses leaven. Though unnoticed at first, the leaven eventually transforms the whole mass.[52] So it is that these biblical principles regarding the shared partnership of the genders were designed to go beyond the issues of prayer and prophecy, beyond what we wear or don't wear on our heads, in order to leaven all of life.

In closing, Paul returned once again to our creation as human beings, restating how we depend upon one another: "For as woman came from man, so also man is born of woman. But everything comes from God."[53] Because we have interdependent origins, we shouldn't be squabbling, as the Corinthians were, over who is more important. Everything we have is a gift from God.[54] Men and women have been created by the same wise and loving God to minister together. We shouldn't be sniping at one another, despising one another, feeling superior, or excluding one another. There is no place for this in the family of God, according to Paul. In the Lord, the sex war is over.

13.

PRAYING AND PROPHESYING

(Part Two of 1 Corinthians 11:2–16)

By David Hamilton

N ow that we've considered his thoughts on the right attitude, let's see what Paul said about the right attire (the "B" parts of the A-B-A-B interchange). These verses not only speak of hairdos and attire but also contain some of the clearest statements supporting women in public ministry. We'll see that Paul expected men and women to participate together in the ministry of the church.

DON'T OVERLOOK THE OBVIOUS

Every man who prays or prophesies with his head covered dishonors his head. And every woman who prays or prophesies with her head uncovered dishonors her head—it is just as though her head were shaved. If a woman does not cover her head, she should have her hair cut off; and if it is a disgrace for a woman to have her hair cut or shaved off, she should cover her head. A man ought not to cover his head, since he is the image and glory of God; but the woman is the glory of man.[1]

In these verses, Paul talked about appropriate attire for those who ministered in public. Some Christians have interpreted these verses as absolute commandments for all times and all places, preaching against young men wearing their hair long or demanding that women not cut theirs. Others have focused on women wearing veils or head coverings in church.

Before we look at what these hair fashions meant in first-century Corinth, we should be careful to note the obvious thing about this passage: Paul told *both* men and women what to wear while ministering in public because *he expected both men and women to minister in public.*

The Full Scope of Ministry

Paul said, "Every man who prays or prophesies..." and "every woman who prays or prophesies...." He wasn't talking about something done on the sidelines of church activity. "To pray and to prophesy" summarized the full scope of the Jewish concept of priestly ministry. To pray is to speak to God on behalf of God's people. To prophesy is to speak to God's people on behalf of God. Prayer may be private or public, but prophecy is almost always public. Because of Paul's parallel statements to men and women in this passage, it is clear that a woman's ministry of prayer and prophecy is as public as a man's.

Prophecy is more than predicting the future with the help of the Holy Spirit. The prophets of the Old Testament did that, but they also preached to, exhorted, judged, pled with, railed at, begged, encouraged, taught, edified, warned, and wooed people with the Word of God. Paul said the prophetic and apostolic ministries were foundational to all others.[2] He showed how broad prophecy could be in 1 Corinthians 14:3 when he said, "But everyone who prophesies speaks to men for their strengthening, encouragement and comfort."

So we see that prophecy included a wide range of ministerial activities and that Paul assumed that women as well as men would be prophesying. In fact, women prophesying alongside men was to be a feature of the church, according to the prophet Joel. On the day the church was born, that's exactly what happened as those filled with the Spirit, "the twelve" and "the women," along with others, began to minister publicly.[3] Peter reminded their audience that this was supposed to happen, quoting Joel's words: "In the last days, God says, I will pour out my Spirit on all people. Your *sons and daughters* will prophesy, your young men will see visions, your old men will dream dreams. Even on my servants, *both men and women*, I will pour out my Spirit in those days, and they will prophesy."[4]

WOMEN PROPHETS IN THE TALMUD

The New Testament's inclusion of men and women in public ministry was not without Old Testament precedent. The Talmud says, "Forty-eight prophets and seven prophetesses prophesied to Israel… 'Seven prophetesses'. Who were these? Sarah, Miriam, Deborah, Hannah, Abigail, Hulda and Esther."[5] In fact, Paul recognized yet another Old Testament prophetess when he quoted Rebekah in Romans 9:12.[6] Despite this, the Talmud said it brought shame to the synagogue if a woman read the Torah in public.[7]

Paul, on the other hand, didn't think women were "second-best" ministers. No, he treated them as peers in preaching the Gospel. It's quite clear from 1 Corinthians 11 that women were praying and prophesying in the early church. If Paul had intended to prohibit women from public ministry, he wouldn't have taken the time to correct *the manner* in which they were ministering. Why would Paul spend time pruning a custom that he wanted to uproot?[8]

WHOM DID PAUL CORRECT?

Notice that Paul spent almost equal time in 1 Corinthians 11:4–7 correcting men and women for improper attire. In the Greek, there are sixty-eight words in these four verses: thirty-one of them (46 percent) are directed to men, while thirty-seven of them (54 percent) are to women.

Why *did* the great apostle show such concern about fashion? Does God really care how long someone's hair is or whether a woman wears a hat in church? As we listen to Paul's side of an imaginary telephone conversation, it's impossible to say with certainty what was going on in the Corinthian church in this regard. We can't be absolutely sure what abuses Paul was dealing with. The church in Corinth was an incredible melting pot of ethnic groups, social classes, and converts from a wide variety of religions. For each of these groups, men and women's hairstyles were different, and what the people wore on their heads held different meanings.

Hats On, Hats Off

Jewish men usually wore their hair long and covered their heads when in the synagogue. The most religious men kept their heads covered at all times. Jewish married women kept their long hair covered, for the rabbis taught that a woman's long hair was sexually enticing.

Greek men, on the other hand, could wear their hair long or short, though by this period, the style was generally short. Whether Greek men were on the street or in the temple, their heads were uncovered. Long hair was considered a sign of beauty for Greek women, who nonetheless kept their heads covered in public.

Roman men wore their hair short and uncovered, but like the Jews, they covered their heads in worship. Roman women had a wide variety of hairstyles and head coverings. In fact, styles changed so often that Roman statues sometimes featured changeable hairdos to keep the person's image up-to-date![9] Generally speaking, the Romans regarded the veil as a sign of a free, married woman and wouldn't allow any slave or former prostitute the right to wear this attire of the aristocrats.

Gender Bending and Idolatry

These customs had exceptions, but the exceptions were usually a sign of mourning, sexual immorality, or frenzied religious rituals. Prostitutes in apostolic times were known to advertise themselves by means of their uncovered heads, "an invitation to lust."[10] This would have been a very common sight in Corinth, the city famous for its army of harlots.

Gender reversals in sexually abandoned festivals became part of several pagan religions.[11] One of these was the cult of Dionysus. In this religion, men dressed as women with long hair and veils, and women cut their hair short and wore men's clothing. One vase from ancient Corinth is decorated with a picture of a female worshiper of Dionysus, dancing in pants equipped with an artificial male organ.[12]

With all of this as part of the mix in Corinth, what was Paul addressing in 1 Corinthians 11? Were ex-prostitutes worshiping Jesus the same way they had worshiped Aphrodite, with their heads uncovered? Was Paul telling men not to wear their hair long or cover their heads because some were cross-dressing, as they had done in worship of Dionysus? Or could Paul have insisted on women wearing veils as a way of giving honor to slave women and ex-prostitutes, who would have been denied that right in Corinth? Did Paul tell the men not to cover their heads in worship as an outward sign that they were no longer under Jewish law or worshiping as Roman men did in their temples?

Perhaps it is not necessary for us to re-create all the precise historical issues when it comes to Corinthian hair do's and don'ts. Recall Loren's teaching in chapter 2 on absolute truths and relative statements. Paul made it very clear that his teaching on hairstyles was dependent on the particular culture. Note that he said those instructions should be followed only "*if* it is a disgrace for a woman to have her hair cut or shaved off."[13] If it is not a disgrace in your culture, these words do not apply.

RIGHT ATTITUDES SHOULD DICTATE RIGHT ATTIRE

When it comes to what practices Paul was addressing, we have more questions than answers. Undoubtedly, Paul's instructions and the reasons for them were very clear to his original audience. With the passing of time, the particular issues the people were grappling with have become less clear to us. But what we can see clearly is that Paul urged the believers to have the right heart attitude, which would dictate right practices. Looking through this Epistle, we can see Paul's overall themes.

- 1 Corinthians 1–4   unity instead of divisiveness
- 1 Corinthians 5–7   sexual purity rather than immorality
- 1 Corinthians 8–10   worshiping God rather than worshiping idols

Paul could have been addressing one or two or all three of these heart attitudes when he told the people what to wear on their heads.

SHE'S THAT AND MORE!

Paul concluded this section of his letter by saying that a man should uncover his head when he ministers because "he is the image and glory of God; but the woman is the glory of man."[14] What was this about? Did Paul mean that only man, and not woman, was made in the image and glory of God?

To fully appreciate this statement we need to consider a few things about the Greek of this phrase. Paul used the gender-specific word *aner* (man) rather than the gender-inclusive word *anthropos* (person). This stands out, since elsewhere he was so careful and deliberate about speaking of creation in gender-inclusive terms.[15] Did Paul limit the image and glory of God to the male? The Creation account in Genesis 1:26–27 says that male and female were made in the image of God, and Paul couldn't have been contradicting that. What Paul was actually saying was, woman is the glory of God...*and* of man! The key to understanding this verse lies in the little Greek word *de*.

A GREAT AFFIRMATION OF WOMEN

The common Greek conjunction *de*[16] has no exact English equivalent. Though sometimes it's translated as "but," it's usually better translated as "and" or "and also." If Paul had wanted to make a contrast between the nature of men and women, highlighting their differences, he probably would not have used the soft word *de* but would have used the strong word *alla* to say, "But..."

Paul purposely used *man/aner* to provoke his audience into rethinking their attitudes regarding gender. He wasn't saying that the male is the glory of God in contrast to the female, who is not. That's impossible, for God didn't glory in His Creation of humanity until He had made the female to join the male. God looked at the male standing there alone and said, "It is not good."[17] Only when the two stood together as partners did God exclaim, "Very good!"[18] Since Paul referred to this exact episode just two verses later in 1 Corinthians 11:9, he clearly had it in mind.

To better understand Paul's use of the conjunction *de*, we could paraphrase this verse as, "Whereas the male is the glory of God along with the female, the female is also the glory of the male!" Paul was showing the men of Corinth that even as Adam gloried in Eve's creation, breaking into song when he first saw her, they should glory in the women who ministered in their midst. Women weren't dishonorable inferiors to be used or avoided, as the Greeks, Romans, and Jews taught. They were valuable, even glorious peers, and should be treated respectfully as full partners in ministry. Paul was telling the men not to despise the women but to value, to honor, to appreciate, to treasure, indeed to glory in the women who ministered in their midst. Thus Paul's phrase "*and* the woman is the glory of man" is one of the most affirming phrases about women in the Scriptures.

Two Things to Notice in Paul's Postscript

> Judge for yourselves: Is it proper for a woman to pray to God
> with her head uncovered? Does not the very nature of things
> teach you that if a man has long hair, it is a disgrace to him,
> but that if a woman has long hair, it is her glory? For long hair
> is given to her as a covering.[19]

These verses are the final "B" section in Paul's A-B-A-B structure.
Here Paul concludes his discussion about what men and women
should wear on their heads while praying and prophesying. Briefly,
there are two things to notice.

First, Paul began with the imperative "Judge for yourselves."[20] This
was the only imperative in this passage that is directed to everyone, to
both males and females without distinction.[21] His command was genuine. Paul didn't want blind obedience. He wanted the people to
become spiritually mature and make responsible decisions based on
the principles he had already given. He posed several questions in
verses 13–15, but he didn't give prepackaged answers. He left the people with the questions to engage their thinking and to make up their
own minds about what to wear while praying and prophesying.

Second, what does the phrase "Does not the very nature of
things"[22] mean in relation to men or women having long hair? Paul
couldn't have meant that *physical* nature teaches this. Physical nature
teaches me, a man, that my hair will grow long if I don't visit the bar-
ber. Is that a disgrace or glory? Physical nature has no answer. And
what of those from tribes in Africa where their hair is so curly that it
doesn't grow long at all?[23] Does nature teach them the same thing that
it teaches me? Obviously, Paul must have had something else in mind
other than some absolute, universal hair code. So what is this all
about? Paul was talking about culture, about what was considered *natural* in Corinthian society.

Keep in mind that in 1 Corinthians 11:6, Paul didn't say a woman
should cover her head no matter what. He said to do so "*if* it is a disgrace for a woman to have her hair cut or shaved off" [emphasis
added]. Paul's way of ministering was both incarnational (identifying
with culture) and prophetic (transforming culture). On one hand,
Paul's teaching radically challenged and transformed culture by means
of the Gospel. On the other hand, Paul didn't ignore culture; he was

very respectful of people and their culture. Indeed, he had pointed this out just a few verses earlier when he said:

> So whether you eat or drink [and we could add: cover your head or leave it bare, have long hair or short] or whatever you do, do it all for the glory of God. Do not cause anyone to stumble, whether Jews, Greeks or the church of God—even as I try to please everybody in every way. For I am not seeking my own good but the good of many, so that they may be saved. Follow my example, as I follow the example of Christ.[24]

PRAY AND PROPHESY

Paul wrapped it up by saying, "If anyone wants to be contentious about this, we have no other practice—nor do the churches of God."[25] What was Paul referring to when he said, "we have no other practice"? Was he talking about women having long hair or wearing something on their heads in church? That seems highly unlikely, since he had just told them to judge for themselves what to wear in ministry.

Paul was talking about the practice of men and women praying and prophesying in public, ministering as coworkers in Christ. He was defending this practice, giving women rights that Corinthian culture had denied them. The practice the churches of God upheld was men and women sharing in the ministry of the church as equal before God and yet completely interdependent. This is the practice we are to embrace without contention, for the Gospel of Jesus Christ calls men and women to minister side by side.

14.

Should Women Keep Silent?

(Part One of 1 Corinthians 14:26–40)

By David Hamilton

Some scriptures seem to be known by everyone, and 1 Corinthians 14:34 is certainly among them. In fact, if you bring up the topic of women preachers, many Christians can quote Paul's words: "Women should remain silent in the churches. They are not allowed to speak, but must be in submission, as the Law says."[1]

So what *did* Paul mean when he told the women to keep silent? If he was indeed saying that women should not minister publicly, he was contradicting what he said earlier when he gave instructions for women's dress code *while prophesying!* There must be an explanation. As we examine these verses, we will see that Paul was definitely not teaching against women ministering publicly. Rather, he was correcting the *way* in which women were ministering in the Corinthian church.

One other word before we begin: If this passage were without difficulties, there wouldn't have been centuries of controversy around it. However, I trust that the Holy Spirit is available to guide us into all truth as together we search for understanding.

Clue #1: What's the Context?

Before delving into any scripture, one needs first to look at the context surrounding the verse. Keep in mind that this verse is part of a passage that concludes a seven-part series on ministry in the church, as outlined at the beginning of chapter 12. Paul didn't toss out haphazard ideas. He was a controlled, disciplined writer and nowhere more so than in this intricate passage. Any understanding of this verse regarding women keeping silent has to be viewed in the context of what has gone before. This includes 1 Corinthians 11:2–16, which, as we've seen before, strongly affirms men *and* women praying and prophesying in public gatherings of the church.

CLUE #2: MUCH HINGES ON PUNCTUATION

Since ancient Greek had no punctuation marks, modern translators have to determine where one sentence ends and another begins. Sometimes these punctuation choices lead to very different meanings. The crucial punctuation question in 1 Corinthians 14:33 is whether to place the period before or after "as in all the congregations of the saints." The translators of the NIV and some other translations place the period beforehand, rendering verses 33 and 34: "For God is not a God of disorder but of peace. As in all the congregations of the saints, women should remain silent in the churches."[2] Other translators place the period before "women," so that the verses read, "For God is not a God of disorder but of peace, as in all the congregations of the saints. Women should remain silent in the churches."[3]

See how important the placement of one little period can be? It makes a major difference whether Paul was making a universal principle that women were to keep silent "as in all the congregations of the saints" or not! Because of some textual issues of ancient manuscripts[4] as well as Paul's positive opinion of women in ministry, it should be clear that the phrase "as in all the congregations of the saints" goes together with the thought that "God is not a God of disorder." So to clarify our study of this passage, we will modify the punctuation of the NIV to read: "For God is not a God of disorder but of peace, as in all the congregations of the saints. Women should remain silent in the churches."[5] This punctuation is further confirmed by yet another clue: the way Paul structured his writing in this passage.

CLUE #3: THE AUTHOR'S STRUCTURE IS IMPORTANT

Seeing *how* Paul pulled his thoughts together makes it clear exactly *what* he was saying. In 1 Corinthians 14:26–40, Paul blended two literary devices with which we're all familiar because they are a part of our everyday lives, even though we might not recognize their technical names—particularization and chiasm.

Particularization

Particularization is a common form of communication. In it a writer simply makes a general statement and then proceeds to illustrate it with several specific examples. In this passage, Paul used particularization and gave it a special twist by repeating his general principle or main idea three times: placing it once at the beginning (14:26), then again in the middle (14:33), and once again at the end of the passage (14:40). His main idea was that since God is a God of order, all should participate in Christian worship in an orderly and edifying way. Paul then proceeded to illustrate this principle by giving examples of what orderly worship should look like. The examples he chose were those who speak in tongues, those who prophesy, and the women of the church. They are found in verses 27–32 and 34–39 and show how Paul's main idea is to be applied.

Chiasm

To make this even more interesting, Paul wrote this particularization within a chiasm! What a mouthful. What on earth is a chiasm? A chiasm is a pattern in which the writer makes a point, then makes two or more other points: Idea A, Idea B, Idea C, Idea D, then backpedals through the points in reverse order: Idea D, Idea C, Idea B, Idea A.

The author can use a few points in a chiasm or many. But in all chiasms, the second half is a mirror image of the first half. Another way to look at this kind of writing is to compare it to an arch, with the centerpiece forming the keystone of the argument, like this:

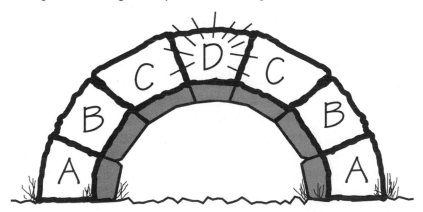

Paul liked using chiasms. So did many writers of old—Greek, Roman, and Jewish. Indeed, God the Creator has filled the world with chiastic structures. The human body, for example, is a chiasm. If you stretch out your hands to either side you create a chiasm:

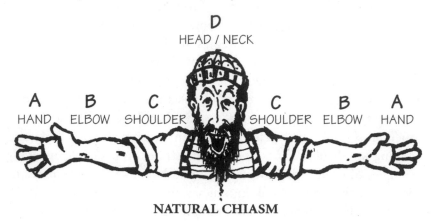

NATURAL CHIASM

The most important idea is in the center of the chiasm. If we were to cut off our fingers, it would be a painful loss, but we would survive. If, on the other hand, we were to cut off our neck, we would die.

THE STRUCTURE AND THE TEXT

Now let's look at this passage of 1 Corinthians 14:26–40, diagramed on the opposite page, and see how Paul wove together both particularization and chiasm to bring correction to the Corinthian church. Notice also that he put his words about women in the center, showing he thought they were the most important idea in this passage.

CLUE #4: WAS PAUL QUOTING AN OPPOSITE OPINION?

You might have noticed that in the diagram I modified the NIV punctuation by putting quotation marks around the sentence about it being disgraceful for a woman to speak in church. Keep in mind that there were no quotation marks in the original because punctuation didn't exist in ancient Greek. So all punctuation has been added at the studied discretion of modern translators.

I believe there are three indications that Paul was not giving his opinion in verse 35b but was quoting the opinion of some of the Corinthian believers:

1. Structure—it fits within his chiasm.

1 CORINTHIANS 14:26–40[6]

C1

[34] Women should be silent in the churches. They are not allowed to speak, but must be in submission, as the Law says. [35] If they want to inquire about something, they should ask their own husbands at home.

B1

[29] Two or three prophets should speak, and the others should weigh carefully what is said. [30] And if a revelation comes to someone who is sitting down, the first speaker should be silent. [31] For you can all prophesy in turn so that everyone may be instructed and encouraged. [32] The spirits of prophets are subject to the control of prophets.

A1

[27] If anyone speaks in a tongue, two—or at the most three—should speak, one at a time, and someone must interpret. [28] If there is no interpreter, the speaker should be silent in the church and speak to himself and God.

C2

"For it is disgraceful for a woman to speak in the church." [36] Nonsense! Did the word of God originate with you? What! Are you the only people it has reached? [37] If anybody thinks he is a prophet or spiritually gifted, let him acknowledge that what I am writing to you is the Lord's command. [38] If he ignores this, he himself will be ignored.

B2

[39] Therefore, my brothers, be eager to prophesy,

A2

and do not forbid speaking in tongues.

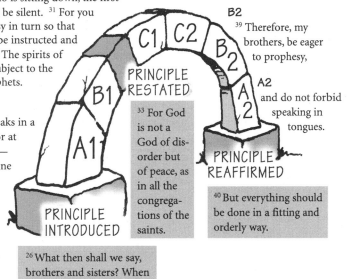

PRINCIPLE RESTATED

[33] For God is not a God of disorder but of peace, as in all the congregations of the saints.

PRINCIPLE INTRODUCED

[26] What then shall we say, brothers and sisters? When you come together, everyone has a hymn, or a word of instruction, a revelation, a tongue or an interpretation. All of these must be done for the strengthening of the church.

PRINCIPLE REAFFIRMED

[40] But everything should be done in a fitting and orderly way.

2. The concept he was arguing in this passage.

3. Paul's repeated use of quotations throughout 1 Corinthians.

Paul quoted from many sources as he ministered to the Corinthian church in this Epistle. He quoted Old Testament Scripture[7] and the words of Jesus.[8] He referred to the words of the Greek dramatist

Menander[9] and a proverb that is probably of rabbinic origin.[10] Paul even quoted the words of unbelievers[11] and of believers[12] in Corinth. Since the NIV translators clearly recognized all of these as quotations, they used quotation marks. I believe they missed this one, especially in light of a Greek word made up of a single letter.

CLUE #5: A TINY GREEK WORD MAKES ALL THE DIFFERENCE

Christian scholars have struggled to determine exactly where Paul was quoting others' words. An important indication that he was quoting another's opinion was his use of a tiny word: ἤ. Paul used this small Greek word forty-nine times in 1 Corinthians.[13]

Though it's used in various ways, at times Paul used ἤ as an emotional rebuttal[14] "to express disapproval of existing situations."[15] It's called an "expletive of disassociation" by Greek scholars. The closest equivalent to ἤ in English would be "What?" or "Nonsense!" or "No way!" This was what Paul probably meant when he put ἤ at the beginning of a question. He introduced fourteen questions in 1 Corinthians with ἤ. The NIV has usually left ἤ untranslated. This is understandable, for the word carries more emotional than intellectual content.

But if we were to insert "What?" or "Nonsense!" or "No way!" wherever we see ἤ in front of Paul's questions, we'd have a much clearer idea of what Paul meant. Notice his use of ἤ in the questions he directed to his Corinthian correspondence:

— 1 Corinthians 1:13   ἤ (No way!) Were you baptized into the name of Paul?

— 1 Corinthians 6:2   ἤ (What?) Do you not know that the saints will judge the world?

— 1 Corinthians 6:9   ἤ (Nonsense!) Do you not know that the wicked will not inherit the kingdom of God?

— 1 Corinthians 6:16   ἤ (No way!) Do you not know that he who unites himself with a prostitute is one with her in body?

— 1 Corinthians 6:19   ἤ (What?) Do you not know that your body is a temple of the Holy Spirit, who is in you, whom you have received from God?

—	1 Corinthians 7:16	Or ἤ (What?) how do you know, husband, whether you will save your wife?
—	1 Corinthians 9:6	Or ἤ (Nonsense!) is it only I and Barnabas who must work for a living?
—	1 Corinthians 9:7	ἤ (No way!) Who tends a flock and does not drink of the milk?
—	1 Corinthians 9:8	ἤ (What?) Doesn't the Law say the same thing?
—	1 Corinthians 9:10	ἤ (No way!) Surely he says this for us, doesn't he?
—	1 Corinthians 10:22	ἤ (Nonsense!) Are we trying to arouse the Lord's jealousy?
—	1 Corinthians 11:22	Or ἤ (What?) do you despise the church of God and humiliate those who have nothing?
—	1 Corinthians 14:36a	ἤ (Nonsense!) Did the word of God originate with you?
—	1 Corinthians 14:36b	Or ἤ (What?) are you the only people it has reached?

Notice how Paul used this expletive of disassociation twice in rapid succession in 1 Corinthians 14:36. Add this to the more important issue—maintaining the integrity of Paul's elaborate structure, which combined particularization and chiasm—and you can see that Paul was probably quoting a slogan of some of the Corinthian believers. Paul didn't agree with them when they said, "For it is disgraceful for a woman to speak in the church."

THE BOTTOM LINE: ORDER FOR THE SAKE OF EDIFICATION

Look over this passage of 1 Corinthians 14:26–40 again. We've already seen that it is an extremely well crafted, integrated piece of writing. What is its central message? That God is a God of order.

It's easy for us to dismiss Paul's instructions as obvious, especially after two thousand years of orderly Christian worship. Although it seems only common courtesy to speak "one at a time"[16] and to take turns,[17] this wasn't obvious to the new converts in Corinth. Their ideas of what made for a good worship service had been forged in the fires of idol altars. For those who had worshiped Dionysus, Aphrodite, and other popular Corinthian deities, Paul's teaching that "God is not a God of disorder"[18] was quite revolutionary. Many pagan worshipers worked themselves up into an absolute uproar of noise and confusion. For them, spirituality was measured in decibel levels: The more noise, the greater the pleasure of the gods and the more "anointed" the occasion. Since it was never the goal of the pagan cults to edify their believers, order and self-restraint were not valued. Paul intended to change all that.

It All Centered Around What God Was Like

Paul had to lay the most elementary groundwork for the Corinthian Christians. It all centered around the character of God. Because God was a God of order, peace should reign in the worship services. People should participate in a thoughtful and orderly way to build one another up. The goal for group worship wasn't emotional outbursts but was communication that edified everyone. Each man or woman who took part was supposed to have the welfare of the Body of Christ in mind. That was Paul's central idea throughout this portion of his Epistle. "All of these must be done for the strengthening of the church."[19]

Paul then illustrated this general principle by giving three particular examples of those who needed to be corrected and brought back to orderly, edifying participation:

1. those who speak in tongues[20]
2. those who prophesy[21]
3. the women in the church[22]

Paul wasn't prohibiting participation. On the contrary. He wanted all to participate, but in an orderly way for everyone's edification.

Paul had two extremes in the church at Corinth: One was the "anything goes" school of worship. These new converts were disrupting the services, probably bringing in practices from their heathen religions that gloried in noise and confusion. Paul corrected the chaos they were producing. The other extreme in the church at Corinth was the "nothing is permitted" school of thought. These people were trying to restrict participation. Paul wasn't on their side either. He showed in verse 26 that he wanted *everyone* to be involved in the ministry of the church, each one contributing according to his or her ministry gifts.

As we consider these three examples—those who speak in tongues, those who prophesy, and the women in the church—notice that Paul referred to each of these groups twice. He went through the three groups one time, *correcting* each one of them for their disorderly, excessive, and inconsiderate communication. Then he went back through the same three groups in reverse order (since this was a chiasm), *defending* their right to communicate in an orderly fashion, correcting those who would silence them outright.

Thus, the first three examples serve as a corrective to those who were abusing their freedom to minister. The second set of three examples is a protection from those who would restrict or totally do away with the freedom for all to minister. Paul develops his two-pronged argument thus:

1 CORINTHIANS 14:27–39

Now let us turn our attention specifically to Paul's correction of women who were bringing disorder into the Corinthian worship services.

15.

LEARNING HOW
TO MINISTER
(Part Two of 1 Corinthians 14:26–40)

By David Hamilton

*P*aul's first word to women in this passage was corrective. He wrote, "Women should be silent in the churches. They are not allowed to speak, but must be in submission, as the Law says. If they want to inquire about something, they should ask their own husbands at home."[1]

Over the years, Paul's command to the women to be silent has been the focal point of much discussion. However, many overlook the important fact that this command does not stand alone. Paul had already given the exact same command to be silent twice in this very passage. He had told to be silent various individuals and groups who were disrupting the service. Each of these three commands was given so that the Corinthian worship would reflect the character of a "God of peace" and result in the edification of all present.

Paul hammered home again and again the message to remain silent. However, we have lost the impact of his deliberate repetition of this one command by the way it has been translated in the NIV:

— Those who speak in tongues   "should keep quiet" (verse 28)
— The prophets   "should stop" (verse 30)
— The women   "should remain silent" (verse 34)

These appear to be three different commands, but they are not. Paul repeated the exact same word in Greek to each group. He intended for us to see a deliberate continuity of thought between verses 28, 30, and 34. To see the symmetry of Paul's repetition restored, we should translate the text as follows:

— To those who speak in tongues "be silent" (verse 28)
— To the prophets "be silent" (verse 30)
— To the women "be silent" (verse 34)

It is dishonest to single out the command directed to the women and make it more of an absolute than the command given to those who speak in tongues or to the prophets. Why have we been obsessed with the third example of orderly conduct and ignored the first two?

Look at the first two examples. It's obvious Paul's "be silent" wasn't an "absolutely-forever-under-every-circumstance-and-at-all-times" injunction against those who spoke in tongues or those who prophesied. No, in the same passage he wrote, "Be eager to prophesy, and do not forbid speaking in tongues."[2] The ministry gifts were not to be permanently silenced but were to be exercised "in a fitting and orderly way."[3] The same is true regarding the women. Paul was not telling women to refrain from all public ministry. To force such an interpretation does violence to the integrity of the text.

PAUL LINKED BEING SILENT TO TAKING TURNS

In these three verses, "be silent" had to do with taking turns,[4] listening to one another, and being self-controlled[5] "so that everyone may be instructed and encouraged."[6] Those who spoke in tongues and the prophets were to participate at times and be silent at times so that all might "be done for the strengthening of the church."[7] The same would be true for the women in the church.

If we consider this passage carefully, we see that prior to the injunction of verse 34, women had already been told to be silent. Women were most probably among those who spoke in tongues,[8] and they were most definitely among those who prophesied.[9] So when Paul earlier instructed the first two groups to be silent, he was not speaking to a group comprising only male ministers. In fact, the gender-inclusive nature of the church's ministry is clear throughout this passage.

Paul began this portion by stressing, "What then shall we say, brothers [and sisters]? When you come together, *everyone* has a hymn, or a word of instruction, a revelation, a tongue or an interpretation."[10] "Everyone" knew no gender limitations. Paul anticipated that men and women would participate fully in ministry, including the bringing of "a revelation" and "a tongue"[11]—the two main issues at play here.

When you think about it, the fact that Paul was having to correct women in the *way* they were ministering confirms the fact that they *were* ministering. If Paul hadn't given them freedom to minister in the first place, they couldn't have ministered wrongly. It was because they did not know how to exercise this freedom correctly that they now stood in need of his correction.

Why Was Paul Correcting the Women?

It's difficult to re-create the setting of the Corinthian church when we don't have all of the pieces to the puzzle. Several possible reasons exist for Paul's words "Let the women keep silent." Any of the following could have been disrupting the Corinthians' orderly worship:

— Women, like the men, may have been ministering without consideration of others, lacking in self-control.
— Because women were uneducated, they may have been interrupting the service by asking questions inappropriately.
— Some of the women may have been reverting to the model of their pagan worship, disrupting the service with their loud noises.

In pagan religions, the only way women were allowed to participate was by wailing and making high-pitched cries called "ululations." If you have ever traveled in the Middle East, or if you've seen the movie *Not Without My Daughter* or *Lawrence of Arabia*, you have heard ululations of women. It's like no other sound you've ever heard. Women have been making these outcries—both for joy and for grief—for thousands of years. From Homer onward, writers described ululation. Among pagans, the men ministered and offered sacrifices while the women provided the sound effects. Paul now expected all to minister, but in an orderly way, without the chaos of their pagan past.

Paul Told Women to Speak, Too

The purpose of this passage was not to limit ministry but to encourage it. Paul wanted to teach new believers how to minister in this young church. He had already said he wanted all—men *and* women—to be ready to contribute with "a hymn, or a word of instruction, a revelation, a tongue or an interpretation."[12] To promote true ministry, Paul found it necessary to correct wrong forms of ministry with his three "be silents."[13] His primary objective was to get the people to minister.

This objective is why Paul also commanded the people twice in this passage to "speak."[14] There is no indication in the text that these commands to speak were limited to men. Paul was addressing anyone who spoke to God on behalf of the people by means of tongues or who spoke to the people on behalf of God by means of prophecy. And as we know, both men and women participated in these two strategic ministries of the church.[15]

Submit to Whom?

Next, Paul commanded the women to "be in submission,"[16] but he did not specify to whom or to what. This omission is quite surprising when we see that out of the thirty-eight places in the New Testament where this verb appears, this is the only time the object to whom one is to submit is not clearly stated.[17] The only instance!

Of course, some will want to rush ahead to the next verse, where husbands are mentioned, and assume that Paul meant that the women were to submit to their husbands. But hold on a minute! Husband-and-wife relationships haven't been mentioned at all in this passage up to this point. Keep in mind that this is the conclusion of a seven-part series on public worship in the church.[18] Yes, husbands will be talked about in the next verse, but up to now, marriage has not been the subject of the discussion. Ministry has been.

Perhaps Paul had something else in mind. Let's look in the previous verses for the antecedent (the preceding noun that Paul was linking to the new verb *submit*). In other words, to whom or what were these women to submit? Three good possibilities stand out: (1) the churches, (2) God, and (3) themselves. Let's consider each of them.

Possibility 1: The Churches

The last noun mentioned was "the churches," or its parallel, "the congregations of the saints."[19] If this was the antecedent Paul meant, he was telling the women to be submissive to the order of the church or to the leaders of the church as they exercised their ministry gifts. This would be the same as what he told those speaking in tongues or prophesying to do. Both men and women were supposed to submit their participation in ministry to church leadership so that worship could be done in an orderly, edifying way.

Possibility 2: God

If we look farther back in the text for the antecedent, the next noun we find is "God," when Paul said that "God is not a God of disorder but of peace."[20] We all are supposed to give Him unqualified submission, whatever our gender. The implication would be that submitting to God would result in imitating Him, bringing order and peace to correct whatever was going on in the Corinthian church during worship.

It's interesting to see that the phrase "orderly way" in verse 40 and "submit" come from the same root word in Greek. Submission and order are intimately related. Paul was saying that order cannot reign in the church unless everyone has a submissive attitude.

Possibility 3: Themselves

There's still one other possibility for the antecedent of the verb *submit*. If we look even farther back into the text, we find another phrase in which the very same verb for *submit* is used. Paul said in 1 Corinthians 14:32, "The spirits of prophets are subject to the control of prophets."[21] Self-control was supposed to characterize the exercise of spiritual gifts. Paul showed that the prophetic utterances of the Spirit of God were completely different from the uncontrollable outbursts of pagan worship. The prophet was to keep his or her own spirit in submission. Again, women weren't the first group Paul required to be submitted in this way. Paul expected to find such submission in the life of anyone who ministered in the church.

All the previous alternatives seem reasonable. Each fits the context of the passage. And each would be consistent with what we know about Paul's spirit of mutuality and reciprocity between men and women in public ministry. So how do we know which one of the three Paul had in mind? Paul didn't leave us guessing. He defined the expected submission by the phrase "as the Law says."[22] This clearly rules out the possibility that Paul was talking about marriage here, because nowhere in the Old Testament do we find any instruction for wives to submit to their husbands. This might surprise you, but a thorough search of the Hebrew Scriptures yields no command for wives to submit to their husbands.

Some might point to Genesis 3:16, where God said to Eve, "Your desire will be for your husband, and he will rule over you." However, in this passage God wasn't *prescribing* how men and women should relate to each other. This was no command. God was simply *describing* the consequences of sin. God never intended Genesis 3:16 to become our guide for life and relationships. There was no command in this passage for Eve to submit to Adam—Eve was merely told the great impact sin would have on her world.

WHAT LAW WAS PAUL REFERRING TO?

So, we are back to considering the three possibilities—women were being told to submit either to the church, to God, or to themselves. Only one of these emerges with a clear Old Testament foundation. Psalm 37:7 commands, "Be still before the LORD and wait patiently for him." It is interesting to note how this verse was translated in the Septuagint.[23]

> The Greek-speaking Jews who prepared a Greek version of the Hebrew Bible (the Septuagint) saw a remarkable correlation between "silence" and "submission." There are three places in Psalms where the Hebrew text speaks of being silent unto God. In each case…translators rendered this by the Greek verb meaning "to submit oneself." The original implication is one of attentiveness and receptivity to God.[24]

Perhaps when he spoke of submission, Paul simply had in mind the Old Testament idea of "waiting on God, or the thought of humility towards God."[25] If so, Paul was asking of women the same thing he required of men. He was telling the women, "You've been accepted as full partners in the Gospel. You've been given the privilege to minister through prayer and prophecy. In the past you were excluded from participation in the synagogues and in the Greek and Roman temples. But now the double standard is over. You have new freedom in Christ. However, we expect the same thing from you that we expect from the men. You are free to minister, but you must do so responsibly. Stop ministering in a disorderly, disruptive, discourteous, insubordinate way. Your participation in the church must be done in an orderly way, submitting to God so that your ministry edifies the whole Body of Christ."

PAUL DOES A REALLY COOL THING

What Paul said next was extraordinary. "If [women] want to inquire about something, they should ask their own husbands at home." This is often seen as a prohibition on participation, but it's just the opposite! Paul was encouraging the women in their desire to learn. He was urging them not to stay on the sidelines but to equip themselves for full participation in the Body of Christ! These words were a radical break with all of the surrounding cultures. Women had little or no educational opportunities among the Greeks or Romans. The Jews also excluded women from study, including formal religious training.

Paul would have no part in that. He wanted women to have the opportunity to learn. So he commanded them to ask their husbands for teaching. He affirmed a woman's right to learn. He opened doors for women that they had only dreamed of for centuries. However, women were supposed to ask these questions in an appropriate setting, not during the worship service while someone else was praying, prophesying, or otherwise publicly ministering.

Paul's words also had a seismic impact on the men. Implicit in his instructions to the women was his expectation that the husbands would provide their wives with an opportunity for education. Men had never been given that obligation before—not since the beginning of time! There were no institutions where women could go to learn— no women's training schools, no women's colleges. It was up to the husbands of the church in Corinth to reorient their values and spend the time necessary to bring their wives up to speed. Paul made it clear: The men should take personal responsibility for this. If their wives wanted to learn, the husbands should do everything they could to help them.

This was a natural outcome of Paul's teaching in these sections on church life. Time and again Paul addressed the need for new believers to be edified, to learn, and to grow. He didn't want them to be ignorant.[26] He wanted them to use the spiritual gifts to build one another up, strengthening the church,[27] which of course included women. He said he preferred to use those gifts in public that allowed him "to instruct others."[28] He urged them all—men *and* women—to grow toward spiritual maturity, to think as adults,[29] not childishly.[30] His stated goal was that "everyone [regardless of gender] be instructed and encouraged."[31]

Paul was making sure that women were not left out of the process. He knew they were at a disadvantage. Because of their cultures, women were entering the kingdom of God with an educational handicap. Paul's instruction sought to eradicate that. With their husbands' help, women could begin to function as peers.

This might seem a small thing to us today, but it was huge in Paul's day. When Paul made provision for women to be taught, he leavened the dough of culture with a yeast that would grow through coming centuries. He gave women the tools to enter into their God-ordained destinies. Even while he was correcting women who were disrupting public worship, he gave them a way to better their lives. His words weren't harsh authoritarianism, relegating women to some narrow role. On the contrary, they showed Paul's compassionate leadership, opening new doors of opportunity for those whom society had excluded and ignored.

PAUL DEFENDED WOMEN IN MINISTRY

Next, Paul shifted his emphasis from correcting those who were creating chaos (which characterized the first half of his chiasm) to protecting everyone's liberty to minister (in the second half). He corrected those who sought to deny people's right to participate.

If you'll recall from the previous chapter, there were two schools of thought in the Corinthian church. After dealing with the "anything goes" school, Paul next addressed the "nothing is allowed" school. The former had placed no restraint on individual participation in the worship service; the latter allowed for no freedom of participation whatsoever. Paul took up the challenge of the statement "It is disgraceful for a woman to speak in the church."

The Greek word translated "disgraceful" occurs only three times in the New Testament.[32] The fact that Paul used it both here and in the first difficult passage we considered greatly helps us interpret it. In 1 Corinthians 11:7b, we saw how Paul—in the context of women

WOMEN
14:34–35a

WOMEN
14:35b–38

C1

C2

PROPHETS
14:29–32

B1

B2

PROPHETS
14:39a

THOSE
SPEAKING
IN TONGUES
14:27–28

A1

A2

THOSE
SPEAKING
IN TONGUES
14:39b

PAUL CORRECTS
CHAOS

PAUL PROHIBITS
PROHIBITIONS

1 CORINTHIANS 14:27–39

praying and prophesying—went to great lengths to affirm that women were the glory of men, a source of joy, not of embarrassment; of pride, not of dishonor. Clearly, this statement—that women speaking in the church was disgraceful—was not something that Paul endorsed.

A moment earlier, Paul had told women to be silent, but not because the fact that they were speaking was disgraceful. Their speaking was contributing to disorder in the church and standing in the way of people being edified. Paul didn't make *women* taboo. He made *chaos* taboo.

The critics of women participating in the Corinthian church had totally missed Paul's point. They were holding to old concepts from Greek, Roman, and Jewish culture, not to things thought by Christ. Listen to how closely this statement quoted by Paul mirrored the pervasive thoughts of the ancients:

— The Greeks said, "The women in silence obey."[33]
— Aristotle repeated Sophocles' famous refrain, "Silence gives grace to woman."[34]

This attitude toward women was carried over into the Roman era:

— Plutarch said, "Keeping at home and keeping silence"[35] was the appropriate role for women.

— A Roman playwright said, "Married women are to watch silently and laugh silently, check the tinkle of their voices and keep their chatter for their home."[36] And, "A woman's always worth more seen than heard."[37]

This sentiment was echoed by the Jewish rabbis, who said of women:

— "Thy silence is fairer than thy speech."[38]

— "A silent wife is a gift of the Lord."[39]

— "A woman's voice is a sexual incitement,"[40] therefore "[to listen to] a woman's voice is indecent."[41]

PAUL SAYS, "NO WAY!"

What, then, was Paul's response to this dredging up of the old idea that it was disgraceful for women to speak? Paul countered, "ἤ [Nonsense!] Did the word of God originate with you? ἤ [What!] Are you the only people it has reached?"[42]

In other words, Paul refuted the claim of some men to hold exclusive rights to minister. God's Word wasn't going to be limited by narrow, gender-exclusive schemes. Paul had already clearly established the validity of women in public ministry and wasn't going to allow anyone to contradict him on this point: "If anybody thinks he is a prophet or spiritually gifted, let him acknowledge that what I am writing to you is the Lord's command. If he ignores this, he himself will be ignored."[43]

Paul then returned to the other two groups—those who spoke in tongues and the prophets—defending their rights to minister as well.[44] With this he completed his chiasm. He then finished by returning to his central theme in verse 40: "But everything should be done in a fitting and orderly way."

So, should women "be silent"? Yes, just like the men. Should women be prepared to minister with "a hymn, or a word of instruction, a revelation, a tongue of interpretation"? Yes, just like the men. Should women exercise self-control as they minister? Yes, just like the men. Should women seek to educate themselves so that they can better edify others when they minister? Yes, just like the men. "For God is not a God of disorder but of peace."

16.

"Do Not Permit a Woman to Teach"

(Part One of 1 Timothy 2:1–15)

By David Hamilton

Now let's look at the third difficult passage regarding women in ministry. Once again, we begin with the setting. We must first understand the situation Paul was addressing if we are to understand what he was saying to his protégé Timothy. Paul was writing sometime between his first and second imprisonment in Rome. It had been almost ten years since he had founded the church in Ephesus, which Timothy was now pastoring.[1]

A Dark and Frightening Stew

To appreciate the situation that Timothy faced in Ephesus, we need to know something about the city itself. Ephesus had to be intimidating when Timothy first arrived. The huge, golden image of Artemis (called Diana by the Romans) was placed within the columns of her temple so that she could be easily seen from the sea. As Timothy came into port, then walked to the city center on Marble Street, the temple of Artemis loomed over everything. After all, it was the greatest of the seven wonders of the ancient world.[2]

It took 120 years to build the structure Timothy stood and looked up at. Entire mountains were quarried for its foundations. The temple was larger than the playing field of an Olympic stadium. It had one hundred marble columns, each soaring five stories high. Color and gold were lavished everywhere.

The next impression that must have hit Timothy was the squalid moral stew that was Ephesus. The city was the center of a worldwide following for Artemis, the fertility goddess with two dozen bare breasts, also known as the Great Mother of Asia. Ovid wrote that the temple's orgies and religious prostitutes kept a young man's eyes fixed with lust and caused a young maiden's cheeks to redden.[3] Stirred into this were the orgiastic rites of other mystery religions, witchcraft, and the Roman worship of Caesar. In fact, though Ephesus was also known as a polit- ical and educational center, much of its economy was based on its occult activities. Pilgrims came from all over the world to its myriad temples and throngs of occult practitioners.

When Paul and his team came to Ephesus, they made so many converts that the city's economy was threatened. Their evangelistic work stirred up the unholy nest of money interests wedded to Artemis worship, and it all came down on their heads.[4] Paul's team had long gone, but Ephesus remained a great spiritual battleground for Timothy, the young pastor.

PERSECUTION FROM WITHOUT, HERESY WITHIN

As Paul wrote his first letter to Timothy, the church at Ephesus was undergoing tremendous difficulties. The Jews and pagan religious leaders continued persecuting it. As if that weren't enough, false teach- ers within the church were promoting heresy. Timothy definitely had his hands full!

So, let's get the big picture of Paul's letter.

OVERVIEW OF 1 TIMOTHY

As we read through this Epistle of Paul to his "true son in the faith," two things stand out:
— Paul's concern for Timothy
— Paul's concern for the church at Ephesus

These two things are shown in the very way that Paul wrote the let- ter. Paul went back and forth continuously between these two topics— personal instruction to Timothy and teaching on the ministry of the church. As we've seen before, this back-and-forth style of writing is called a literary interchange, or an A-B-A-B structure.

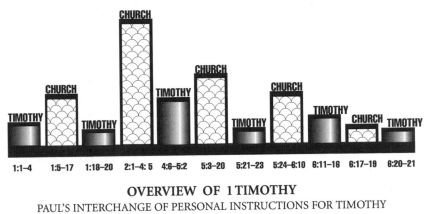

OVERVIEW OF 1 TIMOTHY

PAUL'S INTERCHANGE OF PERSONAL INSTRUCTIONS FOR TIMOTHY
AND GENERAL INSTRUCTIONS FOR THE CHURCH

WHAT PAUL THOUGHT MOST IMPORTANT

The first Epistle to Timothy took shape as Paul alternated between his concern for Timothy and his concern for the church. However, as you look at these eleven parts, it's clear that Paul emphasized one part more than any other. The longest part of his A-B-A-B structure is 1 Timothy 2:1 through 1 Timothy 4:5 in which Paul poured out his concern for the church at Ephesus. It is within this section that we find our difficult passage, 1 Timothy 2:1–15.

As with our other two difficult passages, it will help us first to look at the structure. Paul used particularization and chiasm again, but within an A-B-A-B interchange! The overall principle is, God wants to save everyone. The particular examples are what God wants to do with men and women. Within the last example, women, Paul used a mini-chiasm. He began by talking about women in general, then switched to a particular woman, then switched back to women in general. The graph on the next page should help you visualize it.

What was Paul saying here? Was he really saying that women should not teach, here in a church where Priscilla had been a founding leader? A church where she had spent much time along with her husband, Aquila, correcting the early errors of Apollos, discipling him for leadership?[5] Was Paul, who had asked the church in Rome to receive the woman minister Phoebe with all due honor,[6] now contradicting himself, telling Timothy never to allow women to be leaders in the church?

Before we answer these questions, let's look at the very important foundation that Paul laid in the first seven verses of 1 Timothy 2.

MIRROR STRUCTURES
1 TIMOTHY 2:1–15

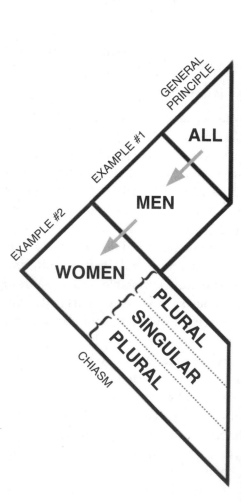

ALL

¹ I urge, then, first of all, that requests, prayers, intercession and thanksgiving be made for everyone— ² for kings and all those in authority, that we may live peaceful and quiet lives in all godliness and holiness. ³ This is good, and pleases God our Savior, ⁴ who wants all persons to be saved and to come to a knowledge of the truth. ⁵ For there is one God and one mediator between God and humanity, the person Christ Jesus, ⁶ who gave himself as a ransom for all humans—the testimony given in its proper time. ⁷ And for this purpose I was appointed a herald and an apostle—I am telling the truth, I am not lying—and a teacher of the true faith to the Gentiles.

MEN

⁸ I want men everywhere to lift up holy hands in prayer, without anger or disputing.

WOMEN

⁹ Likewise, I want women to dress modestly, with decency and propriety, not with braided hair or gold or pearls or expensive clothes, ¹⁰ but with good deeds, appropriate for women who profess to worship God.

A WOMAN

¹¹ A woman should learn in quietness and full submission. ¹² I do not permit a woman to teach or to have authority over a man; she must be silent. ¹³ For Adam was formed first, then Eve. ¹⁴ And Adam was not the one deceived; it was the woman who was deceived and became a sinner. ¹⁵ᵃ But she will be saved through the childbearing

WOMEN

¹⁵ᵇ —if they continue in faith, love and holiness with propriety. 7

GOD'S FOREVER DREAM

Paul began this passage saying, "I urge, then, first of all...."[8] The word *then* could also be translated "therefore," linking what Paul had just said with what was to come.

Look at the first chapter of 1 Timothy. Here was a church in deep trouble. Her persecutors were having a heyday from outside the church, and false teachers were wreaking havoc from within. The natural tendency would have been to withdraw into some self-protective mode. But Paul said that this was the time to be proactive. It was a time of great opportunity, a time to pray.

Opposition is no cause to retreat. Paul reflected this attitude when writing of his own experience in Ephesus: "A great door for effective work has opened to me, and there are many who oppose me."[9] That's the proper reaction when you find yourself being bombarded in the midst of heated spiritual warfare. Pray, realizing that God is opening a great door of opportunity for you.

Paul gave the believers at Ephesus four different words for prayer. How should they pray? In every possible way! They were to leave no stone unturned in the place of prayer. No one was to be excluded from their prayers, either. There were no limits to this kind of praying. There was no one alive on earth beyond the power of their prayer.

Why pray so intensely? Paul said, "...that we may live peaceful and quiet lives in all godliness and holiness."[10] Those who have known what it's like to live under persecution can really appreciate this. Those who have lived through the pain of a church torn apart by controversy and false teaching can also relate to Paul's heart cry. This was a desperate cry for survival. It was the hope of believers going through anguishing times while longing for peaceful and quiet lives.

The Greek word for *quiet* that Paul used here will be key to understanding verses later on in this chapter.[11] For now, let us note that it summed up the desired goal for all believers, male and female. But Paul urged prayer not just so that believers could enjoy peaceful lives but because they should feel what God feels and want what He wants.

THE HEART OF THE HEART OF THE HEART

"This is good, and pleases God our Savior, who wants all [persons] to be saved and to come to a knowledge of the truth."[12] These words are the core of this passage, the central reason for the whole Epistle, indeed the heart of the entire New Testament. In fact, they give us a glimpse into the very heart of God. They are among the most intimate, most tender words in the entire Bible. You reveal your dreams and deepest longings only to your closest friends. You wouldn't make yourself that vulnerable to anyone else. By sharing these words with us, God bares His heart, drawing us in close as His dearest friends, His most trusted confidantes. Wow!

You may have noticed that I changed one word from the NIV to better reflect the original Greek. Throughout the first seven verses of 1 Timothy 2, Paul did not use *aner,* the Greek word for "men." Instead, he used *anthropos,* the gender-inclusive Greek word best translated as "person" or "human." He continued using *anthropos:* "For there is one God and one mediator between God and humanity, the [person] Christ Jesus, who gave himself as a ransom for all [humans]...."[13]

Why is this important? Are we trying to be politically correct here? No. These are the words Paul actually chose. Paul was going out of his way to make it clear that God's love was for *every human being.* Even when he referred to Jesus, Paul used *anthropos*/person instead of *aner*/man. Jesus became a human so that He could be the mediator for every man and woman.

In this one sweeping statement, many lies of the ancient teachers were swept away. Woman was not a separate creation. She wasn't subhuman or merely an occasion for temptation. She was an equal recipient of God's love and Jesus' extravagant sacrifice.

IF YOU RUSH PAST THIS, YOU MISS THE ENTIRE MEANING

All of God's will—His most intense longing, His forever dream, the driving passion of His heart—is summed up in these verses. Everything God has ever done from the Garden to the present has been motivated by this dream. This is why God chose Abraham, why He gave Abraham's children the Law and the Promised Land. This is why He faithfully pursued them in His love, generation after generation, correcting them when they strayed, delivering them when they returned to Him. This is why He sent them His messengers—judges and prophets—one after another, after another, after another. This is why He sent His only Son as the ransom for humanity's sins. All of His acts have been motivated by His desire to redeem every person, every human, every *anthropos.* Everyone, everyone, everyone.

What a shame that so many rush over these words to tackle the difficult issues raised later. They miss this intimate glimpse into the heart of God's love. But they also misunderstand the words that follow. For unless we keep this perspective of God's forever dream before us, we miss it all.

PAUL TALKED TO THE MEN

Paul urged the whole church to pursue God's dream for all to be saved. Then he turned to the men of the church and told them their part: "I want men everywhere to lift up holy hands in prayer, without anger or disputing."[14] For the first time in this passage, he used the Greek word for "males," *aner.* He told the men what he wanted to see in their lives.

Paul's desire grew out of God's desire to see all persons saved. God's dream had spurred the apostle into action.[15] Now the apostle spurred all the men in the Ephesian church into action. They were to pray with holy hands, without anger or disputing. They were to pray in the opposite spirit of those attacking the church from without and from within. The men of the church were to live differently than both the unredeemed pagans persecuting them and the unrepentant teachers of heresy.

NEXT, PAUL SPOKE TO ALL THE WOMEN / "A WOMAN" / ALL THE WOMEN

As Paul turned to speak to women regarding their responsibilities in the church, he began a mini-chiasm. First he spoke to the women in general, then he gave specific instructions to one woman, then he spoke again to all the women. He began by saying, "Likewise, I want women to dress modestly, with decency and propriety, not with braided hair or gold or pearls or expensive clothes, but with good deeds, appropriate for women who profess to worship God."[16]

The NIV begins this verse with "I also." It would communicate Paul's intent more clearly if *also* were translated "likewise" or "in the same way."[17] This word in the Greek is like a literary equal sign. Some have tried to use this passage to say that the roles of men and women are different in the church. But Paul deliberately chose this word to highlight the similarities, not the differences, of men's and women's roles. Though the text does not specifically exhort women to pray, it is implied or suggested by the way Paul chose to begin this sentence. This is probably another example of Paul's use of ellipsis.[18] Paul wanted both men and women to pray and live in such a way that they promoted God's forever dream.

The main idea of this passage was that Paul wanted everyone to pray.[19] He wanted the men to pray, and *in the same way* he wanted the women to pray. It was logical, clear writing for him to tell both groups to pray in a godly manner—men, in holiness and without anger, and women, with decency and propriety.

Chrysostom was one of the early church commentators who understood this and added the words "to pray" to this verse to complete its meaning.[20] If this is correct, "the translation [of 1 Timothy 2:9] will be, 'In the same way I desire that women should pray, dressed in becoming manner.'"[21]

Why the Fuss over Gold, Pearls, and Braided Hair?

When we look at these words of Paul, they seem quaint, even legalistic. Was Paul the great apostle of freedom caught up in petty taboos? What's wrong with braided hair, gold, and pearls?

Just as Paul urged the men to live their lives by a different standard, here he was warning the women to avoid things that would detract from their witness. We've seen that Ephesus was a sensuous, immoral city. Furthermore, in New Testament times, ostentation in dress was in itself considered a mark of promiscuity.[22] One author of antiquity said, "A wife who likes adornment is not faithful."[23] Not only that, the Romans prized pearls above all other jewels.[24] Wearing pearls was considered the most ostentatious display of vanity.[25] Paul wanted Christian women to focus on inner virtues and live in a way that was "appropriate for women who profess to worship God."[26]

This word *profess* is key within this passage. In the original, it conveys a sense of proclamation, profession, and expertise.[27] In fact, it is one of eight Greek verbs in the New Testament formed by adding a prefix to the word for *messenger*. All of these verbs have to do with communication. Paul used seven of the eight in his letters:[28]

— to tell[29]

— to announce[30]

— to herald[31]

— to profess[32]

— to evangelize[33]

— to proclaim[34]

— to declare[35]

You can see that the word *profess* and its linguistic cousins are linked to the very heart and soul of Christian ministry. You can't profess something in silence, nor can you profess something in private. When Paul said the women in the church should dress appropriately because they *professed* God, he was showing that they were involved in public ministry, communicating the Gospel to others.

A FALSE TEACHER SILENCED

Now Paul changed the tone of his voice and the focus of his attention. He spoke to a particular woman: "A woman should learn in quietness and full submission. I do not permit a woman to teach or to have authority over a man; she must be silent. For Adam was formed first, then Eve. And Adam was not the one deceived; it was the woman who was deceived and became a sinner. But she will be saved through the childbearing."[36]

Structure Gives a Clue

The structure of Paul's communication has been very clear so far. Paul laid out the general principle—God's redeeming love for all humanity and our need to pray.[37] Then he gave two examples of how redeeming love should look when it's lived out: first for the men of the church[38] and then for the women.[39] In verse 10, Paul spoke to women involved in spreading the Gospel. As he did so, he remembered one woman who had perhaps played a prominent role in the church at Ephesus. So in verse 11, he stopped speaking in broad, general terms ("everyone," "men," "women") and addressed the case of this one woman. How can we say that? This is based on a very clear grammatical shift in the Greek. From verse 11 to the middle of verse 15, the plural nouns are gone. They're all singular: "a **woman**," "**she** must be silent," and "**she** will be saved through the childbearing." Then, in the second half of verse 15, Paul returned to the plural, "if **they** continue in faith, love and holiness with propriety." So, as Paul spoke to the women again, his grammar formed a small chiasm:

— verses 9–10:   "women" (plural)
— verses 11–15a: "a woman" (singular)
— verse 15b: "women" (plural)

One Certain Woman

Why did Paul make this dramatic switch from plural to singular and back to plural? I suggest that he had a specific Ephesian woman in mind as he wrote these words to Timothy. The context suggests that she was a vocal promoter of the false teachings troubling the Ephesian church. Perhaps she was one of the leaders of this heretical group. Besides the shift in grammar to the singular, several other clues point strongly to such a scenario.

Clue #1: The Pronouns Paul Used

In several places where Paul told Timothy to deal with false teachers, he used gender-inclusive pronouns. Words like these indicate that women were also involved:

— "if *anyone* teaches false doctrines…"[40]
— *"some,"* both men and women, "had wandered away" from a "sincere faith" and "have shipwrecked their faith," because in abandoning their faith they "followed deceiving spirits and things taught by demons…"[41]
— "command *certain [ones—both men and women]* not to teach false doctrines."[42]

Paul told Timothy to silence false teachers—male *and* female.

Clue #2: Women Involved in Heresies

Paul urged Timothy to avoid "old wives' tales,"[43] which suggests older women were among the false teachers. Younger women were swept into it, too, for Paul spoke of young widows who were "saying things they ought not to."[44] Paul said that women who had succumbed to the false teaching were "weak-willed women…loaded down with sins…swayed by all kinds of evil desires, always learning but never able to acknowledge the truth."[45]

Obviously, Paul did not see heresy as the domain of one gender. Both men and women had participated in the heresy that was tearing the Ephesian church apart. Paul declared that these "evil [persons] and impostors will go from bad to worse, deceiving and being deceived."[46] His words were designed to correct this situation.

Clue #3: False Teachers, Named and Unnamed

Though Paul spoke of the group that had been led astray, he also referred to several individuals most responsible for this deception:

 — Hymenaeus[47]
 — Alexander[48]
 — Philetus[49]

He also told Timothy that Phygelus, Hermogenes, and Demas had deserted him.[50] It should not be surprising that here, in 1 Timothy 2:11–15a, Paul advised Timothy what to do about a particular woman who had joined forces with those propagating a false gospel. Why didn't Paul mention her by name? There were other times when Paul didn't mention an individual by name but made it clear about whom he was talking. He did this when writing to the church in Corinth about a man committing incest,[51] and when writing to Titus concerning an unnamed yet specific person: "Warn a divisive person once, and then warn him a second time. After that, have nothing to do with him. You may be sure that such a man is warped and sinful; he is self-condemned."[52]

The context suggests that Paul had a particular person in mind. Paul's words to Titus in Crete are particularly helpful as we consider the unnamed woman in the Ephesian church. Like Timothy in Ephesus, Titus had been left in Crete to "straighten out what was left unfinished"[53] and confront a group of false teachers who, according to Paul, "must be silenced."[54] The "divisive person"[55] was apparently the ringleader of those who were "teaching things they ought not to teach."[56] Paul didn't need to mention him by name because both he and Titus knew exactly who was at the heart of the problem in Crete.

Perhaps Paul did not name these individuals—the contentious person in Crete, the man committing incest in Corinth, and the woman teaching heresy in Ephesus—because he hoped they would be restored. His pastoral heart longed for each of these people to be reconciled to the church. Maybe he avoided using their names to make it easier for them after they repented. This would have been in keeping with the process Jesus gave us for restoring believers who sin.[57]

It isn't surprising that Paul told Timothy to silence this woman without naming her. What is surprising, even shocking, is the way he named the men involved in the heresy—Hymenaeus, Alexander, and Philetus. Perhaps Paul had given up on them.

Clue #4: Back to Eve

Still another clue points to the existence of a deceived woman promoting heresy in the Ephesian church. Paul gave the reason this woman should be silenced by immediately pointing to another deceived woman—Eve.

Paul explained what Timothy was to do with this deceived woman. Then, just to make it really clear to him, Paul used the word *for* or *because*[58] to compare her situation to that of Eve in the Garden. He reminded Timothy that Adam sinned with his eyes open, but Eve did so because she was deceived. Paul held Adam more accountable for his sin because Adam wasn't deceived when he decided to disobey God.[59] However, Eve's sin was the fruit, not of knowing disobedience but of deception.[60] One of the major themes of this entire passage was stopping the deception in the Ephesian church. Eve was deceived, and so was this woman who was to be silenced. Both were acting on false beliefs.

What these two women had in common was that they both had believed a lie. As a result, they both had sinned. The sin of both had affected the lives of a large number of people in a very negative way.

Paul wanted to put an end to this: an end to the sin, an end to the deception, and an end to the conditions that made deception possible. He realized that deception is a fertile field in which sin can easily grow. He understood that the women of his day were more prone to being deceived because they had been excluded from educational opportunities. Paul intended to put an end to this deception. This could be the first step in restoring not only the deceived woman but also the entire church of Ephesus.

17.

PAUL'S GRACIOUS SOLUTION

(Part Two of 1 Timothy 2:1–15)

By David Hamilton

Now let's go back and look closer at what Paul said Timothy should do about this woman in Ephesus. Even though the woman was deceived and had deceived many, Paul gave wonderful, redeeming instructions on how to deal with her.

Paul's first word was that "a woman should learn."[1] This phrase would better reflect the original Greek if it were translated "*must* learn." This is not just a suggestion but an imperative. It is very important to realize that this is the *only* direct command Paul gave in this whole chapter. "Paul did not simply say that woman '*may* learn' or '*should* learn' or that woman should be '*allowed* to learn.' Woman *must* learn. By implication, [this woman] must be instructed."[2] Timothy was expected to make sure that this woman was given an education.

What a gracious response toward someone who had been causing so much harm! Paul realized that the problem lay primarily in the fact that like all the women of her day, this woman had been excluded from the opportunity to learn.[3] Whether this woman was a Gentile or a Jew, she would have been at an educational disadvantage. This had made her more susceptible to false teaching. Because Paul understood this, he extended more grace to her than he did to Hymenaeus, Alexander, and Philetus. These three men had sinned knowingly. So Paul "handed [them] over to Satan."[4] But he handed the woman over to a teacher. Which would you prefer?

The antidote to deception is learning the truth. Therefore, Paul demanded that this woman be taught, opening a door of opportunity that society had shut. As we have already seen, this was a revolutionary stance for Paul, who completely broke with the double standard of the Greeks, Romans, and Jews. The Gospel not only permitted but also *required* equal educational opportunity for women.

Paul went on to say how this woman should learn: "in quietness and full submission."[5] Again, this qualification on how she should learn was not a rebuke; he was not saying that she should just sit down and shut up. The noun used in verses 11 and 12 is related to the word used in verse two of this same chapter, where Paul said that the goal of all believers was to live "peaceful and quiet lives." "'Quietness' implies compliance with the law rather than resistance, and harmony with one's neighbors rather than wrangling and hostility...peace rather than argumentation."[6]

Paul wasn't requiring anything different of this woman than what he required of every church member in Ephesus throughout this passage. It was the same quality the men should have when they prayed "without anger or disputing"[7] and the women should have, behaving "with decency and propriety."[8]

TO LEARN LIKE THE STUDENTS OF THE RABBIS

In fact, the phrase "silence and submission" was a frequent formula in the Near East for a model student. "Before, throughout, and after Paul's time, the rabbis were agreed that silence was an admirable attribute for the pious scholar."[9] "As Simon, the son of Gamaliel, explained, 'All my days I grew up among the sages, and I have found nothing better for a person than silence.'"[10]

Any pupil must have a teachable attitude. This is normal for every disciple. Paul's words made it clear that it was no different for a woman than it was for a man who wished to learn. "A woman [like a man] cannot learn if she does not listen and yield to the instructor."[11] This is the same attitude James described when he said, "Everyone should be quick to listen, slow to speak."[12] This attitude makes for the very best of students. Paul's desire for the woman whom he commanded to learn in quietness and submission in verse 11 was that she become nothing less than that—the very best student. She was "to be learning in the same manner as did rabbinic students," for silence was considered "a positive attribute for rabbinic students."[13]

Another important thing to note is the way Jewish rabbis linked learning and teaching—you could not have one without the other. A student was taught in order that he could teach others.[14] According to the rabbis, "[Scripture states]: to learn, to teach, to observe and to do; consequently there are four [duties associated with each commandment]."[15] All of these were expected of every Jewish man. But women were for the most part excluded from this obligation and privilege.[16]

The rabbis did not get the idea of excluding women from learning and teaching from the Old Testament. But they did learn from Scripture that learning, doing, and teaching were linked together. For instance, Ezra "devoted himself to the *study* and *observance* of the Law of the Lord, and to *teaching* its decrees and laws in Israel."[17] Teaching was the normal end product of learning.

Paul, however, commanded this woman to learn but not to teach. Why? Because she had been teaching false doctrine. Therefore, Paul set aside the normal link between learning and teaching in her case. For a season she was being disciplined, corrected. She couldn't be allowed to continue spreading false doctrine. It was time for her to abstain from teaching altogether and dedicate herself to study alone.

OTHERS WHO WERE SILENCED

Paul silenced this woman not because she was a woman but because she was teaching false doctrine to others. First Timothy 2:12 forbade her "to teach a heresy which was creating serious problems for the church. She [was] certainly not the only one whose teaching must be stopped, however."[18] It was a matter not of gender but of deception, as it had been throughout his letters to Timothy. Paul...

— wrote about "evil **persons**," men and women who were "deceiving and being deceived."[19]

— told Timothy to "command certain **ones** [both men and women] not to teach false doctrines any longer."[20]

— warned Timothy that "[s]**ome** [both men and women] have wandered away...and turned to meaningless talk. They want to be teachers of the law, but they do not know what they are talking about...."[21]

— said that **they** had to be silenced, otherwise "their teaching will spread like gangrene."[22]

WHY DOES SHE GET ALL THE PRESS?

Paul told Timothy to silence false teachers. Whether male or female, they must be stopped—Hymenaeus, Alexander, Philetus, this unnamed woman, or anyone else.

Isn't it amazing? Even though Paul dealt with several men in a similar way, it's the woman who has received all the attention. Why does she get so much press? Paul handed Hymenaeus and Alexander "over to Satan, to be taught not to blaspheme,"[23] in other words, to stop them from speaking untruths about God. Paul silenced them. False teaching is false no matter who—male or female—is giving it, and it must be stopped.

PAUL WAS NOT SILENCING GODLY WOMEN

"There is nothing in this passage to support the silencing of godly women, or forbidding their teaching in church, their call to any form of Christian service, or the use of all the gifts the triune God has bestowed upon them."[24] How do we know that the words in verses 11 and 12 were not a universal prohibition against women teaching? Recall that just two verses earlier, in 1 Timothy 2:10, Paul spoke of those things that were "appropriate for *women who profess* to worship God." Paul expected believing women to be communicating their faith in both deed and word.

We also see Paul's attitude toward women teachers when he reminded Timothy of his spiritual heritage, "the truths of the faith and of the good teaching that you have followed."[25] Where did Timothy get this "good teaching"? From two godly women. Paul said, "I have been reminded of your sincere faith, which first lived in your grandmother Lois and in your mother Eunice and, I am persuaded, now lives in you also."[26] Paul urged Timothy to "continue in what you have learned and have become convinced of, because you know those from whom you learned it, and how from infancy you have known the holy Scriptures, which are able to make you wise for salvation through faith in Christ Jesus."[27] If Paul didn't approve of women teaching the Bible, he certainly missed a golden opportunity to correct Timothy here! Instead, he put a spotlight on these two women for the important role they played, teaching this future leader.

Some may say that this was different because Timothy was obviously young when his mother and grandmother taught him. Indeed, I know of no churches that prohibit women from teaching little boys in Sunday school. But if these words in 1 Timothy 2:11 and 12 were absolute prohibitions against all women teachers, nothing was said about making exceptions on the basis of age. Nor was subject matter mentioned. Paul didn't say, "Do not permit a woman to teach theology, but other subjects are okay." If this is an absolute against women teaching males, then women schoolteachers must not teach boys how to read, or write, or do arithmetic. In fact, mothers engaged in home-schooling their sons must be stopped, too!

Ridiculous? Yes. Recall Loren's words in chapter 2 that related how foolish it is to convert Bible statements relative to a situation into absolute truths.

PAUL WANTED RELIABLE WOMEN TO TEACH

Another indication of Paul's attitude toward women teachers was given in 2 Timothy 2:2. Paul told Timothy, "And the things you have heard me say in the presence of many witnesses entrust to reliable [persons, that is, men *and* women] who will also be qualified to teach others."[28]

If Paul had intended to prohibit women in teaching ministry, he missed another great opportunity here. There would have been no better place to use the Greek word *aner*, "males," rather than *anthropos*, "persons," to settle the issue once and for all. But no. Paul used the gender-inclusive "persons...qualified to teach." This was no accident. It was the deliberate, inspired Word of God. "Far from prohibiting them from teaching, it appears to be a strong exhortation that responsible women should make the proclamation of the truth a very high priority! Those of either sex who are able to teach hereby receive a summons to make known the unsearchable riches of Jesus Christ."[29]

WHAT ABOUT AUTHORITY?

Now let's look at the second part of 1 Timothy 2:12. The meaning of the Greek word[30] that is translated "to have authority" in the NIV is cloudy. Why? For one thing, it's a word that appears only once in the New Testament. Also, this word appears very little in other ancient literature. This makes it difficult for experts to agree on its meaning.[31] Scholars continue to debate whether this Greek word carries a positive meaning (such as rightly using authority to serve others) or a negative one (such as domineering, manipulating, even murdering others). The main thing for us to note is that this is not the normal New Testament word for authority.[32] It was an unusual word for an unusual situation.

In any case, we have to go back to the context of what Paul was talking about. A godless woman was teaching false doctrines and leading in a harmful way. It follows that she should not be allowed to hold a position of authority in the church. She didn't meet the qualifications for spiritual leadership that Paul gave Timothy.[33] Because she was not above reproach, either in word or in deed, disciplinary action was called for.

That's Not the Christian Way

It's worth mentioning that Paul didn't say anything anywhere in his letters to Timothy about a man having authority over a woman. In fact, among the redeemed, no one is to exercise authority in an authoritarian way over another person of either gender. Paul made it clear that the false teachers were the ones trying to control people. Jesus said that His followers were to be radically different from the way the world ran things:

> Jesus called them together and said, "You know that those who are regarded as rulers of the Gentiles lord it over them, and their high officials exercise authority over them. Not so with you. Instead, whoever wants to become great among you must be your servant, and whoever wants to be first must be slave of all. For even the Son of Man did not come to be served, but to serve, and to give his life as a ransom for many."[34]

About Eve

We've already seen how Paul compared this woman to Eve, for they both had been deceived. But there are a couple of other considerations as we look at 1 Timothy 2:13–14, "For Adam was formed first, then Eve. And Adam was not the one deceived; it was the woman who was deceived and became a sinner." These words could indicate one of two things:

1. On the one hand, Paul may have been refuting **the content** of the false teaching. There are indications that the false teachers

were distorting the truth about how God created the world.[35] Perhaps the worshipers of the mother goddess Artemis were denying the biblical Creation story, saying that woman was the source or head of man.[36]

2. On the other hand, Paul might have simply been referring to **the way that Eve became deceived**. If we look at the order of events in the Garden, God created man, then told him not to eat from the tree of knowledge.[37] Only later did God create woman.[38] So when the serpent questioned Eve, "Did God really say...?"[39] Eve had to rely on secondhand information relayed to her by Adam.

Eve didn't become deceived because of some inherent weakness in women. God said that everything He created was good, including the first woman. No. If Eve was deceived, it was because Adam didn't teach her well. If he had done a good job as a teacher, Eve would have known exactly what God had and hadn't said to Adam. The very fact that Adam silently "stood by her side during the whole sorry episode"[40] places the blame squarely on his shoulders for not faithfully passing on the Word of the Lord. No wonder God first addressed Adam when their transgression came to light.[41]

Whichever view you take, it points out the need for good teaching. Good teaching answers the distortions of heresy. The story of Adam and Eve shows how important it is to faithfully teach others so that no one falls into deception. That is why Paul's one command in this chapter was: The woman must learn.

SAVED THROUGH THE CHILDBEARING

Some would try to take Paul's instructions to Timothy to mean that women are more easily deceived than men, therefore not to be trusted as Bible teachers. Paul never said that. He wasn't defining universal gender traits here. He was simply talking about two women who had been deceived, then had fallen into sin—nothing more. To try to stretch this into some statement of inborn strengths and weaknesses in men and women twists the text.

Eve's deception led to sin, according to verse 14, as did this woman's deception in Ephesus. So Paul said (still in the singular), "[S]he will be saved through the childbearing." What does this mean? Was Paul saying that this deceived woman would be reconciled to the

Lord and to the church if she had a baby? If having a child were a requirement for women to be saved, what would that mean for single women or for childless wives?

The phrase "the childbearing" is unique. It isn't found anywhere else in the New Testament. Although a variety of interpretations have been proposed, one thing that is important to notice is that this word isn't a verb. On the contrary, it's a noun, dramatically preceded by the definite article ("*the* childbearing") to point to one particular childbearing.

I believe that Paul was still drawing parallels with Eve, the other deceived woman who was in need of salvation. In Eden, God prophesied of "the childbearing" when He said: "I will put enmity between [the serpent] and the woman, and between [the serpent's offspring] and hers; he will crush [the serpent's] head, and [the serpent] will strike his heel."[42] That's how the Gospel was first proclaimed, the Messiah first promised. And Paul repeated the promise here, saying that this unnamed Ephesian woman could still be saved through Him, the promised Child born to redeem all persons.

Paul began this passage with the most glorious affirmation of God's loving heart for the lost. "The childbearing" refers to the one mediator between God and persons, the person Christ Jesus, the promised seed of Eve, the Child born of a woman.[43] The issue at stake here was salvation, not motherhood. Women aren't saved by getting pregnant and having babies. They're saved by the child who was born—Jesus! Throughout this passage, Paul was talking about how men and women are redeemed, not about how they procreate. The central truth of this entire passage is Jesus and God's desire for all to be saved through the promised childbearing.

Jesus was the focus throughout Paul's letter to Timothy. Paul began by writing, "Here is a trustworthy saying that deserves full acceptance: Christ Jesus came into the world to save sinners."[44] By pointing to Jesus, Paul hoped to win over the unbelieving persecutors and correct the false teachers. Jesus was at the heart of this difficult passage, for it was only through His death and Resurrection that God's forever dream could come true, only through Him could believers "live peaceful and quiet lives."[45] It was all about Jesus.

Paul's pastoral heart was reaching out to this particular woman in Ephesus who had caused so much trouble. Paul was saying that she could be saved through the childbearing—that is, through Jesus. She must learn. What must she learn? She must learn about Jesus so that she might be fully restored to God through Him.

BACK TO THE PLURAL

Then Paul extended his pastoral concern to all women. In mid-sentence, he went back to the plural, saying that Jesus was what all women needed. Salvation would be theirs "if they continue in faith, love and holiness with propriety."[46] This was the rounding off of Paul's mini-chiasm. Even as he wanted "a woman" to be saved, he wanted all women to be saved. What a fitting conclusion to a passage that began by declaring that God wants all persons to be saved through the person of His Son Jesus.

This list of four spiritual characteristics—faith, love, and holiness with propriety—is amazingly similar to the four Paul laid out at the very beginning of his letter to Timothy: "The goal of this command is love, which comes from a pure heart and a good conscience and a sincere faith."[47] Why is this important? It's important because this was a radical departure from everything these people had been taught before. Both Jews and Gentiles defined virtue for women by an entirely different standard. But not Paul. He expected the same response to the Gospel, the same moral standard for both men and women. He followed through on what Jesus had already demonstrated. The ancient double standard of law and behavior was dead. Membership in the family of God was now offered equally to men and women. And service for God was no longer an exclusive male domain but a shared enterprise.

18.

Women Leaders Too

(1 Timothy 3:1–13)

By David Hamilton

We have seen in the past few chapters that Paul definitely was *not* against women preachers, women teachers, or women leaders in the church. In fact, Paul threw the door open for women in public ministry. We will see this again as we look at his teaching on leadership qualifications.

Refer to the figure "Overview of 1 Timothy" on page 207. The passage we will now look at forms part of Paul's heart message to Timothy. Paul turned from dealing with an ungodly woman leader to address what it meant to be a godly leader—both for men and for women. He said, "If anyone sets [his or her] heart on being an overseer, [he or she] desires a noble task."[1] We won't go into 1 Timothy 3:1–13 in the same depth as we did 1 Timothy 2:1–15, but we'll quickly look at several important things.

First, notice that Paul once again used the word *anyone* when talking about those who wanted to be leaders. I have added "his or her" and "he or she" in brackets because this is true to the grammar Paul used.[2]

Second, look at the structure of this passage of 1 Timothy 3:1–13. It's identical to the structure of the one we just studied. Both start with a general principle, then give two particularizations of that principle, then within the second particularization offer a tiny chiasm.

In 1 Timothy 2:1–15, the general principle was that God wanted all to pray and live quiet, peaceful lives. The first example was how the men should behave. The second example was how the women should behave. The miniature chiasm within that second example was plural-singular-plural: all women, a woman, all women.

Now in this next passage, 1 Timothy 3:1–13, Paul gave the general principle that anyone who desired to be a leader desired a good thing. The first example of leaders was overseers, or bishops (verses 2–7). The second example was deacons (verses 8–13). And within that second example, Paul gave a tiny chiasm—male, female, male. Notice how these passages mirror each other in structure.

MIRROR
STRUCTURES

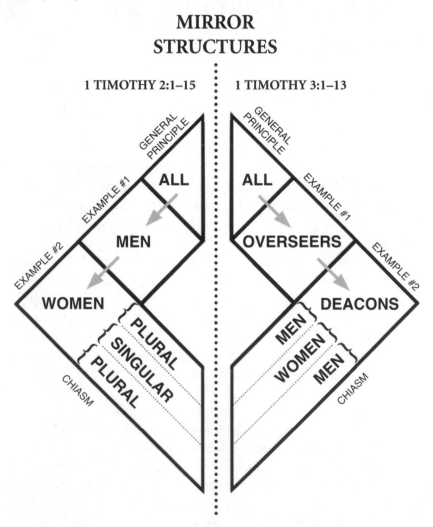

1 TIMOTHY 2:1–15   1 TIMOTHY 3:1–13

"In Like Manner the Women"

"Women likewise must be serious, not slanderers, but temperate, faithful in all things."[3] When Paul turned to speak of women with leadership responsibilities, he again used the word *likewise*. Recall that he did the same thing in 1 Timothy 2:9. Both there and here, this word bridged his discussion as he moved from men to women. Without exception, Paul treated men and women the same, as coworkers in the Gospel. He was absolutely committed to equality. Keep in mind that *likewise* is similar to a literary equal sign; it means "in the same way." What was Paul just speaking about? Men serving as deacons. Then he turned and said, "In like manner the women...."

Deacons or Wives?

The Greek word *gune*[4] that Paul used here may be translated as either "women" or "wives," just as *aner* can be translated as either "men" or "husbands." You have to study the context to understand which meaning fits better. The NIV renders a very poor translation of this verse. It says, "In the same way, their wives are to be women worthy of respect, not malicious talkers but temperate and trustworthy in everything." By choosing to translate *gune* as "wives," it has to add the pronoun *their* and a whole phrase that is nonexistent in the Greek—"are to be women." In doing this, the NIV translators slant the text for the reader, allowing for only one possibility. This choice of words exposes a prejudice against women leaders in the church that is not found in Paul's words. What the Greek literally says is, "Likewise/in the same way, women/wives are to be worthy of respect, not malicious talkers but temperate and trustworthy in everything."

So what did Paul mean? Wives or women? Look at what he was talking about. Was he talking about marriage or about leadership? How do the women in 1 Timothy 3:11 relate to the men of 1 Timothy 3:8–10? Are these women their wives, or are they colleagues in ministry?

Compare again the literary structures of 1 Timothy 2:1–15 and 1 Timothy 3:1–13. Notice how 3:11 parallels 2:11–15a. Each forms the heart of the respective mini-chiasms. It's as if Paul set out to describe the role of godly women leaders in the church as the ultimate antidote to an ungodly woman leader. Paul did not react against all women because of the errors of one woman. He responded in a way that corrected the individual while paving the way for many women to be leaders. The qualities Paul put down in 1 Timothy 3:11 are the very ones that will prevent another tragedy like the one he was dealing with earlier in 1 Timothy—false doctrine being taught by unscrupulous leaders, both male and female.

The ultimate restoration of that regrettable situation (the unnamed woman in 1 Timothy 2:11–15a) was not to ban all women from public ministry. No. Instead, in 1 Timothy 3:11, Paul was stating the qualities neccesary for godly women to be released into public ministry. This is exactly the same thing Paul did to counter the harmful influence of the men who were promoting heresy—Hymenaeus and Alexander.[5] Just because these two men misused their teaching gifts, Paul didn't eliminate all men from roles of leadership. No, to prevent further problems, he likewise set down guidelines for men leaders.[6] Thus, we see that Paul dealt with men and women evenhandedly, correcting those of both genders who fell into heresy, instructing men and women in the ways of spiritual leadership so that they would not "fall into disgrace and the devil's trap."[7]

Are the women of verse 11 deacons or the wives of deacons? The structure of the letter and the content of Paul's message suggest that Paul fully intended women to serve in the leadership of the church. After all, hadn't Paul begun the ministry in this city with Priscilla and her husband, Aquila? Nowhere in his writings do we see Paul withholding leadership responsibilities from godly women. On the contrary, we know from his comments concerning Phoebe in Romans 16:1–2 that he saw her as a fellow servant of the Lord, affirmed her as a deacon, and commended her as an exemplary leader of the church.

Paul's word to us is not one that makes harsh divisions between men and women, neither with the way they are saved nor with the way they are released into ministry. On the contrary, before the Cross, the playing field is leveled. If we are to fulfill God's forever dream—reaching everyone with the opportunity to be reconciled to Him—every one of us must pray, profess our faith, and live peaceful and quiet lives. Every one of us should follow God's leading into whatever ministry He chooses. This is true for men and **likewise** for women.

A FINAL WORD

by David Hamilton

I am a missionary. I also grew up in a missionary home in South America, raised by a strong and loving missionary team—my mom and dad, Keith and Marilynn Hamilton. They are the ones who taught me that God and His Word are the foundation for everything in life. They showed me by their example that the most important work on earth is taking the Gospel of Jesus Christ to the lost.

What could be more important than understanding God's revelation on how to carry out the most important work on earth? We must hear God's voice clearly on this subject of women in ministry so that we can cooperate with Him. We must never find ourselves working against His purposes, quenching His spirit at work in those whom He has called to extend His kingdom.

We must also see that God revealed His Word in time and space. That means, in order to truly understand His Word, we need to know something about the world where that revelation broke through.

The ideas of man spring from the soil of his time and his culture, but not the ideas of God. In fact, the revelation of God often stands in direct opposition to what the majority of people believe. Nowhere was this more true than in the subject of women: what was believed about their roles and their basic value at the time the Scriptures were being written. That is why in this book, we took steps back into history to understand the barriers and humiliation that women faced.

We saw how the Greeks, Romans, and even the Jews forged chains that would last for thousands of years, saying women were a curse, that they were less valuable than men, that they were to be avoided, or at least, carefully quarantined.

I trust you were able to see how dark the despair of women was, and the brightness when Jesus pierced that darkness.

Whether Jesus was dealing with a crippled woman in the synagogue, or giving the most important messages of Christianity to individual women, such as Martha and the Samaritan woman at the well, He was restoring God's original perspective of women. He was showing they were not an embarrassment, not objects of lust, nor creatures to be looked down on. He simply related to them as persons created in the image of God, capable of doing things considered extraordinary in their day. He sent the woman at the well to evangelize her whole village. He even had women traveling and ministering alongside Him and the twelve male disciples.

We also saw how the apostle Paul followed in Jesus' footsteps. The apostle's treatment of women as peers and coworkers couldn't be further removed from the oft-repeated image of Paul as a woman-hater. Instead, Paul affirmed the public ministry of women in 1 Corinthians 11:2-16. He endorsed them as they spoke to God on behalf of the people in prayer, and spoke to the people on behalf of God in prophecy.

In 1 Corinthians 14:26–40, Paul urged all—men and women—to contribute actively to the corporate worship of the church, that all might be mutually edified. Paul stressed that God was a God of order, so he corrected three groups who were bringing disorder into their gatherings: those who spoke in tongues, those who prophesied, and the women. But even though he corrected them in the abuse of their freedom, he did not silence any of those three groups permanently nor take away their freedom to minister. In fact, he made provision for the education of women—a radical departure from all the cultures of the New Testament world.

In 1 Timothy 2:1–15, Paul told Timothy how to fight against persecution from without and heresy from within the church at Ephesus. In the midst of this difficult situation, Paul gave one of the most glorious glimpses into the heart of God. God's forever dream was shown: that He desires to see all persons saved and to come to a knowledge of the truth. Paul then instructed Timothy concerning "a woman" who had held authority in the church but had been led astray by false teachers. He told Timothy he couldn't allow this woman to teach nor to hold authority over men. But even for her, Paul showed pastoral concern. He commanded Timothy to provide teaching to restore her to the knowledge of the truth. Then he finished by encouraging all who were above reproach, both men and women, to assume leadership responsibilities in the church.

In all three of these passages—often used to limit women in ministry—we saw that Paul expected women to be fully involved in the public proclamation of the Gospel. When he gave correction it was for the manner in which women (and men) were ministering. Nowhere did Paul prohibit women from sharing in leadership. In fact, he actively encouraged it. He urged men to reconsider how they valued women. He affirmed the authority of women. He opened doors of educational opportunities for women. He invited, indeed he urged all—both men and women—to be involved in the ministry and the leadership of the church.

Now it's time for us to examine our own hearts and apply the truth we've seen in Scripture, deciding what steps we need to take in our lives, in our work, in our churches and groups, and in our homes. In James 1:23–24, it says that those who read God's Word without applying it are like those who look in a mirror and go away, forgetting what they have seen. What could be more useless than that? Instead, we need to study the Bible, then change our attitudes and practices to bring ourselves in line with it.

In the years since Jesus and Paul, the church has often failed to live according to the high standards set out in Scriptures. Throughout the centuries, God through His Spirit has attempted again and again to bring renewal and correction to His people. But we have continually fallen short of the model that our Savior and His servant Paul set for us. We have been guilty of wandering from New Testament truths even as the rabbis of old strayed from the teaching God gave them in the Old Testament.

In fact, like the rabbis, we have often done so with strong religious conviction and dogmatic zeal! Our teaching and treatment of women have often had more in common with the ancient Greek and Roman philosophers who set up the double standard and first coined the phrase: "Women, you can't live with them and you can't live without them!"[1] Instead of shaping our culture according to the Bible, we have allowed our culture to shape us and even color how we read the Bible. We have erred, and our failing has debilitated our witness, making generations of women believe that the God of the Bible is against them.

There are a multitude of quotations from church history that reveal the persistence of the hatred of women. Thinkers in the early church quickly turned away from the high value of women shown in the New Testament. A typical statement was one made by Tertullian:

You [women] are the Devil's gateway. *You* are the unsealer of
that forbidden tree. *You* are the first deserter of the Divine law.
You are she who persuaded him whom the Devil was not
valiant enough to attack. *You* destroyed so easily God's image
man. On account of *your* desert, that is death, even the Son of
God had to die.[2]

What an awful thing to say about half of the ones whom God created in His image! Yet that attitude persisted into the Middle Ages and
beyond. Sometimes influential men of the church even went back to
the Greek philosophers to support their views that women were intrinsically weaker, more easily deceived, and a trap for men. Bonaventure,
a medieval saint, copied Aristotle when he said: "Woman is an embarrassment to man, a beast in his quarters, a continual worry, a never-
ending trouble, a daily annoyance, the destruction of the household, a
hindrance to solitude, the undoing of a virtuous man, an oppressive
burden, an insatiable bee, a man's property and possession."[3]

We could quote a lot more of such statements made by men closer
to our era, but enough has been said. All we need to do now is to look
back and grieve over how far we have strayed from God's original purposes. We need to recognize and mourn our historical, corporate error.
It is to all of our shame that such words were penned in the name of
the One who came to set women and men free.

As we recognize our broken past—both as a people and as individuals—we must repent, in order that Christ's values, His standards
built upon His foundational ideas, may be made clear to the world.
Repentance is always the starting point to apply God's Word. God help
us to humbly repent, like David of old, who said:

Who can discern his errors?
Forgive my hidden faults.
Keep your servant also from willful sins;
may they not rule over me.
Then will I be blameless
innocent of great transgression.
May the words of my mouth and the meditation of my heart
be pleasing in your sight,
O LORD, my Rock and my Redeemer.[4]

It is time for us to rethink some of our oldest beliefs and traditions. It is time for us to repent for whatever ways we have hindered God's work and misread His Word. It is time for us to release women to be all that God has called them to be.

It is time.

A FINAL WORD

By Loren Cunningham

I was sitting on an airplane bound for Jakarta, editing the manuscript for this book on my laptop. A Muslim woman sat next to me, garbed from head to toe according to the dictates of her religion. As I pecked away, she kept peering over my shoulder, trying to read the words on my screen. That's a picture of what's happening right now. Multiplied millions of women all over the world are looking over the church's shoulder, longing to see the freedom Jesus purchased for them at Calvary.

The world has tried to call women to freedom, but with a spirit of rebellion and bitterness that has only deepened the wounds. Only as the church of Jesus Christ takes the lead in a spirit of humility will we see captives set free.

We also need to see women in the church set free to obey God in their gifts and callings. My passion comes from four decades of ministry, leading cross-cultural mission efforts in every country on earth. My heart's desire is to see the mightiest missionary workforce in history unleashed.

I trust as you have read this book that you have heard our hearts. To me, this is the leading subject in the Body of Christ and in the societies of the world today. It is the issue that can unite or divide homes, churches, communities, and society at large. We didn't enter into such an important field of study without the fear of the Lord upon us. We don't expect everyone to agree with our conclusions. We do hope it has been clear in its presentation.

You could say this book has been thirty years in the making. I began teaching on the right of women to preach the Gospel that long ago, stirred by the many examples around me. My mother, Jewell Cunningham, now in her nineties, has been an ordained minister for more than seventy years. Some of my earliest memories are of hearing her preach the Word. She served alongside my father, T. C. Cunningham, as copastor in a number of churches. Then their ministry broadened, taking them to more than one hundred nations as missionary statesmen.

It wasn't just Mom who served as a sterling example of a woman called by God. My wife, Darlene Scratch Cunningham, is a leader, a leader of leaders, and a trainer of leaders. I don't know of a woman training more international missionaries than Darlene. I cannot imagine being able to found Youth With A Mission without Darlene as my coleader. Nor can I imagine YWAM without the many strong women among us. The mission we founded in 1960 was privileged to pioneer the releasing of young people, laypersons, and short-term workers into missions. We were among the first to send out large numbers of missionaries from non-Western countries. But I believe the largest category of all remains to be fully released.

Youth With A Mission has been blessed with women "generals," such as Elizabeth Baumann Cochrane, who began our work in Nepal, suffering imprisonment there to help open that country to the Gospel. Another is Deyon Stephens, who helped her husband, Don, found Mercy Ships and continues to serve the nations of the world. Nancy Neville is a small giant who helped launch the missions movement in the Southern Cone of South America. These are just a few examples of so many I could name. We have women serving in the highest levels of YWAM oversight, as well as countless more stalwarts serving in every rank, doing true exploits in the kingdom of God. They give me the faith to believe for more.

We did not deal with marriage or family in depth in this book. That will deserve fuller treatment in an upcoming work. However, we do believe marriage is to be a partnership of equals, as God designed in the Garden.

We did not write this book for the millions of women who are happy and secure in their roles. Our passion was for the hundreds of millions of women who are not free. It was for their sake, and for the final completion of the task of taking the Good News to them, that we wrote this book.

Almost a hundred years ago, Frederik Franson wrote:

> It is amazing how one can get such a false idea that not all God's children should use all their powers in all ways to save the lost world. There are, so to speak, many people in the water about to drown. A few men are trying to save them, and that is considered well and good. But look, over there a few women have untied a boat also to be of help in the rescue, and immediately a few men cry out: standing there idly looking on and therefore having plenty of time to cry out: "No, no, women must not help, rather let the people drown."[5]

As we release women, we'll mobilize the hundreds of thousands of people needed to complete the Great Commission. We'll see God's blessing on unity and servant leadership. We'll see more anointing of the Spirit. We'll see a strong Body of Christ, no longer weakened because we fail to discern it.

We must seek God's wisdom in this. Jesus worked within culture to transform it. We must do the same. The greatest changes will not come in our generation, but in the one that is about to emerge. God is setting the stage. The final chapter is about to be written. Everything will be restored when He comes. Until then, we should be sensitive to the Spirit and what He is doing in our time.

If you are a leader...

Be a good steward by releasing the gifts of those who serve with you: women and men, younger people and older ones, and those from backgrounds different from yours. The more people you release, the more God will bless you and your ministry. Give and it shall be given unto you. Rejoice in those whom God has gifted. Promote them. Help them fulfill their destiny.

If you believe differently...

Agree to hear our hearts as we have written this book. We want to seek God's wisdom together with others in the church. We do not want to blast a trumpet in the ear of the Body of Christ. We want to work together to see God's will done on earth.

If you have held women back...

Repent of hurtful attitudes. Let us all ask the Lord to forgive us for hindering His work in any way. Let us humbly ask God's forgiveness for the way we have made women or anyone else into second-class citizens in the kingdom of God. Let us lead the way into reconciliation and healing.

If you are a woman called by God...

Decide that you will obey the Lord. I began this book sharing my dream that little girls and young women and older women would be set free to obey the call of God. Obedience is the bottom line. Ask yourself: Am I fulfilling the call God has placed on my life? Am I obeying Him in my generation? Am I doing what He has called me to do?

If we are committed to obeying God, nothing can stand in our way. However, we must guard our hearts against bitterness. We cannot do God's will the devil's way. We must maintain a servant heart, responding in the opposite spirit to criticism. When anyone stands against us and our call, perhaps out of a genuine, but misguided desire to protect the status quo, we have the responsibility to avoid responding in anger. Instead, we must learn to release the anger we feel because of injustice and wrongs done against us. If we fight our own battles, we will end up confused and defeated. If we allow the Lord to defend us and our ministry, He will make a way where there is none.

Don't give up. No one can keep you from obeying God's call. Has a missionary organization denied you entrance, significant ministry, or leadership because of your gender? Join another. Or start your own. Are you a woman called to preach? If others deny you the right to preach in their pulpit, preach on the streets outside, as John Wesley and George Whitefield did. Or plant your own church. If you guard your heart and attitude, God will bless your ministry.

It is not your job to change everyone's mind. It is your job to obey the Lord and do whatever He is calling you to do. Keep yielded to Him and open to others, free in your spirit from any feelings of rejection or bitterness. Obey God and let Him take care of the results. It will eventually become clear to everyone that God has His hand on you.

You will be one of the daughters who prophesy in the last days.

You will be one of the host of women proclaiming the Good News.

What is God calling you to do?

Recommended Resources

We recommend the following books for those who wish to pursue the study of women in leadership and ministry. There are differences of opinion held between people of good faith and conviction. You will find these books worthwhile reading, though we might differ with them on various points.

Are Women Human? by Dorothy L. Sayers, William B. Eermans Publishing Company, Grand Rapids, 1971.

Beyond Sex Roles: What the Bible Says About a Woman's Place in Church and Family, by Gilbert Bilezikian, Baker Book House, Grand Rapids, Second Edition, 1993.

Beyond the Curse: Women Called to Ministry, by Aida Dina Besançon Spencer, Thomas Nelson, Nashville, 1985.

Equal to Serve: Women and Men Working Together Revealing the Gospel, by Gretchen Gaebelein Hull, Fleming H. Revell Company, Tarrytown, 1991.

Fashioned for Intimacy: Reconciling Men and Women to God's Original Design, by Jane Hansen, Regal Books, Ventura, 1997.

Female Ministry: Woman's Right to Preach the Gospel, by Catherine Booth, The Salvation Army Supplies Printing and Publishing Department, New York, 1859, reprinted 1975.

From Jerusalem to Irian Jaya, by Ruth A. Tucker, Zondervan, 1983, (note especially chapter 9, "Single Women Missionaries: Second Class Citizens.").

God and Women: A Fresh Look at What the New Testament Says About Women, by Dorothy Pape, Mowbrays, London, 1977.

Guardians of the Great Commission: The Story of Women in Modern Missions, by Ruth A. Tucker, Academie Books, Zondervan Publishing House, Grand Rapids, 1988.

I Suffer Not a Woman: Rethinking I Timothy 2:11-15 in Light of Ancient Evidence, by Richard and Catherine Clark Kroeger, Baker Book House, Grand Rapids, 1992.

In the Spirit We're Equal, by Susan C. Hyatt, Hyatt Press, 1998. Mailing address: P.O. Box 764463, Dallas, Texas 75376.

Paul, Women and Wives: Marriage and Women's Ministry in the Letters of Paul, by Craig S. Keener, Hendrickson Publishers, Peabody, 1992.

Paul, Women Teachers, and the Mother Goddess at Ephesus: a Study of I Timothy 2:9-15 in Light of the Religious and Cultural Milieu of the First Century, by Sharon Hodgin Gritz, University Press of America, Lanham, 1991.

The Bible Status of Woman, by Lee Anna Starr, New York Lithographing Corporation, New York, 1955.

What Paul Really Said About Women: An Apostle's Liberating Views on Equality in Marriage, Leadership, and Love, by John Temple Bristow, Harper and Row, San Francisco, 1988.

Who Said Women Can't Teach? by Charles Trombley, Bridge Publishing, Inc., South Plainfield, 1985.

Women as Risk Takers for God, by Lorry Lutz, Baker Book House, Grand Rapids, 1999.

Women, Authority and the Bible, by Alvera Mickelsen, InterVarsity Press, Downers Grove, 1986.

Women in the Maze: Questions & Answers on Biblical Equality, by Ruth A. Tucker, InterVarsity Press, Downers Grove, 1992.

I Commend to You Our Sister: An Inductive Study of the Difficult Passages Related to the Ministry of Women: 1 Corinthians 11:2–16, 1 Corinthians 14:26–40, and 1 Timothy 2:1–15, Master's Thesis by David J. Hamilton for the College of Christian Ministries, University of the Nations, 1996.

ENDNOTES

CHAPTER 1

[1] Acts 2:17–21.

[2] Joel 2:28–29.

[3] "The women who proclaim the good tidings are a great host" Psalm 68:11b, as correctly translated by the NASB, which manages to reflect the Hebrew original most accurately.

[4] Jewell Cunningham, *Women Called to Preach* (Lindale: C & R Publications, 1989), 42.

[5] Matthew 9:37, John 4:35.

[6] Current Population Reports, U.S. Census Bureau, Commerce Department, 1996.

[7] *Statistical Abstract of the U.S. 1997* (Washington: National Data Book, U.S. Department of Commerce, Economics and Statistics Administration, Bureau of the Census, October 1997), 79, table 97.

[8] *Sourcebook of Criminal Justice Statistics,* 1995.

[9] Gavin de Becker, *Protecting the Gift* (New York: The Dial Press, Random House, 1999), 15.

[10] Bureau of Justice Statistics, Reports 98–100, 1996. See http://www.ojp.usdoj.gov/bjs

[11] Sheryl Watkins, "Women: Five Barriers Facing Women in the Developing World," *Today* (Federal Way: World Vision, April–May 1997), 4–7.

[12] Barbara Ehrenreich, "For Women, China Is All Too Typical," *Time,* (September 18, 1995), 130.

[13] Geraldine Brooks, *Nine Parts of Desire: The Hidden World of Islamic Women* (New York: Anchor Books-Doubleday, 1995), 50.

[14] Jean P. Sasson, *Princess* (New York: William Morrow, 1992).

[15] Ibid., 101–102.

[16] Ibid., 181–185.

[17] Ibid., 208–209.

[18] Ehrenreich, "For Women," *Time,* 130.

[19] *Nightline* by ABC News, transcript from television broadcasts on February 16 and February 17, 1999.

[20] Nicholas D. Kristof, "Stark Data on Women: 100 Million Are Missing," *The New York Times* (November 5, 1991), C-1, C-12.

[21] Ibid.

[22] Ibid.

[23] Ibid.

[24] "25 Years of Thumps," *New Woman* (October 1995), 234.

[25] Quoted with a footnote in Ruth A. Tucker, *From Jerusalem to Irian Jaya: A Biographical History of Christian Missions* (Grand Rapids: Academy Books, The Zondervan Corporation, 1983), 233.

[26] 1 Peter 4:17.

[27] Genesis 1:27.

[28] Transcribed from "Women in the Church I and II," seminar by Pastor David Johnson on cassettes 1527 and 1528 from Growing in Grace, a ministry of Church of the Open Door, 6421 - 45th Avenue North, Crystal, MN 55428.

[29] 1 John 3:8.

[30] John 12:1–8.

[31] Matthew 26:6–13.

[32] Matthew 28:10, John 20:17.

[33] "The Role of Women in Ministry as Described in Holy Scripture," a position paper adopted by the General Presbytery of the Assemblies of God, Dr. Zenas J. Bicket, Commission Chairman, published in *Pentecostal Evangel* (October 28, 1990), 12–17.

[34] Vinson Synan, "Women in Ministry," *Ministries Today* (January/February 1993), 46.

[35] Ibid.

[36] Jon Trott, *Cornerstone Magazine* (Volume 25, Issue 108), 23. This was a review of Rebecca Merrill Groothuis, *Women Caught in the Conflict: The Culture War Between Traditionalism and Feminism*, published by Baker Books. Despite earlier endorsements of women in ministry by evangelical pioneers, the movement was influenced away from this stance by later writers. Perhaps the leading antifeminist evangelical writer was C. I. Scofield, whose *Scofield Reference Bible* was published in 1909. Scofield believed that women were unfit for leadership. Soon his views prevailed among evangelicals.

[37] Trott, review of *Women Caught in the Conflict* in *Cornerstone Magazine*, 23.

[38] Transcribed from "Women in the Church I and II" (see note 28).

[39] Synan, "Women in Ministry," *Ministries Today*, 46.

[40] Ibid.

[41] Ralph D. Winter, "Women in Missions," *Mission Frontiers* (August 1999).

[42] Ibid.

[43] Ruth A. Tucker (author and professor at Trinity Evangelical Divinity School in Deerfield, Illinois), quoted in Julia Duin, "Women in the Pulpit," *Charisma* (November 1994), 26.

[44] Tucker, *From Jerusalem to Irian Jaya*, 233.

[45] J. Herbert Kane, *Life and Work on the Mission Field* (Grand Rapids: Baker Books, 1980), 143.

[46] Winter, "Women in Missions."

[47] Melody and Keith Green, *Women's Right to Preach the Gospel* (Lindale: Pretty Good Printing, 1980).

[48] Kane, *Life and Work*, 143.

CHAPTER 2

[1] 1 Corinthians 13:9–12.

[2] Romans 12:2, Ephesians 5:26.

[3] Romans 2:28–29.

[4] 2 Corinthians 3:18.

[5] Acts 17:30.

[6] Matthew 22:34–40.

[7] Leviticus 19:18.

[8] Ephesians 6:9.

[9] Philemon 16–17.

[10] Matthew 28:19.

[11] Even though it was outlawed in Mauritania, slavery still exists there, since the uneducated do not know that their enslavement is against the law.

[12] John 8:32.

[13] Matthew 28:19–20.

[14] Matthew 13:33.

[15] Romans 1:17.

[16] Richard N. Ostling, "Theologian Presses Revision of Calvin's Role in Christianity," the *Washington Times* (August 14, 1999), C-10.

[17] "William Carey's Amazing Mission: No Obstacle Too Great," *Glimpses* (Christian History Institute, Issue #45, 1993).

[18] An excellent source of information on how the revivals of nineteenth-century America gave birth to the women's suffrage movement is the book *In the Spirit We're Equal* by Susan C. Hyatt (Dallas: Hyatt International Ministries, 1998). See especially pages 172–180.

[19] Judges 13:5. See also Numbers 6:1–21.

[20] 1 Corinthians 11:14.

[21] 2 Corinthians 3:6.

[22] 1 Corinthians 1:17 NKJV.

[23] Revelation 22:18–19.

[24] John 16:13.

[25] John 7:17. Also John 8:47.

[26] 1 Peter 1:16.

[27] Psalm 145:17 NASB.

[28] 2 Chronicles 19:6.

[29] 2 Timothy 2:15.

[30] Joel 2:28–29.

[31] Acts 2:17–18.

[32] Angus Kinnear, *Against the Tide* (Fort Washington: Christian Literature Crusade, 1997), 44, 48, 50, 56, 59, 62, 104, 138, 156.

[33] Ibid., 179.

[34] Philippians 2:6.

CHAPTER 3

[1] The elder alluded to the story in Numbers 22:21–31 in which God spoke to Balaam through his donkey.

[2] 1 Chronicles 16:22.

[3] 1 Thessalonians 5:19 NASB.

[4] Psalm 139:15 NKJV, Genesis 1:27.

[5] Romans 11:29.

[6] Isaiah 49:1–2, emphasis added.

[7] Jeremiah 1:5.

[8] Esther 4:14.

[9] Galatians 1:1, 15.

[10] John 1:6.

[11] Philippians 3:12.

[12] Acts 4:19.

[13] Romans 12:6–8, 1 Corinthians 12:8–10, 1 Corinthians 12:28, Ephesians 4:11.

[14] 1 Corinthians 12:8.

[15] 1 Corinthians 12:8.

[16] 1 Corinthians 12:9.

[17] 1 Corinthians 12:9, 28.

[18] 1 Corinthians 12:10, 28.

[19] Romans 12:6; 1 Corinthians 12:10, 28; Ephesians 4:11.

[20] 1 Corinthians 12:10.

[21] 1 Corinthians 12:10, 28–30.

[22] 1 Corinthians 12:10, 28–30.

[23] Acts 19:11.

[24] 1 Samuel 19:23–24.

[25] John 11:49–51.

[26] Matthew 7:22–23.

[27] Romans 12:4–8, 1 Corinthians 12:27–31, Ephesians 4:11.

[28] 1 Corinthians 12:27–31, Ephesians 4:11.

[29] Romans 12:6, 1 Corinthians 12:10, 28–29, Ephesians 4:11.

[30] Ephesians 4:11.

[31] Ephesians 4:11.

[32] Romans 12:7, 1 Corinthians 12:27–31, Ephesians 4:11.

[33] Romans 12:7.

[34] Romans 12:8.

[35] Romans 12:8.

[36] Romans 12:8.

[37] Romans 12:8.

[38] 1 Corinthians 12:28.

[39] 1 Corinthians 12:28.

[40] Romans 10:14.

[41] 1 Peter 4:9–11, Exodus 35:30–35, Zechariah 14:20–21.

[42] Ephesians 4:4–6.

[43] Galatians 3:28.

[44] Acts 11:17.

[45] Judges 4–5.

[46] Judges 5:7. Though sung with Barak, the use of first person makes it clear that Deborah authored the song.

[47] 2 Peter 1:20–21 NRSV.

[48] Micah 6:4.

[49] Exodus 15:20.

50 2 Corinthians 8:23.

51 Matthew 20:25–28, Mark 10:42–45.

52 Romans 16:2 NASB.

53 David Joel Hamilton, *I Commend to You Our Sister* (master's thesis, University of the Nations, 1996), Appendix O, 736–739.

54 Gordon D. Fee, *The New International Commentary on the New Testament: The First Epistle to the Corinthians* (Grand Rapids: William B. Eerdmans Publishing Company, 1991).

55 Genesis 1:26.

56 Luke 8:1–3.

57 John 16:12.

CHAPTER 4

1 Luke 2:36. While many English translations say "prophetess," there was no female version of this Greek word. Women were simply called "prophets."

2 2 Kings 22:14, 2 Chronicles 34:22.

3 Isaiah 8:3.

4 See Acts chapters 1 and 2, noting especially 1:14–15, 2:11, and 2:18.

5 Joel 2:28–29.

6 1 Timothy 2:12.

7 David Joel Hamilton, *I Commend to You Our Sister,* (master's thesis, University of the Nations, 1995), Appendix T.

8 2 Timothy 3:16.

9 Acts 18:26.

10 Hamilton, *I Commend to You Our Sister* (see note 7), Appendix X.

11 Romans 5:14–17, 1 Corinthians 15:22.

12 Worldwide membership figures: Mormons (Church of Jesus Christ of Latter Day Saints—10 million, Jehovah's Witnesses—more than 4 million, Scientology—more than 8 million, Unification Church—no numbers available, Christian Science—3,000 branch churches in more than 50 countries but no membership statistics available.

13 2 Timothy 1:5–6.

14 Transcribed from Jack Hayford, "What on Earth Is Happening in Heaven's Name?" a message on cassette #03928 by SoundWord Tape Ministry of The Church on the Way, First Foursquare Church, 14300 Sherman Way, Van Nuys, CA 91405-2499.

15 For more on this topic, see Loren Cunningham with Janice Rogers, *Is That Really You, God?* (Seattle: YWAM Publishing, 1984).

16 John 4.

17 1 Corinthians 15:13–14.

18 1 Kings 17:7–23, 2 Kings 4:8–37.

19 "The Preacher's Daughter," *Time* (May 1, 2000), 56–57.

20 Ibid.

21 Ralph D. Winter, "Women in Missions," *Mission Frontiers* (August 1999).

22 Psalm 68:11 NASB.

CHAPTER 5

[1] "Plato," Microsoft ® *Encyclopedia Encarta,* 1993.

[2] Eva Cantarella, *Pandora's Daughters: The Role and Status of Women in Greek and Roman Antiquity,* trans. Maureen B. Fant (Baltimore: John Hopkins University Press, 1981), 33.

[3] Homer, *The Iliad, Volume I: Books I–XII,* trans. A. T. Murray (Cambridge: Loeb Classical Library, Harvard University Press, 1965), 8.161–166.

[4] Homer, *The Iliad, Volume II: Books XIII–XXIV,* trans. A.T. Murray (Cambridge: Loeb Classical Library, Harvard University Press, 1968), 15.1–33.

[5] "Wives of Zeus," Microsoft ® *Encyclopedia Encarta,* 1993.

[6] Hesiod, *The Theogony* in *Hesiod, the Homeric Hymns and Homerica,* trans. Hugh H. Evelyn-White (Cambridge: Loeb Classical Library, Harvard University Press, 1936), 507–616.

[7] Semonides, "Fragment 7." Quoted in Sarah B. Pomeroy, *Goddesses, Whores, Wives, and Slaves* (New York: Schocken Books, 1975), 49–52.

[8] Ibid.

[9] Ibid.

[10] Socrates lived 469–399 B.C.; Plato lived 428–348/79 B.C.; Aristotle lived 384–322 B.C.; Alexander the Great lived 356–323 B.C.

[11] "Women will use every means to resist being led out into the light, and they will prove much too strong for the lawgiver. So that elsewhere, as I said, women would not so much as listen to the mention of the right rule without shrieks of indignation; but in our State perhaps they will." Plato, *Laws,* trans. R. G. Bury (Cambridge: Loeb Classical Library, Harvard University Press, 1926), 780e–781d.

[12] Plato, *Laws,* 804d–805a. Also Plato, *The Republic,* trans. Paul Shorey (Cambridge: Loeb Classical Library, Harvard University Press, 1953), 5.3 (451d–452b) and 5.4–6 (454b–456c).

[13] Plato, *The Republic,* 5.3 (451d–452b).

[14] Ibid., 5.6–7 (456e–457d).

[15] Ibid., 5.3 (451d–452b). Emphasis added.

[16] Plato, *Laws,* 780e–781d and 790a.

[17] Plato, *Timaeus* in *Plato, Volume VII: Timaeus, Critias, Cleitophon, Menexenus, Epistles,* trans. R. G. Bury (Cambridge: Loeb Classical Library, Harvard University Press, 1941), 91a–d.

[18] Plato, *The Republic,* 5.4–6 (454b–456c).

[19] Aristotle, *Aristotle, Volume XIII: The Generation of Animals,* trans. A. L. Peck (Cambridge: Loeb Classical Library, Harvard University Press, 1963), 4.3 (767b 4–8).

[20] Ibid., 2.3 (737a 25–30).

[21] Ibid., 4.6 (775a 12–16).

[22] Aristotle, *Physiognomics* in *Aristotle, Volume XIV: Minor Works,* trans. W. S. Hett (Cambridge: Loeb Classical Library, Harvard University Press, 1963), 809b.

[23] Aristotle, *Aristotle, Volume XXI: Politics,* trans. H. Rackham (Cambridge: Loeb Classical Library, Harvard University Press, 1972), 1.2.12 (1254b).

[24] Aristotle, *The Generation of Animals,* 1.20 (728a 18–21).

[25] Aeschylus lived 525–456 B.C.; Sophocles lived 496–406/5 B.C.; Euripides lived 485– 406 B.C.; Aristophanes lived 450–380 B.C.; and Menander lived 342–292 B.C.

[26] Pomeroy, *Goddesses and Slaves,* 240. She cites specific examples from six of Euripides' plays: *Andromache, Orestes, Troades, Iphigeneia at Aulis, Alcestis,* and *Hippolytus.*

[27] Aristophanes, *The Lysistrata* in *Aristophanes, Volume III: The Lysistrata, The Themophorizusae, The Ecclesiazusae, The Plutus,* trans. Benjamin Bickley Rogers (Cambridge: Loeb Classical Library, Harvard University Press, 1963), 367–368. Emphasis in the original.

[28] Aeschylus, *Seven Against Thebes,* 181–202. Quoted in Mary R. Lefkowitz and Maureen B. Fant, *Women's Life in Greece and Rome: A Source Book in Translation* (Baltimore: John Hopkins University Press, 1992), 28.

[29] Euripides, *Medea,* 285, 319–320. Quoted in Pomeroy, *Goddesses and Slaves,* 106.

[30] Euripides, *Ion,* 1025, 1330; *Alcestis,* 304–319, 463–465. Quoted in Pomeroy, *Goddesses and Slaves,* 106.

[31] Menander, *Menander: The Principle Fragments,* trans. Francis G. Allinson (Cambridge: Loeb Classical Library, Harvard University Press, 1944), 535K, 703K, 702K.

[32] Euripides, *Hippolytus* in *Euripides, Volume IV: Ion; Hippolytus; Medea; Alcestis,* trans. Arthur S. Way (Cambridge: Loeb Classical Library, Harvard University Press, 1935), 664–668.

[33] Euripides, *Orestes* in *Euripides, Volume II: Electra; Orestes; Iphigeneia in Taurica; Andromache; Cyclops,* trans. Arthur S. Way (Cambridge: Loeb Classical Library, Harvard University Press, 1978), 605–606.

[34] Sophocles, *Tereus,* 583. Quoted in Lefkowitz and Fant, *Women's Life,* 12–13.

[35] Euripides, *Iphigeneia at Aulis* in *Euripides, Volume I: Iphegenia at Aulis; Rhesus; Hecuba; The Daughters of Troy; Helen,* trans. Arthur S. Way (Cambridge: Loeb Classical Library, Harvard University Press, 1912), 1374–1394.

[36] Hippocrates, *On Virgins,* 8.466. Quoted in Lefkowitz and Fant, *Women's Life,* 242.

[37] Pliny the Elder, *Pliny, Volume VIII: Natural History, Books XXVIII–XXXII,* trans. W .H. S. Jones (Cambridge: Loeb Classical Library, Harvard University Press, 1958), 28.23.77–85.

[38] Aristotle, *The Generation of Animals,* 1.20 (728a 18–21).

[39] Plato, *Timaeus,* 91a–d.

[40] Euripides, *Medea,* 569–75. Quoted in Lefkowitz and Fant, *Women's Life,* 28.

[41] Euripides, *Hippolytus,* 616–652.

[42] Pomeroy, *Goddesses and Slaves,* 57.

[43] Athenaeus of Naucratis, *The Deipnosophists, Book XIII Concerning Women* in *The Deipnosophists, Volume VI,* trans. Charles Burton Gulick (Cambridge: Loeb Classical Library, Harvard University Press, 1959), 13.910–911. See also 13.568d–569f.

[44] "These prostitutes were, in a sense, the 'civil servants of sex,' and the laws protecting them resembled those that protected and regulated the lives of all the state's slaves. Free enterprise, in the matter of bordellos, remained legal, so that besides the slaves who prostituted themselves for the benefit of the state, there were also independent prostitutes. Their trade was subject to a special tax, the *pornikon,* which fed the town's coffers." Ginette Paris, *Pagan Meditations: Aphrodite, Hestia, Artemis* (Dallas: Spring Publications, 1986), 52–53.

[45] Lee Anna Starr, *The Bible Status of Women* (New York: New York Lithographing Corp., 1955), 163.

[46] Plutarch, "The Dialogue on Love" in *Plutarch's Moralia, Volume IX,* trans. W.C. Helmbold (Cambridge: Loeb Classical Library, Harvard University Press, 1969), 768d–769e.

[47] Plutarch, "Advice to the Bride and Groom" in *Plutarch's Moralia, Volume II,* trans. Frank Cole Babbit (Cambridge: Loeb Classical Library, Harvard University Press, 1928), 145c.

[48] Pomeroy, *Goddesses and Slaves,* 79–80.

[49] Ross Shepherd Kraemer, *Her Share of the Blessings: Women's Religions among Pagans, Jews, and Christians in the Greco-Roman World* (New York: Oxford University Press, 1992), 28.

[50] Michael Grant, *Readings in the Classical Historians* (New York: Charles Scribner's Sons, 1992), 194.

[51] Isaeus, *Against the Estate of Aristarchus,* 10.10G. Quoted in Lefkowitz and Fant, *Women's Life,* 64.

[52] Ross Shepherd Kraemer, "Women's Authorship of Jewish and Christian Literature in the Greco-Roman World" in *Women Like This: New Perspectives on Jewish Women in the Greco-Roman World,* ed. Amy-Jill Levine (Atlanta: Society of Biblical Literature, Scholars Press, 1991), 221–242.

[53] Lefkowitz and Fant, *Women's Life,* 163–164.

[54] Alvin John Schmidt, *Veiled and Silenced: How Culture Shaped Sexist Theory* (Macon: Mercer Press, 1990), 141.

[55] Perictione, *Fragments,* 4.28.70. Quoted in Pomeroy, *Goddesses and Slaves,* 134– 136.

[56] Demosthenes, "Theomnestus and Apollodorus Against Neaera" in *Demosthenes: Private Orations, Volume III,* trans. A. T. Murray (Cambridge: Loeb Classical Library, Harvard University Press, 1939), 122. Also found in Athenaeus of Naucratis, "Concerning Women," 13.572d–574c.

CHAPTER 6

[1] Dio Cassius, *Dio's Roman History, Volume VII: Books LVI–LX,* trans. Earnest Cary (Cambridge: Loeb Classical Library, Harvard University Press, 1924), 332.

[2] Aulus Gellius, *Attic Nights,* 1.6. Quoted in Lefkowitz and Fant, *Women's Life,* 103.

[3] Terence, *The Mother-in-Law* in *Terence, Volume II: Phormio; The Mother-in-Law; The Brothers,* trans. John Sarguent (Cambridge: Loeb Classical Library, Harvard University Press, 1912), 1.114–133.

[4] Cantarella, *Pandora's Daughters,* 143.

[5] Ovid, *The Art of Love, Books I–III* in *The Art of Love and Other Poems,* trans. J. H. Mosley (Cambridge: Loeb Classical Library, Harvard University Press, 1969), 1.643–646.

[6] Cantarella, *Pandora's Daughters,* 124. See also Pomeroy, *Goddesses and Slaves,* 165.

[7] Leanna Goodwater, *Women in Antiquity: An Annotated Bibliography* (Metuchen: Scarecrow Press, 1975), 10–11.

[8] Titus Livy, *Livy, Volume I: From the Founding of the City, Books I and II*, trans. B. O. Foster (Cambridge: Loeb Classical Library, Harvard University Press, 1939), 1.4.1–9.

[9] Numa Denis Fustel De Coulanges, *The Ancient City* (Garden City: Doubleday Anchor Books, 1882), 42–43.

[10] Ibid., 87.

[11] Gaius, *Institutes*, 1.144. Quoted in Lefkowitz and Fant, *Women's Life*, 98–99.

[12] Fustel De Coulanges, *The Ancient City*, 97–98.

[13] We are told by Dionysius that "Romulus permitted them to punish both these acts with death, as being the gravest offenses women could be guilty of, since he looked upon adultery as the source of reckless folly, and drunkenness as the source of adultery." Dionysius of Halicarnassus, *The Roman Antiquities* in *Dionysius of Halicarnassus, Volume VII: The Roman Antiquities, Books XI–XX*, trans. Earnest Cary (Cambridge: Loeb Classical Library, Harvard University Press, 1950), 2.25.4–7. We are also told by Valerius Maximus that a certain "Egnatius Metellus...took a cudgel and beat his wife to death because she had drunk some wine. Not only did no one charge him with a crime, but no one even blamed him. Everyone considered this an excellent example of one who had justly paid the penalty for violating the laws of sobriety. Indeed, any woman who immoderately seeks the use of wine closes the door on all virtues and opens it to vices." Valerius Maximus, *Memorable Deeds and Sayings* 6.3.9–12, quoted in Lefkowitz and Fant, Women's Life, 96.

[14] Plutarch, *Bravery of Women* in *Plutarch's Moralia, Volume III*, trans. Frank Cole Babbit (Cambridge: The Loeb Classical Library, Harvard University Press, 1931), 243E–244A.

[15] Cato the Elder, *On the Dowry*. Quoted in Aulus Gellius, *Attic Nights*, 10.23. Quoted in turn in Lefkowitz and Fant, *Women's Life*, 97.

[16] Livy, *From the Founding*, 1.4.1–9.

[17] Romulus, *The Laws of Kings*, 4. Quoted in Lefkowitz and Fant, *Women's Life*, 94.

[18] Pomeroy, *Goddesses and Slaves*, 46.

[19] Ibid., 228.

[20] Plato, *The Republic*, 5.7–10 (458c–461e).

[21] Hilarion, *Oxyrhynchus Papyrus*, 744. Quoted in Lefkowitz and Fant, *Women's Life*, 187.

[22] Cato the Elder. Quoted in Livy, *From the Founding*, 34.1.1–8.3.

[23] Cicero, *The Republic* in *Cicero, Volume XVI: De Re Publica; De Legibus*, trans. Clinton Walker Keyes (Cambridge: Loeb Classical Library, Harvard University Press, 1943), 1.43.67.

[24] Cantarella, *Pandora's Daughters*, 114.

CHAPTER 7

[1] Genesis 1:27.

[2] The Hebrew *adam* preceded by the definite article refers to the human race: It is the Hebrew equivalent of the Greek *anthropos*, a gender-inclusive term that includes all human beings, both men and women. "Who is 'the Adam'? 'The Adam' is a 'they.' The clause, 'he created him' is parallel to the following clause, 'he created them.' 'The Adam' is a 'male and female.' Thus 'the Adam' could be translated

'human' or 'humanity.'" Aida Dina Spencer, *Beyond the Curse: Women Called to Ministry* (Nashville: Thomas Nelson, 1985), 21.

[3] Genesis 2:7.

[4] Genesis 2:19.

[5] Genesis 1:4, 10, 12, 18, 21, 25.

[6] Genesis 2:18.

[7] Genesis 1:31.

[8] Refer to chapter 5.

[9] Genesis 2:22.

[10] B. Sanhedrin 38a.

[11] Genesis 2:18.

[12] Hamilton, *I Commend to You Our Sister,* Appendix S. *'Ezer* is used twenty-one times in the Hebrew Scriptures. Sixteen of these occurrences are linked to God. They are Exodus 18:4; Deuteronomy 33:7, 26, 29; Psalm 20:2, 33:20, 70:5, 89:19, 115:9, 115:10, 115:11, 121:1, 121:2, 124:8, 146:5; and Hosea 13:9.

[13] Psalm 121:1–2.

[14] Ruth A. Tucker, *Women in the Maze: Questions & Answers on Biblical Equality* (Downers Grove: InterVarsity Press, 1992), 37–38.

[15] Spencer, *Beyond the Curse,* 25.

[16] Ibid., 27–28. Emphasis in the original.

[17] Genesis 2:23.

[18] Genesis 2:24.

[19] Genesis 1:26. Emphasis added.

[20] Genesis 1:28. Emphasis added.

[21] Genesis 3:12 KJV.

[22] Starr, *The Bible Status of Women,* 21–22.

[23] Genesis 3:5.

[24] Genesis 3:1.

[25] Genesis 3:2.

[26] Genesis 3:4.

[27] Spencer, *Beyond the Curse,* 31. For a similar perspective, see also Katherine M. Haubert, *Women as Leaders: Accepting the Challenge of Scripture* (Monrovia, MARC, 1993), 18; Richard Kroeger and Catherine Clark Kroeger, *I Suffer Not a Woman: Rethinking 1 Timothy 2:11–15 in Light of Ancient Evidence* (Grand Rapids, Mich.: Baker Book House, 1992), 20–21; and Charles Trombley, *Who Said Women Can't Teach?* (South Plainfield, Bridge Publishing, 1985), 100.

[28] Genesis 3:6. Emphasis added.

[29] Genesis 3:16–19.

[30] Genesis 3:7, 12, 16.

[31] Genesis 3:15.

[32] See Hamilton, *I Commend to You Our Sister,* 48–49.

[33] Starr, *The Bible Status of Woman,* 55.

CHAPTER 8

[1] See Judges 4:1–5:31, 2 Kings 22:11–20, 2 Chronicles 34:19–28.

[2] See Genesis 38:6–30, Judges 19:1–30.

[3] Lewis Browne, ed., *The Wisdom of Israel* (New York: Modern Library by Random House, 1945), 177–178.

[4] Luke 11:46 RSV.

[5] John Temple Bristow, *What Paul Really Said About Women: An Apostle's Liberating Views on Equality in Marriage, Leadership, and Love* (San Francisco: Harper and Row, 1988), 21.

[6] Judith Romney Wegner, *Chattel or Person? The Status of Women in the Mishnah* (New York: Oxford University Press, 1988), 219, notes 6 and 10.

[7] B. Yevamot 103b. The same teaching is repeated in B. Avodah Zarah 22b and B. Shabbat 146a.

[8] M. Sotah 3.8.

[9] B. Bava Batra 58a.

[10] M. Horayot 3.7.

[11] Wegner, *Chattel or Person?*, 220–221, note 26. Emphasis in the original.

[12] B. Kiddushin 49b. A *kab* is a unit of measure.

[13] M. Teharot 7.9.

[14] B. Shabbat 33b.

[15] B. Sanhedrin 100b. Quoted in Rachel Biale, *Women and Jewish Law: An Exploration of Women's Issues in Halakhic Sources* (New York: Schocken Books, 1984), 275–276, note 13.

[16] M. Kiddushin 4.12.

[17] *Testament of Reuben* 5:1–5. Quoted in David M. Scholer, "Women's Adornment: Some Historical and Hermeneutical Observations on the New Testament Passages," *Daughters of Sarah*, 6:1 (January–February 1980), 4.

[18] B. Berakhot 24a.

[19] B. Gittin 90a–b.

[20] B. Nedarim 20b.

[21] B. Sanhedrin 39a. Quoted in Browne, *The Wisdom of Israel*, 211–212.

[22] B. Kiddushin 31b. The Shechinah is the glorious presence of God.

[23] Wegner, *Chattel or Person?*, 7–8.

[24] Ibid., 48.

[25] M. Gittin 9.10. In her comment on this passage, Wegner says, "The salient feature of mishnaic divorce is its unilateral form. A husband has legal power to divorce his wife, but a wife has no power to divorce her husband....The schools of Hillel and Shammai, although agreeing that divorce is a unilateral transaction, differ on the scope of a husband's grounds." Wegner, *Chattel or Person?*, 45–46.

[26] Matthew 19:5, Mark 10:7–8a.

[27] Matthew 19:6, Mark 10:8b–9.

[28] M. Kelim 1.8–9.

[29] J. Sukkah 5a. Quoted in Spencer, *Beyond the Curse*, 49. See also Bristow, *What Paul Really Said*, 49–50.

[30] B. Sanhedrin 39a.

[31] Paula Hyman, "The Other Half: Women in the Jewish Tradition" in *The Jewish Woman: New Perspectives*, ed. Elizabeth Koltun (New York: Schocken Books, 1976), 110.

[32] B. Megillah 23a.

[33] Biale, *Women and Jewish Law*, 29.

[34] B. Berakhot 17a.

[35] Spencer, *Beyond the Curse*, 47.

[36] T. Berakhot 2.12. Quoted in Saul Berman, "The Status of Women in Halakhic Judaism" in *The Jewish Woman: New Perspectives,* ed. Elizabeth Koltun (New York: Schocken Books, 1976), 119.

[37] Kraemer, *Her Share*, 95ff.

[38] B. Berakhot 17a. Spencer notes that the Greek name for this "house of study" is *andron,* meaning "of males" (Spencer, *Beyond the Curse,* 49). Women "were not admitted into Jewish schools" (Spencer, *Beyond the Curse,* 57). Roslyn Lack states, "The very structure of the academy tended to exclude [women]. Scholars would often travel long distances to spend months and years of study with their mentors and colleagues, while wives (of necessity?) remained at home....The semimonastic *ambiance* of the academy together with that climate of camaraderie in intellectual discourse essential for a real grasp of the Talmud precluded the participation of women—except in rare instances—in Talmudic debates and decisions" (quoted in Spencer, *Beyond the Curse,* 47).

[39] B. Niddah 45b. This statement is made in a commentary on Genesis 2:18 (The LORD God said, "It is not good for the man to be alone. I will make a helper suitable for him"). It is based on a play on words in the original language: *make* and *understanding* are derived from the same root word in Hebrew.

[40] Rachel Adler, "The Jew Who Wasn't There" in *On Being a Jewish Feminist: A Reader,* ed. Susannah Heschel (New York: Schocken Books, 1983), 15.

[41] Rabbi Hillel. Quoted by Adler in "The Jew Who Wasn't There," 15.

[42] M. Sotah 3.4–5.

[43] J. Sotah 19a. Quoted by Richard N. Longnecker, "Authority, Hierarchy and Leadership Patterns in the Bible" in *Women, Authority and the Bible,* ed. Alvera Mickelsen (Downer's Grove: InterVarsity Press, 1986), 70.

[44] Philo, *Philo, Supplement I: Questions and Answers on Genesis,* trans. Ralph Marcus (Cambridge: Loeb Classical Library, Harvard University Press, 1953), 1.45.

[45] Philo, *Genesis,* 1.33 and 1.46.

[46] Philo, *The Embassy of Gaius,* 40.319. Quoted in Spencer, *Beyond the Curse,* 51.

[47] Philo, *On the Special Laws* in *Philo, Volume VII,* trans. F.H. Colson (Cambridge: Loeb Classical Library, Harvard University Press, 1953), 2.24–25.

[48] Philo, *Philo, Supplement II: Questions and Answers on Exodus,* trans. Ralph Marcus (Cambridge: Loeb Classical Library, Harvard University Press, 1953), 1.7. Compare with Aristotle, *The Generation of Animals,* 2.3 (737a 25–30); 4.3 (767b 4–8); and 4.6 (775a 12–16).

[49] Philo, *Genesis,* 1.37.

[50] Philo, *Genesis,* 4.15.

[51] Sirach 25:24 RSV.

[52] Sirach 42:12–14 RSV.

[53] Ezekiel 18:4, 20.

[54] Romans 3:22b–24.

CHAPTER 9

[1] Elsie Boulding, *The Underside of History: A View of Women Through Time* (Boulder: Westview Press, 1976), 358.

[2] John 6:37.

[3] Dorothy L. Sayers, *Are Women Human?* (Grand Rapids: William B. Eerdmans, 1971), 47.

[4] John 8:2–11.

[5] Leviticus 20:10, Deuteronomy 22:22.

[6] Starr, *The Bible Status of Women,* 175.

[7] John 8:7.

[8] Leonard Swidler, *Biblical Affirmations of Women* (Philadelphia: Westminster Press, 1979), 173–174.

[9] Mark 10:5–12.

[10] Hamilton, *I Commend to You Our Sister,* 87ff.

[11] Genesis 2:24, Mark 10:7.

[12] Genesis 2:24, Mark 10:8.

[13] Deuteronomy 6:4. Note that the word translated "God" in this verse is the Hebrew *Elohim.* In Hebrew *El* means "God" and the ending *-ohim* is the Hebrew plural. So, *Elohim*—one of the more common Old Testament names for God—literally means "Gods," thus hinting at the reality of the Trinity. So, this famous verse might be translated, "Hear, O Israel, the LORD our Gods, the LORD one is."

[14] Genesis 1:26–27.

[15] Matthew 19:6, Mark 10:9.

[16] Matthew 19:10.

[17] Mark 10:5.

[18] Mark 10:11–12.

[19] Hamilton, *I Commend to You Our Sister,* 107–108. See also M. Ketubbot 8.1–3; M. Kiddushin 1.1–5; M. Yevamot 13.1; and M. Yevamot 14.1. Roman law permitted women to initiate divorce, but this was rejected by Jesus' Jewish contemporaries.

[20] Hamilton, *I Commend to You Our Sister,* 115–116.

[21] Earlier in His ministry, Jesus had healed a crippled man in a synagogue (Matthew 12:9–14, Mark 3:1–6, Luke 6:6–11). The similarity between these two healings is remarkable. Jesus responded to the needs of a woman in exactly the same way He did to a man's.

[22] Luke 13:16.

[23] See Matthew 1:1, 3:9; Luke 3:8, 16:19–31, 19:9.

[24] The phrase "daughter of Abraham" appears only three times in rabbinical teaching, and then only as an allegory for the entire nation. See B. Hagigah 3a, B. Sanhedrin 94b, and B. Sukkah 49b.

[25] Hamilton, *I Commend to You Our Sister,* Appendix J.2. Jesus refers to Himself as "Son of Man" eighty-three times according to the text of the *Textus Receptus*: thirty-one times in Matthew, fourteen times in Mark, twenty-six times in Luke, and twelve times in John.

[26] Jesus was the son of no human male. He was not the son of a man. But because He was born of a woman, He was a human child of divine origin: both fully human and fully God.

[27] Hebrews 2:14–18.

[28] Hamilton, *I Commend to You Our Sister,* Appendix V. The top three terms Jesus used to refer to God were *Father* (189 times), *God* (173 times), and *Lord* (46 times). Fifteen other nouns are employed by Jesus to refer to God with less frequency.

[29] Deuteronomy 4:15–16.

[30] Deuteronomy 32:6; 2 Samuel 7:14; 1 Chronicles 17:13, 22:10, 28:6, 29:10; Psalm 68:5, 89:26, 103:13; Proverbs 3:12; Isaiah 9:6, 63:16a, 16b, 64:8; Jeremiah 3:4,19, 31:9; Malachi 1:6, 2:10. Note that Jesus' use of *Father* when referring to God (189 times) is nearly ten times as frequent as all the authors of the Old Testament put together (19 times).

[31] Deuteronomy 32:18; Psalm 131:2-3; Isaiah 49:15, 66:9–13.

[32] Matthew 13:33; Luke 15:8-10, 13:20–21.

[33] Matthew 22:30, Mark 12:25.

[34] Matthew 28:19–20, Mark 16:15–16. Note that Jesus' disciples baptized believers even during His earthly ministry. See John 3:22–26, 4:1–2.

[35] Hamilton, *I Commend to You Our Sister,* Appendix U. The first three Gospels are known as the Synoptics because they have many shared stories. This appendix compares only the Synoptic Gospels and the many references they make to women. John makes many extended references to women, such as the Samaritan, Martha and her sister Mary, et al., in addition to the 112 passages found in the Synoptics.

[36] Sharon Hodgin Gritz, *Paul, Women Teachers, and the Mother Goddess at Ephesus: A Study of 1 Timothy 2:9–15 in Light of the Religious and Cultural Milieu of the First Century* (Lanham: University Press of America, 1991), 75.

[37] Leonard Swidler, "Jesus Was a Feminist," *Catholic World* (January 1971), 1–8.

[38] Hamilton, *I Commend to You Our Sister,* 116–117 and 123–124.

[39] Matthew 14:21, 15:38.

[40] John 8:20, 10:23.

[41] Luke 10:38–42.

[42] Spencer, *Beyond the Curse,* 58.

[43] Acts 22:3. The fact that Luke authored both of these passages assures us that this is an appropriate parallel.

[44] M. Avot 1.4. Quoted in Spencer, *Beyond the Curse,* 58.

[45] Ibid., 1.5.

[46] Luke 10:42.

[47] John 11:20.

[48] John 11:25–26.

[49] Hamilton, *I Commend to You Our Sister,* Appendix T. Of Matthew's 1,071 verses, at least 29 (2.8%) have women as their source. Of Mark's 678 verses, at least 26 (3.8%) have women as their source. Of Luke's 1,151 verses, at least 114 (9.9%) have women as their source. Of John's 879 verses, at least 57 (6.5%) have women as their source. It is significant that Luke had more verses with women as the source than any of the other Gospels. Luke was Paul's traveling companion and intimate disciple. Had Paul been less sympathetic than Jesus toward women, one would have expected his disciple to avoid their inclusion in his record of the Gospel story. The reverse is true, suggesting to us that Paul's influence on Luke led Luke to highlight Jesus' inclusion of women.

[50] John 11:26. Note also the follow-through question in verse 40.

[51] John 11:27.

[52] Matthew 16:16, Mark 8:29, Luke 9:20.

[53] Matthew 16:18.

[54] John 4:4–42.

[55] John records that she came to the well at "about the sixth hour" (i.e., about noon), an unusual hour, since trips to the well were customarily made in the early morning. Her tardiness was probably due to her nighttime sexual services and her desire to avoid contact with respectable women who would have chided her for her ways.

[56] John 4:24.

[57] John 4:25–26.

[58] Jesus' 26 "I am" statements are found in John 4:26; 6:20, 35, 41, 48, 51; 8:12, 18, 23a, 23b, 24, 28, 58; 10:7, 9, 11, 14; 11:25; 13:19; 14:6; 15:1, 5; 18:5, 6, 8, 37.

[59] John 3:1–21.

[60] Note that the NIV text of Jesus' discussion with Nicodemus (in John 3) uses a total of 449 words. The NIV text of His discussion with the Samaritan woman (in John 4) requires 539 words. So the record of Jesus' time with the female outcast is a full 20 percent greater than that of His encounter with the male leader.

[61] John 4:27.

[62] John 4:28–29.

[63] John 4:39

[64] The only other place we find the title "Savior of the World" is in 1 John 4:14.

[65] Matthew 9:20–22, Mark 5:24–34, Luke 8:43–48.

[66] Mark 5:31.

[67] Leviticus 15:19–30.

[68] Mark 5:26.

[69] Mark 5:30.

[70] Luke 8:47.

[71] Mark 5:34.

[72] Luke 4:18–19, Isaiah 61:1–2.

[73] Acts 1:21–26.

[74] Hamilton, *I Commend to You Our Sister,* Appendix K. The Greek verb *diakoneo* means "to serve, to wait upon, to administer, to minister." It is found thirty-two times in the New Testament. It is related to two nouns: *diakonia,* which means "service, ministry" (used thirty-four times in the New Testament), and *diakonos,* which means "servant, minister, deacon" (used twenty-nine times in the New Testament). Note that neither the seven men in Acts nor the seven women in the Gospels are ever identified with the noun *diakonos.* However, both groups are linked with the verb *diakonia,* making this comparison very compelling. Both the men and the women "deacons" served Jesus in practical ways, both men and women "deacons" supported the ministry out of their personal economic resources, both proclaimed men and women "deacons" bore witness to the Resurrection, etc.

[75] Acts 6:1–6.

[76] Note that the noun *diakonos* is used neither for the seven men in Acts 6:1–6 nor for the women in the Gospel narratives. It is church tradition that leads us to call the men in Acts "deacons." Based on the language of the Scriptures, there is no distinction between the men who ministered (verb *diakoneo*) and the women who ministered (verb *diakoneo*). So if the noun *deacons* appropriately applies to the one group, it could equally apply to the other group.

[77] Matthew 8:14, Mark 1:30, Luke 4:38–39.

[78] Matthew 27:55–56, Mark 15:40–41, Luke 8:2.

[79] Matthew 27:55–56, Mark 15:40–41.

⁸⁰ Ibid.

⁸¹ Luke 8:3.

⁸² Ibid.

⁸³ Luke 10:40, John 12:2.

⁸⁴ Luke 8:1–3. Emphasis added.

⁸⁵Joan Morris, *The Lady Was a Bishop: The Hidden History of Women with Clerical Ordination and Jurisdiction of Bishops* (New York: MacMillan, 1973), 114.

⁸⁶ Luke 23:55. Emphasis added to highlight the article as it appears in the Greek text.

⁸⁷ Luke 24:22, 24.

⁸⁸ Mark 3:14b–15.

⁸⁹ Luke 10:1–17. Although the missionary tour of the twelve (Matthew 10:1–42) obviously involved only six pairs of men, this second tour could have been made up of pairs variously comprised: two men, two women, or a man and a woman. In fact, does not Paul tell us that it was Peter's custom to travel with his wife (1 Corinthians 9:5) later on in his ministry? It seems likely that they may have begun this shared ministry lifestyle at a much earlier stage of life. Perhaps Mr. and Mrs. Peter were one of the thirty-six ministry teams sent out by the Lord at that time. Perhaps Jesus' earlier healing of Peter's mother-in-law (Luke 4:38–39) freed Mrs. Peter up from having to stay by her mother's bedside to take care of her so that she might be able to be more fully involved with her husband in the service of the kingdom.

⁹⁰ John 20:17.

⁹¹ Starr, *The Bible Status of Woman,* 171.

⁹² Matthew 28:9–10.

⁹³ Luke 11:27.

⁹⁴ B. Berakhot 17a.

⁹⁵ Luke 11:28.

⁹⁶ John 2:4, 19:26.

⁹⁷ John 19:25–27.

CHAPTER 10

¹ Acts 17:6 RSV.

² Acts 19:23–41.

³ Acts 21:27–36.

⁴ Ephesians 2:13–16. Note that the phrase translated "one new man" in the NIV may be confusing. Whereas in English the term *man* may be ambiguous, sometimes used to refer to all humanity and sometimes used to refer to only males, the Greek language has two distinct words that eliminate gender confusion. One Greek word (used here in Ephesians 2:15) is *anthropos.* This is a gender-inclusive term and is best translated as "person or human being." The other Greek word is *aner.* This is a gender-specific term and is best translated as "man or male." Therefore, this passage tells us that Jesus is creating a new humanity. Both men and women are included in His redemptive purposes. For further detail, see Hamilton, *I Commend to You Our Sister,* Appendix J.1.

⁵ Acts 22:3.

[6] Paul quotes the words of Epimenides both in speaking (Acts 17:28a) and in writing (Titus 1:12). Similarly, he quotes Aratus and Cleanthes in his speech in the Areopagus of Athens (Acts 17:28b) and Menander in his letter to the Corinthians (1 Corinthians 15:33).

[7] Acts 13:1–28:31, Romans 15:17–29, 2 Corinthians 11:21b–33, and Galatians 1:13–2:10 detail some of Paul's travels.

[8] Acts 9:1–22.

[9] We find this concept of the household code in Greek literature: Aristotle, *Politics*, 1.2.1–2 (1253b), 1.2.21 (1255b), 1.5.1–2 (1259a-b), 1.5.4–8 (1259b–1260a), 3.4.4 (1278b); Homer, *The Odyssey*, 11.404–461; and Perictione, *Fragments*, 4.28.10. We can also read of this concept in Roman literature: Cicero, *The Republic*, 1.43.67, and Artimidorus Daldanius, *Onirocriticus*, 1.24. Likewise, Jewish rabbinic literature bears testimony to this concept of ancient households: M. Bava Metzia 1.5; M. Berakhot 3.3; M. Hagigah 1.1; M. Menahot 9.8; M. Pesahim 8.7; M. Shekalim 1.3,5–6; M. Sukkah 2.8 and 3.10; B. Bava Batra 51b; B. Berakhot 17b, 20a, 45a–b, 47b; B. Gittin 52a; B. Nazir 61a; B. Pesahim 4a, 91a; and B. Sukkah 28a–b. Even Philo ordered his world around this concept of the household: Philo, *On the Special Laws*, 7.14. For the complete text of most of these references and a more detailed look at the subject of the ancient code, see Hamilton, *I Commend to You Our Sister*, 128–138 and related appendixes.

[10] Ephesians 1:10.

[11] Ephesians 2:1–3.

[12] Ephesians 2:4–10.

[13] Ephesians 2:22.

[14] See Paul's sentence structure charted and explained in Hamilton, *I Commend to You Our Sister*, 125–128.

[15] Ephesians 5:18–23. The NIV translation has been modified by the authors.

[16] Though the term *ellipsis* may be unfamiliar to some readers, the use of this grammatical style is common to everyday usage in English as well as in Greek. The definition of an ellipsis, according to Microsoft ® *Bookshelf 98*, is "The omission of a word or phrase necessary for a complete syntactical construction but not necessary for understanding." For example, it is not uncommon to say something like, "I'm going to the store. Bob is, too." Though we don't say it, we understand that "Bob is *going to the store*, too." If "Bob is, too" were read by itself, you'd be clueless as to what Bob was doing. The ellipsis requires you to look back to the preceding statement in order to insert mentally the prior action into the sentence about Bob. Understanding the context is of paramount importance in this everyday example as it is in biblical interpretation.

[17] Ephesians 5:22–6:9. Of the 328 words in the Greek, 40 were directed to the wives, 150 to the husbands, 35 to the children, 16 to the fathers, 59 to the slaves, and 28 to masters. Note that Paul dedicated almost four times as many words to the husbands as he did to the wives. Though we often still focus on the wives, Paul's main objective was to emphasize the responsibilities of the husbands in this passage. That clearly was his focus.

[18] Since the Greek language has very clear verb forms, it is a simple matter of observation to note which verbs are imperatives. In the original Greek of Ephesians, the commands to the *pater familia* (husband/father/master) are five: (i) 5:25—"love your wives," (ii) 5:33—"must love his wife," (iii) 6:4a—"do not exasperate your children," (iv) 6:4b—"bring them up," and (v) 6:9—"treat your slaves

in the same way." Two commands are given to the children: (i) 6:1—"obey your parents" and (ii) 6:2—"honor your father and mother." Only one command is directed to slaves: 6:5—"obey your earthly masters." And there are *no* commands given to the wives.

[19] Ephesians 6:4.

[20] Ephesians 6:9.

[21] Ephesians 5:25.

[22] Ephesians 5:28.

[23] Ephesians 5:29.

[24] Ephesians 5:33.

[25] Ephesians 5:31.

[26] See (in NASB) Genesis 4:19; 6:2; 11:29; 21:21; 24:3–4, 37–38, 40, 51, 67; 25:1, 20; 26:34; 27:46; 28:2, 6, 9; 31:50; 34:21; 36:2; 38:6; Exodus 6:20, 23, 25; Numbers 12:1; Judges 3:6; 14:2–3; 1 Samuel 25:39–40, 43; 2 Samuel 5:13; 12:9–10; 1 Kings 4:15; 16:31; 1 Chronicles 7:15; 14:3; 2 Chronicles 11:18 for examples of this terminology. This distorted concept of marriage was so ingrained in the culture that it shaped the Hebrew language. Some of Israel's most notable heroes—Abraham, Isaac, Jacob, Moses, and David—are to be found in the verses here listed.

[27] Consider Philippians 2:5–11.

[28] Ephesians 6:9.

[29] T. Berakhot 7.16–18. Quoted in Spencer, *Beyond the Curse*, 56.

[30] B. Menahot 43b–44a. A parallel passage may be found in J. Berakhot 9.1.

[31] B. Shabbat 153a. Contrast this with Jesus' teaching in Luke 13:15–16.

[32] B. Yevamot 62a. See B. Kiddushin 68a and B. Shabbat 53a for similar statements.

[33] B. Berakhot 45b. This passage reflects a similar value system to that reflected by Iphigeneia in Euripides' play when she states, "Worthier than ten thousand women one man is to look on the light." Euripides, *Iphigeneia at Aulis*, 1374–1394.

[34] Galatians 5:1.

[35] Richard Boldry and Joyce Boldry, "Women in Paul's Life," *Trinity Studies*, 2 (1972), 20.

CHAPTER 11

[1] William Barclay, *The Daily Bible Study Series: The Letters to the Corinthians*, rev. ed. (Philadelphia: Westminster Press, 1975), 4.

[2] Donald Engels, *Roman Corinth: An Alternative Model for the Classical City* (Chicago: University of Chicago Press, 1990), 28.

[3] Aelius Aristeides: *Orations* 46:23–28. Quoted in Jerome Murphy-O'Connor, *St. Paul's Corinth: Texts and Archaeology* (Wilmington: Michael Glazier, 1983).

[4] Alciphron, Letters of Parasites, 24 (3.60). Quoted in Murphy-O'Connor, *St. Paul's Corinth*, 119–120.

[5] Barclay, *Corinthians*, 2–3.

[6] 1 Corinthians 5:11, 6:10, 11:21.

[7] Menander, *Fragments*, 764K. Note that Paul quoted from Menander's work *Thais* in his correspondence with the Corinthians: "Let us eat and drink, for tomorrow we die" (1 Corinthians 15:33).

[8] Aelius Aristeides, *For Poseidon*, 23. Quoted in Engels, *Roman Corinth*, 89, footnote 95.

[9] Plato, *The Republic*, 3.13 (404d). Quoted in Athenaeus of Naucratis, *Concerning Women*, 13.558a–560a. In turn quoted in Murphy-O'Connor, *St. Paul's Corinth*, 56.

[10] Plutarch, *The Dialogue on Love*, 767F–768A.

[11] Strabo, *The Geography of Strabo, Volume IV: Books VIII and IX*, trans. Horace Leonard Jones (Cambridge: Loeb Classical Library, Harvard University Press, 1927), 8.6.20–23 (378–382).

[12] Athenaeus of Naucratis, *Concerning Women*, 13.572d–574c.

[13] Richard Kroeger and Catherine Clark Kroeger, *Women Elders…Called by God?* (Louisville: Women's Ministry Unit, Presbyterian Church USA, 1992), 36.

[14] Catherine Clark Kroeger, "The Apostle Paul and the Greco-Roman Cults of Women," *Journal of Evangelical Theological Society*, 30.1 (March 1987), 33–34.

[15] 1 Corinthians 2:2.

[16] Acts 18:1–3.

[17] Acts 18:5.

[18] See 1 Corinthians 1:20–28; 6:12; 7:17–24; 9:19–23; 10:18–21, 23, 32–33; 11:17–22; 12:2, 13.

[19] They are referred to not only in this passage but also in Acts 18:18–19, 24–26; Romans 16:3–5; 1 Corinthians 16:19; and 2 Timothy 4:19. See Hamilton, *I Commend to You Our Sister*, Appendix X.

[20] Apollos' Corinthian connection is stated in Acts 18:27–19:1; 1 Corinthians 3:1–4:13, 16:12.

[21] John Chrysostom, "First Homily on the Greeting to Priscilla and Aquila," trans. by Catherine Clark Kroeger, *Priscilla Papers* 5.3 (Summer 1991), 18. Emphasis in the original.

[22] Mimi Haddad, "Priscilla, Author of the Epistle to the Hebrews?", *Priscilla Papers* 7.1 (Winter 1993), 8.

[23] Speaking to women, Tertullian said, "*You* are the Devil's gateway. *You* are the unsealer of that forbidden tree. *You* are the first deserter of the Divine law. *You* are she who persuaded him whom the Devil was not valiant enough to attack. *You* destroyed so easily God's image of man. On account of *your* desert, that is death, even the Son of God had to die." Tertullian, *Concerning the Dress of Women*, 1.1. Quoted in Rosemary Radford Ruether, *Sexism and God-Talk: Toward a Feminist Theology* (Boston: Beacon Press, 1983), 167. Emphasis in the original.

[24] Tertullian. Quoted in Dorothy Pape, *God and Women: A Fresh Look at What the New Testament Says about Women* (London: Mowbrays, 1977), 200.

[25] Gibson states: "The theory that Priscilla wrote the New Testament letter to the Hebrews has been advanced by three scholars—Harnack, Harris and Peake. The source of this book has always been a mystery; in the year 225, Origen said, 'Who wrote the Epistle to the Hebrews, only God knows.' This anonymity is so amazing that it is regarded as one of the hints suggesting female authorship." Elsie Gibson, *When the Minister Is a Woman* (New York: Holt, Rinehart & Winston, 1970), 8–9.

[26] Pape, *God and Women*, 201–202.

[27] Earlier we observed Paul's use of ellipsis in Ephesians 5:22 (refer to chapter 10, endnote 15). Keep in mind that the definition of an ellipsis, according to

Microsoft ® *Bookshelf 98*, is "The omission of a word or phrase necessary for a complete syntactical construction but not necessary for understanding."

[28] Paul also speaks of another house church in Corinth, that of Stephanas (1 Corinthians 1:16, 16:15). Similarly, he speaks of two house churches in Ephesus, one under Priscilla and Aquila's leadership (1 Corinthians 16:19) and one under Onesiphorus' leadership (2 Timothy 1:16, 4:19). He also speaks of the house church in Colosse, led by a woman named Nympha (Colossians 4:15). He also refers to the house church that Priscilla and Aquila led in Rome (1 Corinthians 16:3–5). Note that all of these are parallel expressions; some of them describe men in leadership, and others name women. If one of these phrases is understood to refer to an expression of the church, all of them should be so considered. Similarly, if one of these phrases is understood to point to the house church's leadership, in all honesty, all of them do the same. Thus, we see Paul indiscriminately making reference to men and women in church leadership roles.

[29] Josephus, *Josephus: Volume IV: Jewish Antiquities, Books I–IV*, trans. by H. St. J. Thackeray (Cambridge: Loeb Classical Library, Harvard University Press, 1930), 4.219 (4.8.15). Josephus, like his contemporary Paul, was a Jew born to a prominent family who benefited from Roman citizenship.

[30] Paul mentions two sources of information he had regarding the status of the church in Corinth that spurred him to write this letter. The first is the oral report from Chloe (1 Corinthians 1:11). The other is a letter mentioned in 1 Corinthians 7:1. These two sources might have been one and the same. Chloe's messengers may have given Paul a verbal report and handed him a letter written by Chloe. This is only a possibility and cannot be affirmed with any degree of certainty. However, it is not implausible, for we see in Paul's writings that it was customary to send an oral message by means of the mail carrier who at the same time delivered the written correspondence (see Ephesians 6:21–22, Colossians 4:7–9).

[31] Spencer, *Beyond the Curse*, 119.

[32] 1 Corinthians 16:15b–16; the NIV concludes this paragraph with the phrase "such men deserve recognition" (1 Corinthians 16:18). In Greek there is no word *men* here. Instead, there is a personal pronoun in the masculine plural form. Like the term *brothers*, this form of the pronoun could be gender specific (all male) or gender inclusive (both male and female) in the Greek language. The NIV's rendering of this verse seems to bias the interpetation in only one way, even though the grammar does not indicate that. "Such ones deserve recognition" would be a more accurate translation.

[33] This term in the masculine plural form could be gender specific (all male, thus "brothers," as in the NIV) or gender inclusive (both male and female, thus "brothers and sisters," as in the NRSV) in the Greek language.

[34] See Ephesians 5:21 and the explanation in chapter 10 of this book.

[35] Paul used the same Greek word here that he used for mutual submission in Ephesians 5:21.

[36] Philippians 4:2–3, Romans 16:3.

[37] Romans 16:6, 12.

[38] Hamilton, *I Commend to You Our Sister*, Appendix X.

[39] F. F. Bruce. Quoted in W. Ward Gasque, "Biblical Manhood and Womanhood—Stressing the Differences," *Priscilla Papers* 4.1 (Winter 1990), 9.

[40] Romans 16:1–2.

[41] See Hamilton, *I Commend to You Our Sister,* Appendix L.

[42] 2 Corinthians 10:12.

[43] 2 Corinthians 10:18.

[44] 2 Corinthians 3:1.

[45] 2 Corinthians 12:11.

[46] Paul used the Greek word *diakonos* twenty-one times in his letters. The NIV translates it as *deacon* three times (Philippians 1:1; 1 Timothy 3:8,12), as *minister* three times (2 Corinthians 3:6, Colossians 4:7, 1 Timothy 4:6), as *servant* fourteen times (Romans 13:4a, 4b; 15:8; 16:1; 1 Corinthians 4:1; 2 Corinthians 6:4; 11:15a, 15b, 23; Ephesians 3:7, 6:21; Colossians 1:7, 23, 25), and, oddly, as *promote* once in Galatians 2:17.

[47] See Hamilton, *I Commend to You Our Sister,* Appendix K.

[48] Schmidt, *Veiled and Silenced,* 180. See also Trombley, *Who Said Women Can't Teach?,* 194; and Katherine C. Bushnell, *God's Word to Women: One Hundred Bible Studies on Woman's Place in the Divine Economy* (North Collins: Reprinted by Ray B. Munson, 1978), 366. *The Apostolic Constitutions* (a Syriac document from about A.D. 375) is the first known Christian writing to use the feminine form of *diakonos.*

[49] See Hamilton, *I Commend to You Our Sister,* Appendix X. Paul referred to fourteen individuals with the term *diakonos* or one of its cognate words. Twelve of them are men: Achaicus, Apollos, Archippus, Epaphras, Fortunatus, Mark, Onesimus, Onesiphorus, Philemon, Timothy, Titus, and Tychicus. The thirteenth person is Stephana/Stephanas (1 Corinthians 16:15ff), whose name, as we saw earlier in this chapter, could be that of either a man or a woman. Finally, the last person referred to in this way by Paul is the woman minister Phoebe.

[50] Philippians 2:25–30. Note that in Philippians 2:29, *men* does not occur in the original in association with *honor.* The KJV does a better job of translation here, rendering this phrase, "hold such in reputation." Similarly, the NRSV translates, "honor such people."

[51] The NIV, the NASB, the RSV, TLB, and *The Message* all use some form of *help* or *helper.* The KJV uses *succourer,* the NRSV uses *benefactor,* the NEB says that she "has herself been a good friend," TJB that she "has looked after," and the JBP that she has "been of great assistance." See Hamilton, *I Commend to You Our Sister*, Appendix O.

[52] Mark 9:35.

[53] Josephus, the famed Jewish historian who was Paul's slightly younger contemporary, used this word twenty times in his three major works. The word's usage included protector, champion, and patron as descriptions of governor, Lord, ruler. Josephus even used the word to describe Caesar as "the Lord of the Universe." It would be difficult to find a more lofty expression—it is used to describe the very apex of human leadership. See Hamilton, *I Commend to You Our Sister,* Appendix O.

[54] The Greek verb *egeneithei* is in the aorist passive form. This means that Phoebe became a *prostatis* not by her own action but by the action of another. This is not a self-appointed designation; it is an officially appointed responsibility. "The passive indicates that the appointment or ordination was made by someone else. Paul's mention of himself in the possessive might be understood technically as a genitive of source or cause. Thus, the sentence might be rendered, 'For she has been appointed, actually by my own action, an officer presiding over many,'" according to Kroeger and Kroeger, *Women Elders?,* 17. It should be further noted that "the

very same construction is used to say that Paul was made or ordained a minister" in Ephesians according to Catherine Clark Kroeger, "Toward an Egalitarian Hermeneutic of Faith," *Priscilla Papers,* 4.2 (Spring 1990), 6.

[55] The Greek is *aner*. The thirty-two occurrences in 1 Corinthians are 7:2, 3a, 3b, 4a, 4b, 10, 11a, 11b, 13a, 13b, 14, 16a, 16b, 34, 39a, 39b; 11:3a, 3b, 4, 7a, 7b, 8a, 8b, 9a, 9b, 11a, 11b, 12a, 12b, 14; 13:11; 14:35. See Hamilton, *I Commend to You Our Sister*, Appendix J.1.

[56] The Greek is *gune*. The forty-one occurrences in 1 Corinthians are 5:1; 7:1, 2, 3a, 3b, 4a, 4b, 10, 11, 12, 13, 14a, 14b, 16a, 16b, 27a, 27b, 27c, 29, 33, 34, 39; 9:5; 11:3, 5, 6a, 6b, 7, 8a, 8b, 9a, 9b, 10, 11a, 11b, 12a, 12b, 13, 15; 14:34, 35. See Hamilton, *I Commend to You Our Sister*, Appendix J.1.

[57] 1 Corinthians 1:17.

[58] 1 Corinthians 1:18–2:5.

[59] 1 Corinthians 5:1–5.

[60] 1 Corinthians 5:1 KJV.

[61] 1 Corinthians 5:2.

[62] 1 Corinthians 5:5.

[63] 1 Corinthians 6:12.

[64] 1 Corinthians 6:13, 15, 18, 20.

[65] 1 Corinthians 7:1.

[66] 1 Corinthians 7:7. The Greek is *exousia*.

[67] The bracketed phrase [or her] has been inserted into the text because the Greek pronoun used here is gender inclusive.

[68] 1 Corinthians 7:32, 34.

[69] 1 Corinthians 7:35.

[70] 1 Corinthians 9:5, 15.

[71] 1 Corinthians 7:34.

[72] The translation used here is the NRSV, which does a better job than the NIV in translating the Greek word *anthropos*. The NIV translates it as *men*, which could be understood as gender specific, but *anthropos* is gender inclusive, including both men and women without exclusion.

[73] Day 6, part two: Genesis 1:26–27.

[74] Day 6, part one: Genesis 1:24–25.

[75] Day 5, part two: Genesis 1:21b.

[76] Day 5, part one: Genesis 1:21a.

[77] Refer to chapter 5 in this book.

[78] 1 Corinthians 15:39.

[79] 1 Corinthians 15:21–22 NRSV.

CHAPTER 12

[1] 1 Corinthians 11:3; NIV text modified by authors in order to accurately reflect the Greek articles.

[2] 1 Corinthians 14:34.

[3] 1 Timothy 2:12.

[4] James 1:5.

[5] 1 Corinthians 11:2–16; NIV text modified by authors. The modifications are as follows: In verse 3, "a woman is the man" replaces "the woman is man." In verse

10, "a sign of" has been dropped and "on" has been replaced by "over." The reason for these modifications will be explained in this chapter.

[6] 1 Corinthians 11:3; NIV text modified by authors.

[7] Gretchen Gaebelein Hull, *Equal to Serve: Women and Men Working Together Revealing the Gospel* (Tarrytown: Fleming H. Revell Company, 1991), 252.

[8] Philip Barton Payne, "Response" in Mickelsen, *Women, Authority and the Bible*, 118.

[9] Berkley Mickelsen and Alvera Mickelsen, "What Does *Kephale* Mean in the New Testament," in Mickelsen, *Women, Authority and the Bible*, 100.

[10] Payne, "Response," 121–123.

[11] Refer to chapter 5 of this book. Note that "Alcmaeon of Croton, a near contemporary of Pythagoras, believed that the sperm came from the brain, while Aristotle (like his mentor, Plato) explained that the semen descended from the head through the spinal cord to the genitals and was then sent forth to produce new life." This quotation is from Catherine Clark Kroeger, "Appendix III: The Classical Concept of *Head* as 'Source'" in Hull, *Equal to Serve*, 270.

[12] Catherine Clark Kroeger, "Appendix III: The Classical Concept of *Head* as 'Source'" in Hull, *Equal to Serve*, 270. Kroeger cites a half-dozen occurrences of this usage among the ancients.

[13] *Exousia.*

[14] 1 Corinthians 11:10; the NIV incorrectly inserts the phrase "a sign of" into the text. The Greek does not contain such a phrase. This will be more fully discussed later in this chapter.

[15] In the Greek it has the definite article *the* before man but not before woman. Whereas the NIV says, "The head over the woman is man," the Greek literally says, "The head over a woman is the man." This small but significant correction to the NIV text will greatly help us interpret this challenging passage.

[16] The Greek verb is in the present active tense, which means that it is occurring now.

[17] Philippians 2:10–11.

[18] Acts 17:25, 28. The first quotation Paul cites is from Epiminedes' *Cretica*. The second quotation is found both in Aratus' *Phaenomena* and Cleanthes' *Hymn to Zeus*. Interestingly, Zeus' headship is likewise associated with his supposed creative, life-giving power. The *Orphic Poems*—written in Zeus' honor—state, "Zeus is the head, Zeus the middle, from Zeus are all things made." Quoted in Kroeger, *Head as Source*, 89.

[19] 1 Corinthians 8:6.

[20] Gilbert Bilezikian, *Beyond Sex Roles: What the Bible Says about a Woman's Place in Church and Family,* 2nd ed. (Grand Rapids: Baker Book House, 1993), 138.

[21] Craig S. Keener, *Paul, Women and Wives: Marriage and Women's Ministry in the Letters of Paul* (Peabody: Hendrickson Publishers, 1992), 55.

[22] Galatians 4:4–5.

[23] John 1:1.

[24] John 1:14.

[25] Cyril of Alexandria, *De Recte Fide ad Arcadiam et Marinam.* Quoted in Kroeger, *Head as Source*, 277.

[26] See Hamilton, *I Commend to You Our Sister*, 128ff. In fact, Paul uses *kephale* only nine times outside of 1 Corinthians 11. Once (Romans 12:20) he uses it in a

literal sense. In the other eight occurrences, Paul uses the word metaphorically (1 Corinthians 12:21; Ephesians 1:22, 4:15, 5:23a, 5:23b; Colossians 1:18, 2:10, 2:19).

[27] In all his writings, Paul uses *kurios* ("Lord") 282 times in reference to God/Jesus—this was his most usual way to refer to the divine. In contrast, he employs *soter* ("Savior") very selectively—only twelve times in his letters. He uses "Lord" an amazing twenty-three times for every one time he uses "Savior." Because his use of "Savior" is so rare, it makes its use all the more extraordinary here in Ephesians 5:23.

[28] Ephesians 5:18–22.

[29] See Matthew 3:17, 17:5; Mark 1:11, 9:7; Luke 3:22, 9:35; Philippians 2:9.

[30] See Luke 11:13, 24:49; John 3:34, 14:16, 14:26, 15:26; Acts 1:4–5.

[31] See Matthew 26:39, 26:42; Mark 14:36; Luke 22:42; John 4:34, 5:19, 5:30, 6:38, 8:28.

[32] See John 6:63, 7:37–39, 16:7, 20:22; Acts 1:8.

[33] See John 14:26, 15:26, 16:14–15.

[34] See John 14:26, 15:26, 16:13; Acts 1:4–5.

[35] Catherine Clark Kroeger, "An Illustration of the Greek Notion of 'Head' as 'Source,'" *Priscilla Papers*, 1.3 (August 1987), 5.

[36] 1 Corinthians 11:8–12; NIV text modified by authors. The phrase "a sign of" has been deleted and "on" has been replaced by "over" in verse 10 because these words do not appear in the Greek text. The addition of these words by the NIV and other translations distorts the Scriptures, making it appear that the woman is to be subject to authority rather than to exercise authority. "Sir William Ramsey in his *Cities of St. Paul* states in this connection: 'Most of the ancient and modern commentators say the "authority" which the woman wears on her head is the authority to which she is subject—a preposterous idea which a Greek scholar would laugh at anywhere except in the New Testament where (as they seem to think) Greek words may mean anything that the commentators choose.'" Pape, *God and Women*, 109.

[37] Genesis 2:22; see Hamilton, *I Commend to You Our Sister*, 89ff.

[38] Genesis 2:18; see Hamilton, *I Commend to You Our Sister*, 91ff.

[39] If prior means superior, then frogs are superior to men, since they were created on day 5, whereas man was created on day 6. See Genesis 1.

[40] 1 Corinthians 15:3–11.

[41] See chapter 7 in this book.

[42] 1 Corinthians 11:10; NIV text modified by authors. The phrase "a sign of" has been deleted from verse 10 because it does not appear in the Greek text. See Hamilton, *I Commend to You Our Sister*, Appendix F.1.

[43] The fifteen verses that contain the Greek phrase *exousia epi* are Matthew 9:6, 28:18; Mark 2:10; Luke 5:24, 9:1, 10:19, 19:17; Acts 26:18; 1 Corinthians 11:10; Revelation 2:26, 6:8, 11:6, 13:7, 14:18, 16:9.

[44] See Hamilton, *I Commend to You Our Sister*, Appendix M. The definition of *exousia* as given by Thayer is "1) power of choice, liberty of doing as one pleases; leave or permission; 2) physical and mental power; the ability or strength with which one is endued, which he either possesses or exercises; 3) the power of authority (influence) and of right; 4) the power of rule or government." John Henry Thayer, *A Greek-English Lexicon of the New Testament*, 4th ed. (Milford: Mott Media, 1982), 225. Bauer, Gingrich, and Danker define *exousia* as "1) freedom of choice, right to act, decide, or dispose of one's property as one wishes; 2) ability

to do something, capability, might, power; 3) authority, absolute power, warrant; 4) the power exercised by rulers or others in high position by virtue of their office: a) ruling power, official power; b) the domain in which the power is exercised; c) the bearers of the authority—i) human authorities, officials, government; ii) of rulers and functionaries of the spirit world." Bauer, Gingrich, and Danker, 1979, in *Logos ® Bible Software 2.0.*

[45] 1 Corinthians 11:10; NIV text modified by authors. The phrase "a sign of" has been deleted from verse 10 because it does not appear in the Greek text. Also, "on" has been replaced by "over." See Hamilton, *I Commend to You Our Sister,* Appendix F.1. Emphasis added.

[46] Matthew 22:23–33, Mark 12:18–27, Luke 20:27–40.

[47] 1 Corinthians 11:13. In two other verses, Paul commands the Corinthians to judge: 1 Corinthians 4:5 and 10:15.

[48] Keener, *Paul, Women and Wives,* 42.

[49] 1 Corinthians 11:11.

[50] Bristow, *What Paul Really Said,* 59.

[51] Genesis Rabbah 8.9 and 22.2. Quoted in Madeleine Boucher, "Some Unexplored Parallels to I Cor. 11:11–12 and Gal. 3:28: The New Testament on the Role of Women," *Catholic Biblical Quarterly,* 31.1 (January 1969), 52.

[52] Matthew 13:33, Luke 13:20–21.

[53] 1 Corinthians 11:12.

[54] 1 Corinthians 4:7.

CHAPTER 13

[1] 1 Corinthians 11:4–7.

[2] Ephesians 2:20, 3:5.

[3] Acts 1:12–15 specifically mentions the two publicly recognized groups that formed a regular part of Jesus' ministry entourage: "the twelve" and "the women" (refer to discussion on this in chapter 9) among the approximately 120 believers. It was they who were the first ones to be filled with the Spirit on Pentecost and who ministered publicly through the speaking in tongues. (Acts 2:1–41). Of course, Matthias was the newest member of the twelve, replacing Judas.

[4] Acts 2:17–18. Emphasis added. See Hamilton, *I Commend to You Our Sister,* 149–150.

[5] B. Megillah 14a. See also B. Sotah 12b.

[6] Paul quoted Genesis 25:23. See Hamilton, *I Commend to You Our Sister,* Appendix T.

[7] B. Megillah 23a. Quoted in Biale, *Women and Jewish Law,* 26.

[8] Adoniram Judson Gordon, "The Ministry of Women," *World Missionary Review* (reprint by Christians for Biblical Equality, 1893), 3.

[9] William Sterns Davis, *A Day in Old Rome: A Picture of Roman Life* (New York: Biblo and Tannen, 1962), 93.

[10] Keener, *Paul, Women and Wives,* 30.

[11] Plutarch, "Bravery of Women," 245C-F. Quoted in Lefkowitz and Fant, *Women's Life,* 129–130.

[12] Kroeger, *Greco-Roman Cults,* 37. Kroeger bases her assertions on

Philostratus, *Imagines* 1.2; Aristides, *Rhetoric* 41.9; Euripides, *Bacchae* 836 and 862; Plutarch, *Moralia* 268 C-E; Athenaeus 12.525; Lucian, *Dea Syria* 6.

[13] 1 Corinthians 11:6. Emphasis added.

[14] 1 Corinthians 11:7.

[15] See Hamilton, *I Commend to You Our Sister,* 183–184.

[16] The conjunction *de* is so common that it is used 193 times in 1 Corinthians alone.

[17] Genesis 2:18.

[18] Genesis 1:31.

[19] 1 Corinthians 11:13–15.

[20] 1 Corinthians 11:13.

[21] Two other imperatives are in 1 Corinthians 11:2–16, both of them found in 1 Corinthians 11:6. However, these imperatives are directed only to the women. See Hamilton, *I Commend to You Our Sister,* Appendix F.5.

[22] 1 Corinthians 11:14.

[23] Patricia Gundry, *Women Be Free! Free to Be God's Woman* (Grand Rapids: Zondervan, 1977), 36.

[24] 1 Corinthians 10:31–11:1. The concept "cover your head or leave it bare, have long hair or short," though not in the text, could undoubtedly be included in the phrase "or whatever you do" and may be legitimately inserted, for it is the next subject Paul takes up. The insertion of this phrase here serves to illustrate how we need to think through Paul's principles, learn from the particular examples that he gives us, and then apply those truths to all areas of life.

[25] 1 Corinthians 11:16.

CHAPTER 14

[1] Some evangelical scholars believe that this verse and the following one—1 Corinthians 14:35—were inserted by later scribes, because their location varies in the early manuscripts. I believe we must deal with both verses as genuine for two reasons: First, no known manuscript omits these verses. This points to the location variation as being a simple clerical error of a copyist rather than a deliberate addition to the inspired words of God. Second, I believe we can be confident that God maintained sovereign oversight in the formation of the ancient texts preserved for us. Even if someone other than Paul wrote these words, we should still embrace them as part of the inspired Word of God. The human agency is not the determining factor; God's inspiration is.

[2] The translations that do this are the American Standard Version, the Amplified Bible, the Catholic Bible, the Jerusalem Bible, the Moffatt Version, the New English Bible, the New International Version, the New Jerusalem Bible, the New Revised Standard Version, the Oxford Study Bible, the Revised Standard Version, and Today's English Version.

[3] The translations that do this are the 1886 Revised Version, the 1911 Bible, the Berkeley Version, J. B. Phillips's Translation, the King James Version, the Knox Version, the Modern Language Version, the Modern Reader's Version, the New American Standard Bible, the Scofield Bible, and the Thompson Chain Reference Bible.

[4] The transposition of verses 34 and 35 in several of the ancient manuscripts makes these two verses a grammatical unit separate from verse 33. If the last part of verse 33 was intended to be seen as the opening clause of verse 34, it would have been transposed along with verses 34 and 35 in those manuscripts, but it was not.

[5] 1 Corinthians 14:33–34a; NIV text modified by authors.

[6] 1 Corinthians 14:26–40. NIV text modified by author as follows: In verse 26 "and sisters" has been added to communicate the gender-inclusive nature of *adelphos* when used in its plural form. The three silencing commands (in verses 28, 30, and 34) have all been rendered the same: "should be silent." This reflects the original Greek in that the same verb in the same tense is used in all three occasions, helping us to see Paul's deliberate repetition. Punctuation has been modified in two locations. The phrase "as in all the congregations of the saints" has been linked to the first half of verse 33, and a period has been placed at the end of verse 33. Verse 35 was separated into two sentences to distinguish between Paul's teaching (35a) and his quotation of the erroneous comment made by certain members of the Corinthian church (35b, which has now been placed in quotation marks). Finally, two expletives of disassociation (Nonsense! What!) have been inserted in verse 36 to reflect the untranslated tiny Greek word ἤ. All of these modifications will be explained in the course of this and the next chapter.

[7] The Old Testament quotations in 1 Corinthians are 1:19 (Isaiah 29:14); 1:31 (Jeremiah 9:24); 2:9 (Isaiah 64:4); 2:16 (Isaiah 40:13); 3:19 (Job 5:13); 3:20 (Psalm 94:11); 5:13 (Deuteronomy 17:7, 19:19, 21:21, 22:21, 22:24, 24:7); 6:16 (Genesis 2:24); 9:9 (Deuteronomy 25:4); 10:7 (Exodus 32:6); 10:26 (Psalm 24:1); 14:21 (Isaiah 28:11–12); 15:27 (Psalm 8:6); 15:32 (Isaiah 22:13); 15:45 (Genesis 2:7); 15:54 (Isaiah 25:8); 15:55 (Hosea 13:14). Note that these seventeen quotations are taken from eight Old Testament books that span the three major categories (the Law, the Prophets, and the Writings) of the Hebrew Scriptures.

[8] 1 Corinthians 11:24–25 reflects the words recorded in Luke 22:19–20.

[9] 1 Corinthians 15:33. Paul quoted from Menander's work *Thais*.

[10] 1 Corinthians 4:6. Paul quoted a rabbinic axiom that was later recorded in B. Makkot 23a.

[11] 1 Corinthians 10:28, 12:3, 14:25.

[12] 1 Corinthians 1:12, 3:4, 6:12–13, 10:23, 12:3, 15:35.

[13] ἤ is found in 1 Corinthians 1:13; 2:1; 4:3, 21; 5:10a, 10b, 11a, 11b, 11c, 11d, 11e; 6:2, 9, 15, 19; 7:9, 11, 15, 16; 9:6, 7, 8, 10, 15; 10:19, 22; 11:4, 5, 6, 22, 27; 12:21; 13:1; 14:5, 6a, 6b, 6c, 6d, 7, 19, 23, 24, 27, 29, 36a, 36b, 37; 15:37; 16:6. This, of course, is based on the UBS third edition of the Greek New Testament text. There are some discrepancies with the Textus Receptus, but none of them affect the structural issue being discussed here. Whereas the Textus Receptus does not have ἤ in 1 Corinthians 6:2, it does have four additional references of ἤ: 1 Corinthians 3:5, 5:10c, 5:11f, 11:14, thus totaling fifty-two occurrences.

[14] Linda McKinnish Bridges, *Paul's Use of Slogans in the Rhetorical Strategy of I Corinthians 14:34–36* (Richmond: Baptist Seminary, unpublished paper, 1990), 13.

[15] Bilezikian, *Beyond Sex Roles*, 286.

[16] 1 Corinthians 14:27.

[17] 1 Corinthians 14:31.

[18] 1 Corinthians 14:33.

[19] 1 Corinthians 14:26.

[20] 1 Corinthians 14:27–28, 39b.
[21] 1 Corinthians 14:29–32, 39a.
[22] 1 Corinthians 14:34–38.

CHAPTER 15

[1] 1 Corinthians 14:34–35a. NIV text modified by the authors.

[2] 1 Corinthians 14:39.

[3] 1 Corinthians 14:40.

[4] 1 Corinthians 14:31.

[5] 1 Corinthians 14:32.

[6] 1 Corinthians 14:31.

[7] 1 Corinthians 14:26.

[8] 1 Corinthians 14:2 states that "anyone who speaks in a tongue does not speak to men but to God." This can be one form in which the women are said to have prayed in public (1 Corinthians 11:5, 13). Indeed, we see that speaking in tongues is clearly associated with prayer in 1 Corinthians 14:14–15: "For if I pray in a tongue, my spirit prays, but my mind is unfruitful. So what shall I do? I will pray with my spirit, but I will also pray with my mind."

[9] 1 Corinthians 11:5.

[10] 1 Corinthians 14:26, NIV text modified by authors and emphasis added. As we have noted earlier, *adelphos*, in the plural masculine form as we have it here, may be used to address either a group of just brothers or a mixed group of brothers and sisters. The latter would be the most normal understanding of this word, as Paul had previously addressed women along with the men in these sections regarding public ministry within the church. For that reason, NRSV translates it with nongender terminology "friends."

[11] These two are among various possible forms of ministry expressed in 1 Corinthians 14:26. This list is not intended to be exhaustive but rather is exemplary of the possible diversity of ministry during a Christian worship service. Note that to bring a revelation could have involved either preaching, teaching, or prophesying. It is the public ministry of the Word of God.

[12] 1 Corinthians 14:26.

[13] 1 Corinthians 14:28, 30, 34.

[14] 1 Corinthians 14:28, 29.

[15] 1 Corinthians 11:4–5.

[16] 1 Corinthians 14:34. The Greek verb is *upotasso*.

[17] See Hamilton, *I Commend to You Our Sister*, Appendix R.

[18] See pages 160–161 of this book.

[19] 1 Corinthians 14:33, 34. Although the NIV translates one as "congregations" and the other as "churches," in both instances the Greek noun *ekklesia* is employed.

[20] 1 Corinthians 14:33.

[21] Both the phrase "must be in submission" in 14:34 and "are subject" in 14:32 are translations of the Greek verb *upotasso*. Again we see that Paul is requiring of women only that which he required of all.

[22] Though Paul's appeal to the Law for authority may at first strike us as unusual, we must realize that he does so on two other occasions in this letter: 1 Corinthians 9:8–9 and 14:21.

[23] The Septuagint was the Greek translation of the Old Testament in use during Paul's time.

[24] Kroeger and Kroeger, *I Suffer Not*, 75–76. The three Old Testament references are Psalm 37:7, 62:1, and 62:5.

[25] Bushnell, *God's Word to Women*, 299.

[26] 1 Corinthians 12:1. The word translated in the NIV as "brothers" is *adelphos*. This Greek word in the plural can refer either to a group of males or to a group of males and females. See the NRSV, which says, "Brothers and sisters...."

[27] 1 Corinthians 14:5, 12.

[28] 1 Corinthians 14:19.

[29] 1 Corinthians 14:20.

[30] What a sharp contrast with pagan practice, which always considered women to be intellectual minors, never able to grow beyond mental childhood. See Hamilton, *I Commend to You Our Sister*, 68.

[31] 1 Corinthians 14:31.

[32] 1 Corinthians 11:6, 14:35; Ephesians 5:12.

[33] Aristophanes, *The Lysistrata*, 524–532.

[34] Aristotle, *Politics*, 1.5.4–8 (1259b–1260a). Also, Sophocles, "Ajax" in *Sophocles, Volume II: Ajax, Electra, Trachiniae, Philoctetes*, trans. F. Storr (Cambridge: Loeb Classical Library, Harvard University Press, 1929), 293.

[35] Plutarch, *Bride and Groom*, 142D.

[36] Titus Maccius Plautus, *Little Carthaginian*. Quoted in F. H. Sandbach, *The Comic Theatre of Greece and Rome* (New York: Norton, 1977), 109.

[37] Titus Maccius Plautus, "The Rope (Rudens)" in *Plautus, Volume IV: The Little Carthaginian, Pseudolus, and The Rope*, trans. Paul Nixon (Cambridge: Loeb Classical Library, Harvard University Press, 1951), 1114.

[38] M. Gittin 4.8.

[39] Sirach 26:14 RSV.

[40] B. Berakhot 24a.

[41] B. Kiddushin 70a.

[42] 1 Corinthians 14:36.

[43] 1 Corinthians 14:37–38.

[44] 1 Corinthians 14:39.

CHAPTER 16

[1] The book of Acts concludes by saying, "For two whole years Paul stayed there in his own rented house and welcomed all who came to see him. Boldly and without hindrance he preached the kingdom of God and taught about the Lord Jesus Christ" (Acts 28:30–31). The New Testament is silent as to what happened at the end of these two years. The early church historian Eusebius picks up the story for us. He says, "Luke also, who committed the Acts of the Apostles to writing, finished his narrative at this point by the statement that Paul spent two whole years in Rome in freedom, and preached the word of God without hindrance. Tradition has it that after defending himself the apostle was again sent on the ministry of preaching, and coming a second time to the same city suffered martyrdom under Nero. During this imprisonment he wrote the second epistle to Timothy, indicating at the same time that his first defense had taken place and that his martyrdom was at

hand." Eusebius, *The Ecclesiastical History, Volume II*, trans. J.E.L. Oulton (Cambridge: Loeb Classical Library, Harvard University Press, 1973), 2.22.1–2.

[2] Philo of Byzantium described the seven wonders circa 225 B.C. He praised the temple of Artemis at Ephesus as the greatest of them all, declaring that it was "the only house of the gods. Whoever looks will be convinced that a change of place has occurred: that the heavenly world of immortality has been placed on earth." Philo of Byzantium, *On the Seven Wonders*, 6.1. Quoted in John and Elizabeth Romer, *The Seven Wonders of the World: A History of the Modern Imagination* (New York: Henry Holt and Company, 1995).

[3] Ovid, "The Heroides 20.5–8, 201–212" in *Ovid: The Heroides and The Amores*, trans. Grant Showerman (Cambridge: Loeb Classical Library, Harvard University Press).

[4] See Acts 19:23–41.

[5] Acts 18:26.

[6] Refer to earlier references to Phoebe in chapters 3 and 11.

[7] 1 Timothy 2:1–15. NIV text modified by authors as follows: To more accurately reflect the meaning of *anthropos*, "persons" replaces "men" in verse 3; "humanity" replaces "men," and "person" replaces "man" in verse 5; and "humans" replaces "men" in verse 6. In verse 10, "she" replaces "women" and "the" is inserted before "childbearing" to reflect the Greek grammar more accurately. These modifications will be explained in the course of this and following chapters.

[8] 1 Timothy 2:1.

[9] 1 Corinthians 16:9.

[10] 1 Timothy 2:2.

[11] The adjective *quiet* is *hesuchios*. Its cognate noun *hesuchia* will appear twice later on in 1 Timothy 2:11–12. See Hamilton, *I Commend to You Our Sister*, Appendix N.

[12] 1 Timothy 2:3–4; NIV text modified by authors.

[13] 1 Timothy 2:5–6a; NIV text modified by authors.

[14] 1 Timothy 2:8.

[15] 1 Timothy 2:7.

[16] 1 Timothy 2:9–10; NIV text modified by authors.

[17] See Thayer, *Greek-English Lexicon*, 682. Thayer's lexicon states that this word means "in like manner, likewise."

[18] We first considered the meaning of *ellipsis* when we looked at Ephesians 5:22 in chapter 10 of this book. Once again, the definition of an ellipsis, according to Microsoft ® *Bookshelf 98*, is "The omission of a word or phrase necessary for a complete syntactical construction but not necessary for understanding." For example, it is not uncommon to say something like, "I'm going to the store. Bob is, too." Though we don't say it, we understand that "Bob is *going to the store*, too." In a similar way, Paul's statement, "The men should pray. Likewise the women…" should be understood by the reader to mean, "Likewise the women *should pray…*"

[19] 1 Timothy 2:1.

[20] Gordon, "The Ministry of Women," *World Missionary Review*, 2.

[21] John Chrysostom. Quoted in Charles Kingsley Barrett, "Pastoral Epistles" in *The New Clarendon Bible* (Oxford: Clarendon Press, 1963), 55. Note also Keener, *Paul, Women and Wives*, 102–103: "Although the grammar is not clear on this point, the 'likewise' of 2:9 probably suggests that Paul, who has just instructed the

men how to pray, now turns to instructing the women in the same way. As in 1 Corinthians 11, women are not silenced in church; they are permitted to pray."

[22] Richard Kroeger and Catherine Clark Kroeger, "1 Timothy 2:9–10 Revisited," *Priscilla Papers,* 8.1 (Winter 1994), 4. Because Ephesus was so filled with immorality, Paul's instructions in this regard were especially relevant.

[23] *Sentences of Sextus* 513. Quoted in Gordon Fee, *New International Biblical Commentary: 1 and 2 Timothy, Titus* (Peabody: Hendrickson Publishers, 1988), 71. Another writer of antiquity wrote, "The temperate, freeborn woman must live with her legal husband adorned with modesty, clad in neat, simple, white dress without extravagance or excess. She must avoid clothing that is either entirely purple or is streaked with purple and gold, for that kind of dress is worn by hetaerae [that is, prostitutes] when they stalk the masses of men. But the adornment of a woman who wishes to please only one man, her own husband, is her character and not her clothing. For the freeborn woman must be beautiful to her own husband, not to the men in the neighborhood." Pseudo Melissa, *Letter to Kleareta.* Quoted in Keener, *Paul, Women and Wives,* 106.

[24] Davis, *Old Rome,* 97–98.

[25] Pliny was utterly shocked when some women went to such an extreme that "they even use [pearls] on their feet, and fix them not only to the laces of their sandals but all over their slippers." Pliny the Elder, *Natural History,* 9.56.114.

[26] 1 Timothy 2:10.

[27] Kroeger and Kroeger, "Timothy Revisited," 5.

[28] The one that is not used is *exagello* ("to publish") and is found only in 1 Peter 2:9.

[29] *Anagello* is found in Romans 15:21, 2 Corinthians 7:7.

[30] *Apagello* is found in 1 Corinthians 14:25, 1 Thessalonians 1:9.

[31] *Diagello* is found in Romans 9:17.

[32] *Epagello* is found in Romans 4:2–3; Galatians 3:19; 1 Timothy 2:10, 6:21; Titus 1:2.

[33] *Euagello* is found in Romans 1:15, 10:15a, 10:15b; 15:20; 1 Corinthians 1:17, 9:16a, 9:16b, 9:18, 15:1, 15:2; 2 Corinthians 10:16, 11:7; Galatians 1:8a, 1:8b, 1:9, 1:11, 1:16, 1:23, 4:13; Ephesians 2:17, 3:8; 1 Thessalonians 3:6.

[34] *Katagello* is found in Romans 1:8; 1 Corinthians 2:1, 9:14, 11:26, Philippians 1:16, 1:18; Colossians 1:28.

[35] *Paragello* is found in 1 Corinthians 7:10, 11:17; 1 Thessalonians 4:11; 2 Thessalonians 3:4, 6, 10, 12; 1 Timothy 1:3, 4:11, 5:7, 6:13, 6:17.

[36] 1 Timothy 2:11–15a; NIV text modified by authors.

[37] 1 Timothy 2:1–8.

[38] 1 Timothy 2:8.

[39] 1 Timothy 2:9–10.

[40] 1 Timothy 6:3. Emphasis added.

[41] 1 Timothy 1:6, 6:21, 4:1. Emphasis added.

[42] 1 Timothy 1:3; NIV text modified by authors. Emphasis added.

[43] 1 Timothy 4:7.

[44] 1 Timothy 5:13.

[45] 2 Timothy 3:6–7.

[46] 2 Timothy 3:13; NIV text modified by authors to correctly translate *anthropos.*

47 1 Timothy 1:20, 2 Timothy 2:17.
48 1 Timothy 1:20, 2 Timothy 4:14–15.
49 2 Timothy 2:17.
50 2 Timothy 1:15, 2 Timothy 4:10.
51 In 1 Corinthians 5:1, Paul stated, "[A] man has his father's wife." A few verses later Paul again speaks of "this man" (1 Corinthians 5:5). Though they were not mentioned by name, Paul clearly had a specific man and woman in mind. The notoriety of the case made it unnecessary for Paul to record their names. Both he and the Corinthians knew about whom he was talking.
52 Titus 3:10–11.
53 Titus 1:5.
54 Titus 1:11.
55 Titus 3:10.
56 Titus 1:11.
57 Matthew 18:15–17.
58 1 Timothy 2:13.
59 Twice in his letters, Paul placed the blame for sin's entry into the world at Adam's feet: Romans 5:12–21 and 1 Corinthians 15:22. There is no such parallel statement made regarding Eve in Paul's writings.
60Sin is sin, and as such, it is never excusable. However, the Scriptures recognize the difference between sin committed deliberately and that done unknowingly. Jesus said, "That servant who knows his master's will and does not get ready or does not do what his master wants will be beaten with many blows. But the one who does not know and does things deserving punishment will be beaten with few blows" (Luke 12:47–48a). Paul seems to apply this principle in the differing discipline he gave to Hymenaeus and Alexander on the one hand and to the unnamed woman on the other. Likewise, this explains the differing judgment Paul had of Adam and Eve's actions.

CHAPTER 17

1 1 Timothy 2:11, 2 Timothy 2:17.
2 Spencer, *Beyond the Curse*, 74. The author faithfully reflects the singular of the Greek text by using "woman" until the last phrase, wherein she uses the plural "women." My quotation corrects that, replacing the plural with the singular form in brackets.
3 "The Ephesian women were untaught. Education usually was not a privilege they shared in the Graeco-Roman world. Judaism [likewise] generally did not allow them to receive instruction." Haubert, *Women as Leaders*, 64. See also Hamilton, *I Commend to You Our Sister*, 37–38, 55ff, and 110ff.
4 1 Timothy 1:20.
5 1 Timothy 2:11. See Hamilton, *I Commend to You Our Sister*, Appendix N and Appendix R for a complete study on these two key words. Please note that the phrase does not define "in submission" to whom. Is it to the teacher? To God? Or to the truth taught?
6 Kroeger and Kroeger, *I Suffer Not a Woman*, 68.
7 1 Timothy 2:8.
8 1 Timothy 2:9.

[9] Spencer, *Beyond the Curse,* 79.

[10] M. Avot 1.17. Quoted in Aida Dina Besançon Spencer, "Eve at Ephesus: Should Women Be Ordained as Pastors According to the First Letter to Timothy 2:11–15?" *The Journal of the Evangelical Theological Society* (Fall 1974), 218.

[11] Haubert, *Women as Leaders,* 64.

[12] James 1:19.

[13] Spencer, *Beyond the Curse,* 75.

[14] "That when it is for the purpose of study the matter is different; as it has been taught: Thou shalt not learn to do—but thou mayest learn in order to understand and teach." B. Avodah Zarah 43b.

[15] B. Sotah 37a–b.

[16] See Hamilton, *I Commend to You Our Sister,* 109ff. Also, Biale, *Women and Jewish Law,* 31.

[17] Ezra 7:9–10. Emphasis added.

[18] Kroeger and Kroeger, *I Suffer Not a Woman,* 60.

[19] 2 Timothy 3:13. Note Paul's use of *anthropos.*

[20] 1 Timothy 1:3. Note Paul's use of gender-inclusive pronoun.

[21] 1 Timothy 1:6–7. Note Paul's use of gender-inclusive pronoun.

[22] 2 Timothy 2:17.

[23] 1 Timothy 1:20.

[24] Berkeley Mickelsen, "Who Are the Women in I Timothy 2:1–15? (Part II)," *Priscilla Papers,* 2.2 (Spring 1988), 6.

[25] 1 Timothy 4:6.

[26] 2 Timothy 1:5.

[27] 2 Timothy 3:14–15.

[28] Once again, the NIV's use of "men" here is potentially misleading. The Greek is the gender-inclusive *anthropos* and is thus more accurately translated "persons."

[29] Kroeger and Kroeger, *I Suffer Not a Woman,* 82.

[30] *Authentein.*

[31] Experts do not agree on how this word emerged. "Etymologically, it means either 'to murder' or 'to exercise authority.'" Sharon Hodgin Gritz, *Paul, Women Teachers, and the Mother Goddess at Ephesus: A Study of 1 Timothy 2:9–15* in *Light of the Religious and Cultural Milieu of the First Century* (Lanham: University Press of America, 1991), 134.

This "pivotal word…has implications of killing, beginning, and copulating, [all of which] were elements of the mystery religions practiced in Asia Minor." Kroeger and Kroeger, *I Suffer Not a Woman,* 87.

Within its wide range of meanings are to begin something, to be primarily responsible for a condition or action (especially murder), to rule, to dominate, to usurp power or rights from another, to claim ownership, sovereignty, or authorship. Kroeger and Kroeger, *I Suffer Not a Woman,* 84.

[32] The normal word for authority in the Greek New Testament is *exousia.* See Hamilton, *I Commend to You Our Sister,* Appendix M.

[33] 1 Timothy 3:1–13.

[34] Mark 10:42–45. This same teaching is also recorded in Matthew 20:25–28 and Luke 22:25–27. Note that the Greek words translated "authority" in the Gospel accounts were not *authentein* but words that are a derivative of the more usual *exousia.* See Hamilton, *I Commend to You Our Sister,* Appendix M.

[35] In 1 Timothy 4:3, Paul says, "They forbid people to marry and order them to abstain from certain foods, which God created to be received with thanksgiving by those who believe and who know the truth." The legalistic practices of the false teachers seem to have distorted the truth about how "God created." This may also be why Paul finds it necessary to add the phrase "who gives life to everything" in 1 Timothy 6:13 in order to define the nature of God.

[36] This may be the reason Paul uses the difficult word *authentein* in verse 12. For this reason, the Kroegers translate 1 Timothy 2:12 thus: "I do not allow a woman to teach nor to proclaim herself author of man." Kroeger and Kroeger, *I Suffer Not a Woman*, 189.

[37] Genesis 2:16–17.

[38] Genesis 2:22.

[39] Genesis 3:1.

[40] Trombley, *Who Said?*, 100. See also Hamilton, *I Commend to You Our Sister*, 94.

[41] Genesis 3:9–11.

[42] Genesis 3:15.

[43] See 1 Timothy 2:3–6, Genesis 3:15, Galatians 4:4.

[44] 1 Timothy 1:15.

[45] 1 Timothy 2:2.

[46] 1 Timothy 2:15b.

[47] 1 Timothy 1:5.

CHAPTER 18

[1] 1 Timothy 3:1; NIV modified by the authors.

[2] Note the use of the indefinite pronoun, here translated "anyone." This is a gender-inclusive word in Greek. Note also that there are no other pronouns in the Greek sentence. The "his/her" and "he/she" are implied within the conjugation of the two singular, third-person verbs. There is no distinction between masculine and feminine in this conjugation. The verbs could refer to persons of either gender. There is no grammatical reason why the text should be rendered by one gender's pronoun over that of the other.

[3] 1 Timothy 3:11 NRSV.

[4] See Hamilton, *I Commend to You Our Sister,* Appendix J.1.

[5] 1 Timothy 1:20.

[6] 1 Timothy 3:2–10, 12–13.

[7] 1 Timothy 3:7.

A FINAL WORD

[1] Aulus Gellius, *Attic Nights,* 1.6 Quoted in Lefkowitz and Fant, *Women's Life,* 103.

[2] Tertullian, *Concerning the Dress of Women,* 1.1. Quoted in Rosemary Radford Ruether, *Sexism and God-Talk: Toward a Feminist Theology* (Boston: Beacon Press, 1983), 167. Emphasis in the original.

[3] Emma T. Healy, *Women According to Saint Bonaventure* (New York: Georgian, 1956), 46. Quoted in Ruth A. Tucker, *Women in the Maze: Questions and Answers on Biblical Equality* (Downers Grove: InterVarsity Press, 1992), 156.

[4] Psalm 19:12–14.

[5] Franson, qtd. *Women in the Maze: Questions and Answers on Biblical Equality*, Ruth A. Tucker, InterVarsity Press, Downers Grove: 1992, p. 179.

ABOUT THE AUTHORS

LOREN CUNNINGHAM has been teaching on the subject of women in ministry for over thirty years. Youth With A Mission—the interdenominational international mission he founded with his wife, Darlene—has led in releasing people to obey God's call: young people, laypersons, short-term workers, non-Western missionaries, and women. Having ministered in every nation of the world, Loren knows firsthand how much hinges on the question *Why Not Women?*

Loren has written three other books, *Making Jesus Lord, Daring to Live on the Edge,* and *Is That Really You, God?* He and Darlene currently live in Kona, Hawaii.

DAVID J. HAMILTON is a veteran missionary and scholar who wrote his master's thesis on the difficult Bible passages related to the ministry of women, an extensive work in which he cites some four hundred books and articles.

David recently coauthored *Courageous Leaders Transforming Their World* and served as one of the senior content editors for the *Christian Growth Study Bible.* He has served in Youth With A Mission for more than twenty years, currently as an international associate provost for the University of the Nations, and also as assistant to the president. He and his wife, Christine, have four children.

JANICE ROGERS lives with her husband, Jim, in Lindale, Texas, where they are pioneering a communications training center, Youth With A Mission Woodcrest. They have three grown sons who all are working with YWAM. Janice is also the sister of Loren Cunningham, with whom she has written three other books.

Other Books by Loren Cunningham and David J. Hamilton

IS THAT REALLY YOU, GOD?
Hearing the Voice of God

by Loren Cunningham, $9.99

This practical guide to hearing God's voice shows how an ordinary man who was committed to hearing God and obeying Him became the founder of the largest interdenominational missions organization in the world.

MAKING JESUS LORD,
The Dynamic Power of Laying Down Your Rights

by Loren Cunningham, $9.99

Laying down rights is a concept foreign to our culture and humankind. We live in a world in which the protection and exaltation of individual rights has become an obsession. As Christians we believe that personal rights do hold great value. As a result, we can perform no greater act of faith and worship than to consciously lay down these rights at the feet of the One who has gone before us, Jesus Himself! Loren Cunningham details proven steps to a transformed life of freedom, joy, and intimate fellowship with God.

DARING TO LIVE ON THE EDGE,
The Adventure of Faith and Finances

by Loren Cunningham, $9.99

Living by faith is not the domain of only those Christians called to "full-time" ministry. What is important is not our vocation, but whether we are committed to obeying God's will in our lives. If we are willing to step out in faith, doing whatever God has asked us to do, we will see His provision. A Christian who has experienced this is spoiled for the ordinary.

COURAGEOUS LEADERS,
Transforming Their World

by David Hamilton, James Halcomb, and Howard Malmstadt, $15.99

Our world needs courageous leaders who will recognize the need for God-motivated action and follow through with a God-led plan. Whether their vision for change is local or global, simple or complex, for home, business, or ministry, *Courageous Leaders* will help Christians remain on a true course and reach the goal set before them.

I COMMEND TO YOU OUR SISTER, An Inductive Study of the Difficult Passages Related to the Ministry of Women: 1 Corinthians 11:2–16, 1 Corinthians 14:26–40, and 1 Timothy 2:1–15

by David Hamilton

This work, a master's thesis done in 1996 for the College of Christian Ministries, University of the Nations, is for anyone who wants to take a deeper look into the issue of women in ministry and leadership. It is a rich resource for Christian leaders, pastors, Bible teachers, and students of theology. This thesis has served as a basis for much of the material in this book.

Other Recommended Books from YWAM Publishing

THE LEADERSHIP PARADOX,
A Challenge to Servant Leadership in a Power Hungry World

by Denny Gunderson, $9.99

What is the key to effective leadership? The ability to organize and take charge? The ability to preach and teach? Entrepreneurial skill? A charismatic personality? According to Jesus, none of the above. This refreshingly candid book draws us to the Master's side. From this vantage point, we observe Jesus through the eyes of people who experienced Him firsthand. And through their eyes we discover surprising insights that will challenge us to re-think our leadership stereotypes.

DISCIPLING NATIONS,
The Power of Truth to Transform Cultures

by Darrow Miller, $14.99

The power of the gospel to transform individual lives has been clearly evident throughout New Testament history. But what of the darkness and poverty that enslave entire cultures, even nations? Have Christians underestimated the power of God's truth to transform entire societies? In *Discipling Nations*, Darrow Miller builds a powerful and convincing thesis that God's truth not only breaks the spiritual bonds of sin and death but can free whole societies from deception and poverty. Excellent study of worldviews.

UNVEILED AT LAST,
Discover God's Hidden Message from Genesis to Revelation
by Bob Sjogren, $9.99

Read your Bible as one book with one introduction, one story, and one conclusion. Bob Sjogren unlocks the unifying theme of Scripture from Genesis to Revelation: God redeeming people from every tongue, tribe, and nation.

INTERCESSION, THRILLING AND FULFILLING
by Joy Dawson, $11.99

This book proves that we are surrounded by opportunities to impact our world through the powerful means of intercessory prayer. *Intercession, Thrilling and Fulfilling* spells out the price of obedience, but leaves us in no doubt that the rewards and fulfillment far outweigh that price. We become history shapers and closer friends of Almighty God.

Call 1-800-922-2143 for a full catalog,
or visit our website at www.ywampublishing.com